For our parents

TALENTED TEENAGERS

The roots of success and failure

MIHALY CSIKSZENTMIHALYI
KEVIN RATHUNDE
SAMUEL WHALEN
with contributions by
MARIA WONG

CAMBRIDGE
UNIVERSITY PRESS

PUBLISHED BY THE PRESS SYNDICATE OF THE UNIVERSITY OF CAMBRIDGE
The Pitt Building, Trumpington Street, Cambridge CB2 1RP

CAMBRIDGE UNIVERSITY PRESS
The Edinburgh Building, Cambridge CB2 2RU, United Kingdom
40 West 20th Street, New York, NY 10011-4211, USA
10 Stamford Road, Oakleigh, Melbourne 3166, Australia

First published 1993
Reprinted 1993, 1994
First paperback edition 1997

Printed in the United States of America

Library of Congress Cataloging-in-Publication Data is available.

A catalog record for this book is available from the British Library.

ISBN 0-521-41578-0 hardback
ISBN 0-521-57463-3 paperback

Contents

Part III. The cultivation of talent

Acknowledgments

The research summarized in this volume was often complex and demanding, and would not have been possible without the talents and enthusiastic support of a great many friends and colleagues. First and foremost, we wish to thank the Spencer Foundation for their generous funding of the project during the four years of data collection and analysis. A Spencer Pre-Dissertation Grant to the second author provided supplementary funds for the study of talent and family issues.

We wish also to thank the students, parents, and staffs of Oak Park–River Forest High School and Lyons Township High School. Their willingness to squeeze us into their already crowded schedules reflects the progressive spirit of both communities and their commitment to the talents of all their children. Without the assistance of teachers and staff members in the departments of art, athletics, mathematics, music, and science, as well as of the administrative staff, much of the data collection would have been impossible.

A highly capable research team from the University of Chicago was assembled to carry out the experience sampling phase of the data collection. Their dedication and efficiency were essential to the success of the project. Dr. Judith LeFevre coordinated all activities on the research sites and managed relations with the high school staffs. Dr. Edward Donner took primary responsibility for technical support and data analyses. Their resilience and good humor kept the early data collection on track and encouraged the development of research skills among the junior staff. Maria Wong handled much of the data analysis during later stages of the project, and contributed to instrument development. Other research contributors included Sheila Black, Kathleen Chattin, In-soo Choe, Norma

Davila, Christine Haenchen, Elise Junn, Lisa Lombard, Robert Manning, Emily Ooms, Joanne O'Sullivan, Carolyn Schneider, Mardi Solomon, Susan Webster, Ellen White, Richard Wolf, Farzin Yazdanfar, and Gary Zimmerman.

A number of colleagues reviewed preliminary drafts of the manuscript, including Howard Gardner, Maria Wong, Ulrich Schiefele, and James Stigler. Isabella Csikszentmihalyi gave the working draft its first editorial overhaul and assisted with editing subsequent drafts. We also extend our appreciation to the editorial staff of Cambridge University Press. In particular we thank Julia Hough, who supervised the editorial process with great efficiency.

Finally, we thank our families, and especially Isabella, Vicki, and Susie for their patience and support for a book that was long in the making, and consumed much attention and time. For Casey, Kendell, and Jonathan, we hope the insights from this study may enhance the prospects for their talent development, and for the great talents of their generation. We dedicate this volume to our parents – Alfred and Edith Csikszentmihalyi, Arthur and Elizabeth Rathunde, and Samuel and Anna Mary Whalen – whose abiding commitment to our interests and potential made so much seem possible.

I

Introduction

This volume describes a study of over 200 talented teenagers undertaken in an effort to understand what makes it possible, given similar environmental conditions, for some teenagers to continue cultivating their talent while other equally gifted teens give up and never develop their abilities.[1] It is during adolescence and young adulthood that many individuals who seem destined for great futures in the arts or the sciences seem to lose interest and settle for careers that require average skills.

THE WASTE OF TALENT

Underachievement, or dropping out, on the part of talented youth has been described in fields as different as athletics,[2] art,[3] science,[4] mathematics,[5] mathematics and science,[6] and music.[7] Many reasons have been advanced to explain this phenomenon of disengagement from talent. An obvious one is the possibility that certain neurophysiological changes during puberty interfere with the cognitive organization necessary to perform well at higher levels in mathematics,[8] music,[9] and presumably other fields as well.[10] Thus adolescents will lose interest in their area of talent because they are no longer able to master the required skills. Other explanations place the blame more on the way schools provide information to students.[11] For instance, Stanley and Benbow claim that "boredom, frustration, and habits of gross inattention" are sure to result from the way algebra is taught in high schools, and they conclude that "motivation for mathematics may suffer appreciably in all but those few students devoted to the subject."[12] But many other reasons may also be involved. For example, Albert and Runco, Bloom, and Rimm[13] have shown that children need the support of a great number of individuals and institutions to develop their talent. Without dedicated parents, savvy coaches and mentors, good schools, and challenging opportunities to express their gifts, it is very difficult for teenagers to persist in the demanding discipline that the cultivation of a talent requires.

Yet strongly entrenched myths would seem to contradict the position just stated. Many people believe that "talent will out" regardless of external circumstances. In fact, one can find many examples of individuals who have struggled successfully to fulfill their potential despite great odds. Thomas Edison was expelled from first grade because his teacher thought he was retarded, and for a long time the only person who disagreed with this estimate was his mother. Itzaak Perlman, born to an unmusical family in Israel, is said to have heard, at age 3, a broadcast of a concerto being played by Jascha Heifetz. He kept pointing to the radio when the violin was heard, saying "I want that!" until his parents understood; they enrolled him with a private tutor to learn to play the instrument. Despite having become partly paralyzed, Perlman is considered one of the great virtuosi of his time. Manfred Eigen, who won the Nobel Prize in chemistry in 1967, left school at 15 when he was drafted to serve in a German antiaircraft battery. Soviet troops captured him 3 years later, but he escaped and walked across Germany to enroll at the University of Göttingen, which had an excellent reputation in science. Even though he had never finished high school, Eigen obtained his PhD at age 22. These and many similar stories can be told of the single-minded perseverance with which gifted individuals pursue their talent.

But do we know how many geniuses are never recognized because their talents are blighted before they have a chance to be expressed? The fact is nobody does, and in principle the question is unanswerable. Although we are in doubt, the most reasonable assumption seems to be that talent is much more widely distributed than its manifestation would suggest. The proportion of gifted children appears to be much greater than that of gifted adults; what happens to those children during the hazardous passage through adolescence?

Some of the attrition could be the result of social and economic inequalities: A disproportionate number of disadvantaged children lose heart because they believe that after many years of hard training they will still fail to reap any benefit from their talent. Only substantial changes in the life prospects of disadvantaged ethnic groups will relieve this source of attrition. But privileged children give up developing their gifts as well – and we really don't know whether the attrition among them is any less. Yet it will make a great deal of difference to our children, and to their children, whether they live in a society where talents are valued and developed to their utmost or in one where potentials are left stagnant and unfulfilled.

To get a better sense of the daily hassles that act as deterrents to the development of talent in adolescence, let us look at the weekend of one of the students who took part in the study on which this book is based. Sandy – her name, like those of the other students who helped us, is fictitious – is a bright and lively 14-year-old whose performance in biology has been so outstanding that several teachers nominated her as being talented in science. Much as she likes to study, however, a great deal of her attention, or psychic energy, is taken up by the problems of surviving among family and peers. We pick up her story on a Friday morning at 8:35. She is sitting on the couch in the family room "planning revenge." This is what she wrote in the questionnaire booklet when the electronic pager that we used in our research signaled her to respond:

I hate my mom so much. I was leaving for school, where I should be now. My little brother wanted to take his bike to school, so my mom made me give him my lock. I thought that meant she was going to give me a ride to school, when it came time to go I went upstairs to say "let's go." She started yelling at me saying, "Why didn't you take the bus? Why do you hate me so much? Why do you try as hard as you can to ruin my life?" We got into a big fight and then she started to cry. Then she said to walk to school which is about 2 miles; there is no way I could make it on time. So I am still at home and late to school.

The next page of the booklet was filled out when the pager signaled at 10:15. Sandy had finally gotten to school, but she was not in class; she was "walking through halls, avoiding narks, hiding in bathroom stalls crying." This is what she wrote:

My mom dropped off my baby sister at my grandparents' house. I called my dad from work and he came home. My mom packed up and left us. I feel guilty, I know it's my fault. I should have walked to school. Now that I am here I have not gone to my classes because I am always crying. I hope my mom comes back home.

Fortunately, the family crisis is resolved by evening: Dad gets Mom back home and Sandy is more or less reconciled with her parents, although she is "still depressed and angry about my mom." But the weekend has barely started. On Saturday, Sandy spends some time raking the yard for a neighbor, goes with the family to watch her brother's team lose at soccer, goes shopping for clothes, and by 11:00 p.m. is at her friend Sabrina's house, drinking and "debating the real reason we are here on this planet." Sandy then skips several signals; the next entry is not until 6:30 on Sunday evening:

It's 6:30 now – last night at the party I left for a walk with two guys (some of my brother's friends). We drove down to O'Hare Airport to walk around and do stuff. We got there around 1:00 in the morning. We were having fun, we went to the hotel across the street and we (Eric and me) lost Dennis. Dennis is the one who had the car keys. Anyway we were supposed to get back to my brother by 1:30. So Eric and I were looking around the airport, parking garage, and hotel for a long time. We went back to the car and broke in. Now it was 3:00 a.m. and I knew my parents and my brother must be going crazy by now, I had Eric call them. We then slept in the car. When the sun rose it woke me up. Eric and I did not mean to sleep at all. Eric then went and called my mom. He was supposed to call her at 4:00, and it was about 8:00. So my mom had all the cops out looking for us. My mom came out and got us, I got home by 9:30. I then had to go to church till 11:30, when I got home I slept till 6:00 p.m., then I ate, then I realized I had missed all these beeps, sorry. It was a crazy night.

The last entry for the weekend was made when the pager signaled at 10:00 that evening and Sandy was in the family room watching TV. Her thoughts were concerned with the possibility of catching mononucleosis from having slept so close to Eric in the car. She wrote:

I think I was never up this late before, my first all night out with a boy I did not even know, sleeping together all night, very drunk. I don't know how to act. I think I like Eric a lot, he is 3rd in State gymnastics, and is smart, the only thing I worry about is that he parties too much. Too many drugs. I have never tried drugs.

So concludes a weekend in the life of a talented 14-year-old. Family drama, love, hate, alcohol, drugs, sex, sports, cops, break-in, getting lost in an international airport – all the ingredients of an exciting prime-time show. Certainly Sandy can't complain of leading an uneventful life. But to what extent do such events (which were by no means rare in the daily rhythm of the adolescents we studied) interfere with the concentration necessary to develop the discipline that any talent eventually entails? This is the basic question our study was designed to answer. In Sandy's case the answer is rather clear. Four years after this "crazy" weekend, she graduated from high school in the middle of the pack. She had stopped taking advanced classes in science long before, and her outlook for the future included an easy liberal arts college degree, marriage, and perhaps some fun part-time job. Her teachers thought she was performing far below her potential, that is, somewhat below average for her cohort. For many students this would not be by any means a bad accomplishment, but for Sandy it was a far cry from the exceptional promise she had shown at the end of grade school.

As anyone who keeps track of contemporary mores knows, the demands placed on Sandy's psychic energy were by no means unusual. In fact, perhaps a majority of adolescents by now live in circumstances that are even less conducive to the development of talent. At least Sandy came from a relatively affluent and intact family, was reared in a religious atmosphere, lived in a stimulating suburban community, and went to excellent schools. If she could not invest the energy necessary to develop her rare talent, how many other potentially gifted young people are giving up the opportunity to develop theirs?

The present volume is based on a 5-year longitudinal study that tried to answer the question: How do young people become committed to the development of their talent? Or, to take the mirror image of that question: Why do some young people become disengaged from their talent? We hoped that the results might help parents, teachers, and other interested individuals prevent the losses that the underutilization of rare skills entails. After all, unusual talent is a potential benefit for society as a whole; its loss is a loss for everyone.

But the goal of this volume is still broader. By focusing on talented youth, we do not wish to endorse an elitist view of education. We believe that all children are talented in one way or another, even though their gifts may not be ones formally recognized by teachers or school curricula. As Howard Gardner has convincingly argued, the dimensions of giftedness include body movement, empathy, visual acuity, and so forth.[14] One could argue that any channel through which a mind communicates with the environment could develop into a talent, as long as the culture is willing to recognize and support the given skill.[15] The point is that by studying a number of young people with recognized talents in such traditionally accepted fields as math, science, and music, we can learn much that will be useful to all children. The attrition of talent can be most easily studied among the most talented; but what is learned there will be applicable to every child struggling to develop her or his potential, whatever its level.

MOTIVATION AS THE KEY TO THE DEVELOPMENT OF TALENT

The studies that form the empirical underpinnings of this volume do not cover all possible aspects of the problem of disengagement from talent. Among the most obvious omissions is the cognitive dimension: We did not investigate the contribution of intellectual abilities. The study did not address whether students who continued to develop their talent had a greater facility with formal operations,[16] peculiar hemispheric preferences,[17] faster information processing or reaction times,[18] or superior reasoning skills and intellectual styles.[19]

There were two reasons for omission of the cognitive dimension. First, the great majority of scholars have focused on the question of how gifted and talented children differ from "average" children along cognitive lines. We were afraid to founder in the sea of ink devoted to this question. In comparison – and this is the second reason – little is known about the other dimensions that may interfere with the development of talent. We had good reason to suspect that among these, emotional and motivational issues may be as important as the purely cognitive ones, or more so. The reason so many talented young persons don't become skilled scientists and artists – and that so many more with average endowments never learn to read and count – is not so much that they can't cope with the intellectual challenges as that they simply don't want to bother putting out the effort required to learn.[20] The thesis of our work is in agreement with the conclusions of a recent report by the U.S. Department of Education, which claims that high academic achievers are not necessarily born "smarter" than others, but work harder and develop more self-discipline.

Thus the present study deals mainly with the question: What motivates some teenagers to continue in their area of talent while others drop out? It turns out, however, that this question is not a simple one. Motivation is in part a matter of personality: It involves habitual patterns of thought and action that develop over time and remain more or less stable. Thus to answer the question we had first of all to look at the personality patterns that are characteristic of talented adolescents who become committed to their talent.

These traits are, in turn, related to how persons use their time and invest their psychic energy: Some teenagers as they grow older will spend less and less time studying and more time interacting with friends. Learning to invest attention in difficult tasks is indispensable to the development of any skill. Therefore another answer to our question about motivation directed us to investigate the patterns of activity and time use of talented teens.

The motivation of young people is also deeply bound up with the social environment in which they live. How much time and effort they will devote to study and practice depends in great part on the material and emotional support their parents are able to give. Even though many geniuses have been able to overcome disastrous early family circumstances,[21] it is probable that many more would have flourished if their families had provided a more secure launching pad. How much parents value the development of talent[22] and how supportive they are emotionally[23] seem to be important factors in keeping youngsters focused on their talent. Rathunde has described the kind of family interaction that would best promote children's ability to concentrate their attention on demanding tasks;[24] his conclusions are in line with the results of other researchers in the area.[25]

Later in life, schools also have a great effect on the motivation of students.[26] Occasionally an entire school seems able to arouse in its students a great enthusiasm for learning – for instance, the Bronx High School of Science or the Lutheran and the Model high schools in Budapest, where so many of the great mathematicians and physicists of the first half of this century first became interested in science. Most students who become interested in an academic subject do so because they have met a teacher who was able to pique their interest.[27] Therefore to answer the question of what motivates teenagers' continuing development of those skills that make the growth of their talent possible, we had also to consider families and schools.

But knowing about personality, habits, and families and schools is still not enough to understand motivation. Whether a teenager will want to devote a great deal of time to studying chemistry or music depends also

on the quality of the experience he or she derives from working in the lab
or practicing an instrument. The sum of momentary experiences adds up
either to enjoyment or to boredom and anxiety; which of these prevails
will to a large extent decide a young person's future involvement.

On this score the testimony of individuals who have successfully developed their talent is clear: The main reason they do what they do is that
they enjoy it. In 1934 Schlick pointed out how important enjoyment is in
sustaining the activity of scientists.[28] Galileo Galilei, one of the first true
modern scientists and still considered one of the greatest, used to comment on the fun he was having in setting up his experiments – and this at
a time when fun was taken much less seriously than it is now.[29] Similarly,
when asked why all through his life he kept experimenting with the
measurement of the speed of light, Albert Michelson, who was the first
American to win a Nobel Prize in science, is said to have answered, "It
was so much fun."[30] A Nobel laureate closer to us in time, Francis H. C.
Crick, codiscoverer of the double helix, along with other scientists and
artists interviewed in a recent study, rated "enjoyment of work" as the
characteristic most responsible for his success – ahead of 32 other traits,
such as creativity, competence, and breadth of knowledge.[31] Skilled athletes, artists, artisans, and scientists tend to describe the use of their
talents as highly enjoyable.

All this talk about enjoyment and fun can be misleading, however. It
gives the impression that talented people go from one high to the next,
immersed in a constant stream of pleasurable experiences. Actually, almost the opposite seems to be the case. What characterizes people who
use their skills to the utmost is that *they enjoy the hardships and the challenges of their task.* It is not that they are more likely to encounter pleasant
experiences but that they persevere when they meet difficulties that would
daunt others and occasionally succeed in turning experiences that others
find meaningless or threatening into highly enjoyable ones. How is this
skill that helps in developing talent acquired? It is one of the goals of this
volume to answer that question.

In the last few years, several scholars have become interested in how
intrinsic rewards help motivate gifted children to stay involved in their
work. The studies of Deci and Ryan[32] and Amabile[33] have been especially influential in demonstrating that when people enjoy a given activity and are not distracted by external considerations, they will keep

doing it longer and will approach it more creatively than if the same activity were extrinsically rewarded and not under the person's control. Other scholars have been investigating the role of *interest* in learning – how personal interest in a subject facilitates the recall and cognitive organization of information;[34] how interest helps involvement in science[35] and mathematics;[36] and how it helps scholastic achievement, especially in the sciences.[37]

It would seem obvious that educators concerned with the cultivation of talent would make it a priority to fuel students' interest in learning and help them discover learning's intrinsic rewards. Unfortunately, this is not the case. The priority among most teachers seems to be to cover as much information as possible without regard to whether the students are becoming interested in learning. For instance, getting students interested in mathematics is one of the least important goals of math teachers – compared with such important objectives as "learning mathematical facts and principles and . . . develop[ing] a systematic approach to problem solving."[38] These are surely worthy goals, but how are they to be achieved if the students are not motivated to learn? Not surprisingly, the proportion of students nationwide who say they are interested in mathematics also decreases with each grade level.[39] Despite our relatively heavy investment in education as a nation, we still do not seem to realize that teaching which does not consider the students' priorities is useless. It is wasteful to teach someone who is not interested and so is not motivated.

One of the reasons motivational issues are rather low on the formal educational agenda is that in the past few decades cognitive psychologists have applied the computer analogy of information processing to human learning a bit too easily. The computer will store and use any information programmed into it, providing the plug is in the wall and the right system is booted up. Hence the main issue concerning computer programs is how clear and rational they are. Pursuing the analogy between computers and the human brain, the same considerations of clarity and rationality have become the main goals of educators designing school curricula and instruction. But the analogy misses the fact that students, as distinct from computers, will not process information presented to them unless they are motivated to do so.[40] It is not enough for the information to be clear and rational; it also has to be interesting. Learning has to be engaging and rewarding for students to learn.

Despite the general tendency to ignore motivational factors at the expense of more purely cognitive dimensions, there is enough evidence to show that certain motivational states interfere with learning. Two adverse conditions are especially dangerous: anxiety and boredom. Anxiety occurs primarily when teachers expect too much from students;[41] boredom occurs when teachers expect too little.[42] When curricular expectations are out of sync with students' abilities, not only does motivation decrease, but also achievement.[43]

Because we still do not have a very clear idea of how interest and motivation help children become involved in sustained learning, this volume will focus primarily on that aspect of the development of talent. The studies we conducted differ from previous research in this area in that they focus on the *ongoing experience* of students involved with the development of their talent over the 4 years of high school. We wanted to get a better idea about what happens in the minds of talented teenagers when they are studying – what they think about, how they feel, how much they want to do what they are doing – and whether the quality of their experience predicts the level of their commitment to talent 4 years later, at the end of high school.

THE CONCEPT OF PSYCHIC COMPLEXITY

We were able to measure ongoing experience systematically through the use of the Experience Sampling Method (ESM), a technique developed in our laboratory for the purpose of obtaining accurate measures of thoughts, activities, and mental states.[44] Persons who participate in ESM studies wear an electronic pager and carry a booklet of self-report forms for a week. Each day, at randomly chosen moments, signals activate the pagers, and the respondents then fill out a page of the self-report booklet, describing their behavior and subjective state in minute detail – just as Sandy did over the weekend we summarized earlier in this chapter. In the present study, over 7,000 such self-reports were made, providing a dynamic record of changing moods and motivations.

This effort to develop a *systematic phenomenology* makes it possible to get a closer view of the subjective events that are important in determining whether or not a teenager will want to continue pursuing a particular talent. In addition to the ESM, we conducted extensive interviews and collected data from questionnaires and standardized tests from the students and, whenever relevant, from their parents and teachers as well.

So much for the methods of the study. As for our theoretical perspective, it was informed by a simple assumption: that the development of talent requires a peculiar mind-set, based on habits cultivated in one's early environment that eventually become so ingrained that they end up forming something like a personality trait. We shall call this mind-set a *complex attentional structure*, or a *complex consciousness*, or a *complex self*, depending on which aspects of the process we are mainly concerned with.

The reason to consider a person's attentional structure as the key to the development of talent is that one cannot accomplish any novel or difficult task without concentrating attention on it. Because it takes attention to make anything happen, it is useful to think of attention as *psychic energy*. And like other forms of energy, attention is a limited resource: We cannot deal with more than one demanding task at a time.[45] For example, during the entire 3 days of her "crazy" weekend, Sandy, preoccupied with her mother and with partying, never reported thinking about her studies. While her mind was occupied with these other issues, little talent-related academic learning took place. In the long run, it is safe to predict that teenagers who are unable to exclude daily hassles and the inevitable problems of existence from their minds – at least occasionally and temporarily – will not be able to cultivate their talents beyond an average level.

But what is a complex attentional structure? To answer this question, we need to take a detour through the theoretical framework that informs the present investigation. According to this perspective, which is shared by other theorists of development, psychological growth is best captured by dialectical models and concepts. Dialectical models try to account for two seemingly opposing forces or processes that in fact are interrelated and mutually defining and that combine to propel development to higher levels. The most widely known example of such an approach is the work of Jean Piaget. Cognitive development, thought Piaget, is moved by the complementary processes of assimilation and accommodation. The first refers to the mind incorporating new information into its existing patterns, the second to the mind adjusting itself to new information. There are in addition many other models that will not be reviewed here but that contain a similar logic despite using a diverse range of terms. The specific terminology is less important than the attempt to account for the process of development, which in turn requires thinking about the roles of *constancy* and *change* in ongoing development. Models that are one-dimensional, that is, that fail to account for important contributions from each of these dimensions, will fail to give an adequate account of human development.

In this volume the terms *integration* and *differentiation* will stand for the general dialectical processes of constancy and change. These terms have been widely used in systems theory[46] and have been successfully applied to a variety of disciplines from biology to computer science. An integrated system is one in which the individual parts that make up the system are successfully interrelated and mutually reinforcing. A differentiated system, in contrast, is one in which the individual parts have unique or specialized functions. In a more process-oriented language, to integrate is to bring together parts, to organize or harmonize; to differentiate is to make distinctions among, to discriminate contrasts among, parts.

Such general and vague concepts, of course, have little to offer beyond providing an overarching framework in which one can find a general orientation to complex phenomena and see basic connections among diverse conceptual approaches. For all practical purposes, integration and differentiation have to be defined in different operational terms, depending upon the type of system one is trying to understand. For instance, systems theory has influenced research on the family through such concepts as cohesion and adaptability,[47] where the integration component deals with the mutuality of family members, and the differentiation component, with the flexibility of responses to changes in the family system. But the family is only one important system to consider from the perspective of integration and differentiation; there are several other systems that can be so described.

In this volume, at least four such systems are investigated, ranging from the level of personality (i.e., the system of traits, or habitual patterns of thought and action, described in chapters 4 and 5) to cultural domains (i.e., the informational systems that contain the symbols of math, science, music, etc., discussed in chapter 6) to immediate experience (i.e., the attentional system, or system of consciousness, described in chapter 7) to social systems (e.g., family or classroom environments; see chapters

8 and 9). Each system can be seen through the template of an integration/differentiation model, and we have tried to adapt various measures to operationalize it in each case. With more time or with additional measures and imagination, there is no doubt that we could have found other ways to look at these processes. Nor have we succeeded completely in bringing together these various levels into an "integrated" theory. Much work remains to be done. Nevertheless there is a consistency to the various levels of our analysis and, we believe, a consistent story that emerges in the end concerning optimal conditions for the development of talent. Each of the four levels is described in detail in subsequent chapters; the following is a brief overview of what they have in common.

Common to all levels of analysis is the association of integration with stability (constancy) and of differentiation with change. An optimal system is *complex,* that is, both integrated and differentiated. It is cohesive and stable yet able to adapt and change when necessary. Such notions by themselves add nothing new to other similar conceptions of optimally functioning systems. What is unique in the present approach is the attempt to reach a clearer understanding of the dynamics between stability and change. We have attempted to answer the question: What energizes, or *motivates,* an integrated system to differentiate, and a differentiated system to integrate? A concrete example is: Why do teenagers want to become more independent of their parents yet at the same time want to maintain ties and relations with them? Our approach to answering such a question was to view it from the perspective of subjective experience. In other words, it would be very difficult to compare personality, family, and information systems in terms of their "objective" features. But in a person's experience there is a confluence of these various levels; all information – regardless of its type – is processed through consciousness and "experienced."

Concerning motivation, our perspective was that people will pursue an activity if they enjoy doing it and that people tend to enjoy what they can do well. The idea is not new; Aristotle extolled the enjoyment derived from the achievement of excellence in activity and called it "virtue."[48] It is an idea that early psychologists, especially William James and John Dewey, were well acquainted with. The form in which the idea is expressed in this volume is that of the *flow model of optimal experience.*[49]

FLOW AND COMPLEXITY

Flow is a subjective state that people report when they are completely involved in something to the point of *losing track of time and of being unaware of fatigue and of everything else but the activity itself.* It is what we feel when we read a well-crafted novel or play a good game of squash or take part in a stimulating conversation. The depth of involvement is something we find enjoyable and intrinsically rewarding. This flow experience is relatively rare in everyday life, but almost everything – play and work, study and religious ritual – is able to produce it, provided the conditions are conducive to deep concentration.

But what makes the optimal experience of flow possible? Interview reports collected from over 7,000 individuals of different ages and from different cultures and social classes, as well as several ESM studies, point to the conditions that seem to be present when a person enjoys what he or she is doing for its own sake.[50] First, a deeply involving flow experience usually happens when there are clear goals and when the person receives immediate and unambiguous feedback on the activity. Clear goals and feedback are readily available in most games and sports and in many artistic and religious performances, which is the reason such activities readily provide flow and are intrinsically motivating. In everyday life, and all too often in classrooms, individuals don't really know what the purpose of their activities is, and it takes them a long time to find out how well they are doing.

Another condition that makes flow experiences possible is the balance between the opportunities for action in a given situation and the person's ability to act. When challenges and skills are matched, as in a close game of tennis or a satisfying musical performance, all of the actor's attention needs to be focused on the task at hand. Acting within realistic parameters, people report a sense that, at least in principle, they are able to be in control of the situation. This introduces a further element of the flow experience: the merging of action and awareness. The person becomes so concentrated and involved that the duality between actor and action disappears; the person feels as if on automatic pilot, doing what needs to be done without conscious effort.

The depth of involvement forces one to focus on the present, so that the irrelevant thoughts and worries which in everyday life weigh down our minds tend to disappear. People report forgetting their troubles because the intensity of the experience precludes thinking about the past or the future. This further leads to a loss of self-consciousness, so that a person no longer worries about how good he or she looks or whether others like her or him. In fact, people often mention a feeling of self-transcendence, as when a musician listening to a particularly beautiful melody feels at one with the order of the cosmos, or when dancers feel at one with the rhythm that moves them and the other dancers. In addition, a distortion of the sense of time is often reported, so that hours seem to pass by in minutes.

When most of these dimensions are present in an experience, the activity tends to become *autotelic*, that is, worth doing for its own sake. This is because the flow experience is so enjoyable that one wants to repeat it. If one experiences flow in scuba diving, then one will want to dive again so as to have a similar experience. If one reaches the flow state by solving a mathematical problem, then one will keep seeking out more problems to solve.

Flow leads to complexity because, to keep enjoying an activity, a person needs to find ever new challenges in order to avoid boredom, and to perfect new skills in order to avoid anxiety. The balance of challenges and skills is never static. One cannot do the same thing at the same level of proficiency for a long time and keep on enjoying it. After a while one's skills inevitably will increase, and one will start getting bored by what initially seemed so exciting. At that point, to return into flow one must find new opportunities for action in the activity. Thus the desire to keep enjoyment alive forces us to become more complex – to differentiate new challenges in the environment, to integrate new abilities into our repertory of skills. The most critical task in human development is to learn to create flow in productive, prosocial activities, thereby making it possible to maximize the quality of both personal and social life. This is what Plato meant when he said that the most important task of education is to teach young people to find pleasure in the right things.

The theoretical perspective in this volume has thus evolved from relating the systems logic of complexity based on integration and differentiation to the flow model of optimal experience.[51] The basic hypotheses in the study were derived from the notion that complex systems are related to optimal experience, which in turn is related to the growth of talent. A complex family or personality or domain is believed to enhance talent development by providing conditions conducive to interest or flow.

The reason for expecting that the flow experience will be involved in the development of talent is that flow usually begins when a person takes on challenges that are just at or above her or his skills. This is the phase of change or differentiation; to be enjoyable, this phase must be followed by a stabilizing or integrating phase when skills appropriate to the challenge are developed. The completion of the activity, at the conclusion of a cycle of differentiation and integration, results in stretching or extending the person's being. A student sees a bright star through the telescope for the first time, becomes curious and wants to determine its age, learns how to do a spectral analysis of its light, and works on the analysis for months. By the time the project is finished, that student is no longer what she was before. Her knowledge of astrophysics has become more complex, and she has enjoyed the process.

OUTLINE OF THE VOLUME

In chapter 2 we define the sense in which the term *talent* is used in this volume. The personal, social, and cultural conditions that help or hinder the development of talent will be reviewed in terms of their significance for the chapters that follow.

In chapter 3 the procedures used in the study will be described. This methodological section is important for the scholar who is interested in the details of data collection and analysis but can safely be skipped by the layperson who is more interested in the results of the study. In any case, the reader can always return to this chapter later for clarification.

Chapter 4 consists of a series of contrasts between talented and "average" adolescents. It describes the family background, academic ability, and personality patterns of our sample compared with available norms. The daily patterns of activity and time use of talented teens are presented in chapter 5 and are compared with those of more typical adolescents. Here we begin to identify those daily habits that underlie the complex attentional structures that should lead to the cultivation of talent over time. This concludes part I of the volume, which is focused on the traits that distinguish talented students from their peers.

Part II turns to a description of how adolescents report thinking and feeling when they are involved in their field of talent. Chapter 6 differentiates arts students from science students, because the attentional structures of students in these two academic areas turn out to be very different. Chapter 7 presents case studies describing how it feels to be involved in various talent areas and delves into the question of what motivates adolescents to develop their talents. Chapter 8 deals with the impact various forms of family interaction have on the students' ability to concentrate attention on academic subjects and therefore to develop complex attentional structures. Chapter 9 contains accounts of the types of teaching methods and teachers that seem to be effective in motivating talented adolescents to focus their psychic energy on cultivating their talents.

Some of most important findings of the study are contained in part III. Here we review the results of the longitudinal study concerning engagement and disengagement from talent. Chapter 10 describes how engagement with talent was operationalized – a rather difficult but important task in itself – and shows the variables that are most strongly related to the development of talent by the end of high school. Chapter 11 focuses in greater detail on a group of the most committed students and describes, within the framework of our theoretical perspective, their approach to study and the development of their skills. Finally, chapter 12 summarizes the main findings and reflects on what we have learned both about the phenomenon of talent and about the theory of motivation and optimal experience that underlies our analysis.

The basic goal of this book is to help understand what keeps some young men and women motivated in the difficult pursuit of excellence when so many forces in our culture encourage them to just get by, take shortcuts, and get away with whatever they can. Doing one's best for the sake of doing one's best is not a popular idea these days, and in the relativistic climate of contemporary social science it is not even one that seems to make sense. What, after all, can we mean by the idea of *best*? Shortly after the end of the "me" decade, when greed and selfishness became respectable and doing a good job for its own sake a faintly quaint notion, to worry about the pursuit of excellence may seem anachronistic. Yet we believe that each person knows quite clearly what it means to do one's best, and that everyone, given a chance, would like to savor that experience as often as possible. We hope that this book will help achieve that goal.

NOTES

1 The earliest study that set out to follow a group of "gifted" children (meaning children with high IQs) over time was L. M. Terman's longitudinal research of a group first tested over 60 years ago (Terman, 1925), which still continues (Oden, 1968). Terman's approach differed from ours in focusing exclusively on high intelligence as a measure of giftedness, and on being primarily concerned with psychological traits rather than with the full range of social and cultural variables involved in the development of talent. The same could be said about the difference between this book and current studies of the development of giftedness or talent, e.g., Albert & Runco, 1986; Eccles & Harold, 1992. For a recent collection of research on this topic see Colangelo, Assouline, & Ambroson, 1992.

2 Klint & Weiss, 1986.

3 Getzels & Csikszentmihalyi, 1976. The longitudinal study on which this volume was based followed a group of about 300 young artists over a period of 20 years to find out what characteristics of art students predicted artistic success.

4 Hansen & Neujahr, 1976.

5 Stanley, Keating, & Fox, 1974.

6 O'Donnell & Andersen, 1977.

7 Bamberger, 1982.

8 Julian Stanley, from Johns Hopkins, and Camilla Benbow, now at Iowa State, have pioneered research on the development of mathematical talent, especially as it concerns gender differences. Of their many publications, one might cite Benbow, 1991; Benbow & Stanley, 1983; Stanley & Benbow, 1983.

9 Bamberger, 1986.

10 The theoretical model that describes the interaction of cultural domains, social fields, and talented individuals was first described in Csikszentmihalyi & Robinson, 1986.

11 Janos, 1990.

12 Stanley & Benbow, 1986, p. 368.

13 Albert & Runco, 1986; Rimm, 1991. The most detailed description of the

exhausting social support parents have to provide gifted children is given in Bloom, 1985.

14 Gardner, 1983.

15 Csikszentmihalyi, 1990b; Csikszentmihalyi & Robinson, 1986.

16 Carter & Ormrod, 1982.

17 Aliotti, 1981; Pivik, Bylsma, Busby, & Sawyer, 1982; Torrance, 1978.

18 Jenson, Cohn, & Cohn, 1989; Mohan & Jain, 1983.

19 Henderson & Gold, 1983; Marr & Sternberg, 1986; Terman, 1925; Thornburg, Adey, & Finnis, 1986.

20 Csikszentmihalyi, 1990c.

21 Goertzel & Goertzel, 1962.

22 Van Tassel-Baska, 1989.

23 Dunn, Putallaz, Sheppard, & Lindstrom, 1987.

24 Rathunde, 1988, 1989a,b, 1991b.

25 Albert & Runco, 1987; Green, Fine, & Tollefson, 1988; West, Hosie, & Mathews, 1989.

26 Bloom & Sosniak, 1981; Walberg, 1984. See Janos, 1990, for a review.

27 Csikszentmihalyi & McCormack, 1986. For the history of mathematics education in Budapest and the role that national competitions and inspired teachers played in training an entire generation of outstanding scientists and mathematicians, see Hersh & John-Steiner, in press.

28 Schlick, 1934.

29 Drake, 1978.

30 Chandrasekhar, 1987, p. 25.

31 Griessman, 1987, p. 133.

32 Deci & Ryan, 1985.

33 Amabile, 1983.

34 Dewey, 1913; Evans, 1971; Hidi, 1990; Hidi & Baird, 1986; Schiefele, 1988.

35 Carter, 1982; Cooke, 1980; Tamir & Lunetta, 1978.

36 Geffert, 1985.

37 Barrilleaux, 1961; Frandsen & Sorenson, 1969; Runco & Okuda, 1988; Schiefele, Winteler, & Krapp, 1991; Sjoberg, 1984; Subotnik, 1988a,b.

38 Weiss, 1990, p. 151.

39 Dossey, Mullis, Lindquist, & Chambers, 1988.

40 Csikszentmihalyi, 1988a,b, 1990c.

41 Csikszentmihalyi & Larson, 1984; Csikszentmihalyi & Nakamura, 1986, 1989; Mayers, 1978; Nakamura, 1988.

42 Buescher, 1987; Fimian & Cross, 1986; Galbraith, 1985.

43 Eccles & Midgely, 1989; Janos, 1990; Mayers, 1978; Redding, 1989.

44 Csikszentmihalyi & Csikszentmihalyi, 1988; Csikszentmihalyi & Larson,

1984, 1987; Csikszentmihalyi, Larson, & Prescott, 1977; deVries, 1992; Hormuth, 1986; Kubey & Csikszentmihalyi, 1990; Massimini & Inghilleri, 1986.

45 Csikszentmihalyi, 1978, 1990a; Hasher & Zacks, 1979; Hoffman, Nelson, & Houck, 1983; Kahneman, 1973; Simon, 1969, 1978.

46 Bertalanffy, 1968; Werner, 1957.

47 Olson, Sprenkle, & Russell, 1979.

48 MacIntyre, 1984, p. 160.

49 Csikszentmihalyi, 1975, 1990a.

50 Csikszentmihalyi & Csikszentmihalyi, 1988; Massimini & Inghilleri, 1986. The most extensive archive of flow interviews is the one at the Medical School of the University of Milan; it has been compiled by Professor Fausto Massimini and Dr. Antonella delle Fave and their team of researchers.

51 Csikszentmihalyi, 1990a; Rathunde, 1989a,b.

PART I

Talented teens

2
What is talent?

The term *talent* is steeped in biblical origins. It was a noun denoting a monetary unit, a valuable coin widely used in the Middle East. Its metaphorical meaning derives from the parable of the talents (Matthew 25), a section in the New Testament in which Jesus tells the story of a landowner who upon leaving for a long journey gives each of his three stewards some talents, "to every man according to his several ability," and enjoins them to put the money to good use. When the owner returns from his journey, he asks the stewards to account for the talents they had received. The first two had doubled the coins they received, whereas the third, who was afraid to lose the sum entrusted to him and who had hidden the talent he was given in a safe place, returns the coin to his master. The landowner praises the two stewards who made the most of their talents and scolds the one who simply preserved his.

Even though the culture in which we live has become largely secular, many elements of this parable still reflect our attitudes toward individual differences in ability. We believe that some people are given greater gifts than others: sharper wits, better memories, keener senses. Many also believe that it is not the size of the initial gift that counts, but what each person makes of it. A natural endowment that is not improved upon is wasted, as the opportunity to increase his talent was wasted by the last steward. Some of the concerns reflected in this ancient parable are still with us, and they have informed our study.

The research that resulted in this book involved a group of 208 outstanding students, each of whom was nominated by her or his teachers as having the promise of exceptional talent in one of five areas: art, athletics, mathematics, music, and science. We followed them from the first to the last year of high school. Our task was, first, to determine in what ways they differed from students whose talents were more ordinary. Second and most important, we wanted to find out what made some of these students improve on their native gifts and what made others "waste" theirs.

Experience suggests that a large proportion of the initial group were likely to abandon serious pursuit of their talent area during the 4 years of high school. Experts generally agree that if a young musician or a young scientist loses interest before the end of high school, it is very difficult for her or him to recapture the lost ground later.[1] Of course a promising musician who stops practicing and playing music may turn into a great banker or college president – thus developing an entirely different, and perhaps even more valuable, talent. But at least as far as musical talent is concerned, giving up practicing in late adolescence means giving up the musical talent.

We started our study from the assumption that the development of talent is one of the most important goals in the conservation of human resources. By understanding what makes talented youngsters unique and what contributes to disengagement from talent, we should be in a better position to improve the quality of both individual and social life. But where should we look for such understanding? Before attempting to answer this question, we need to take a closer look at what is meant by talent.

THE ELEMENTS OF TALENT

A basic feature of being human is our astonishing diversity. Some of us are born with genes that will make us grow tall; others are destined to stay relatively short. Some children can acquire perfect pitch without much effort; others never learn to carry a tune. Some are endowed from early childhood with superior spatial visualization; others are obviously athletic or double jointed or gifted with particularly fast reflexes. How such gifts are distributed remains a mystery. Inevitably they must originate with the genes of some ancestor, distant or recent; but in which particular child the ability will show up, in what strength, and in combination with what other traits is at this point utterly unpredictable. As far as the traits we inherit are concerned, chance rules.

This great diversity of potentials is part of the evolutionary strategy of the human race. If we were all more or less alike, humans would grow into narrowly specialized organisms. It would be difficult for us then to adapt to changing conditions, and the rate of cultural change would be much slower and more predictable. We cannot foresee at this point which traits will turn out to be essential next year or in the next generation. Perhaps short, tone-deaf, unathletic persons will be those best adapted to reap the opportunities of the next century and to save humanity from external dangers or from ourselves. Then again, perhaps not. Because the potentials required by future conditions are forever changing, a diverse pool of traits from which to choose as the occasion arises has been the way human evolution has prepared itself for the unpredictable challenges of the future. Diversity is the built-in creative potential of our species.

The common attitude people hold toward "talent" or "giftedness" – such as a very high IQ or a prodigious musical ability – is that these traits are natural advantages with which some individuals had the good fortune to be born. But talent is not a natural category. Talent is a social construction: It is a label of approval we place on traits that have a positive value in the particular context in which we live. In some cultures, epilepsy is considered a divine gift; in others, people who are overweight are admired. In our culture – one increasingly dependent on the manipulation of symbolic information – intellectual skills, especially those that tend toward logic and quantification, are considered valuable talents.

It is useful at this point to introduce some terminology that will help clarify what talent is. We can think of it as being made up of three elements: individual *traits*, which are partly inherited and partly developed as a person grows up; cultural *domains*, which refer to systems of rules that define certain ranges of performance as meaningful and valuable; and social *fields*, made up of people and institutions whose task is to decide whether a certain performance is to be considered valuable or not.

For instance, it would be impossible for a young person to become a talented mathematician, no matter how skilled he or she was in the mental manipulation of relationships and quantities, unless exposed to the domain – to the axioms, rules, and procedures we know as mathematics.

Nor would this person be recognized as talented unless her or his performance was evaluated by individuals and institutions whose expertise in the matter was accepted by society at large.

A good example is the case of the Indian mathematician Ramanujan, who in the 1930s astounded the world with his genius. Ramanujan was born and grew up in a part of India where the domain of mathematics was not highly developed and where the field was not looking for new talent. He was fortunate to have been exposed to the domain sufficiently to be able to express his skills in an acceptable, if idiosyncratic, mathematical form. Working on his own, he rediscovered proofs and theorems that other mathematicians had previously formulated. Had he stayed home, all one would know of him was that he showed a great deal of promise. However, Ramanujan sent some of his calculations to G. H. Hardy, an eminent British mathematician of the day and hence a powerful figure in the field. Hardy decided that Ramanujan had extraordinary talent. He arranged a fellowship for him at Cambridge and when Ramanujan arrived there, mentored him until the full potential of his skill was developed. The rest is history: We now know Ramanujan as one of the greatest mathematical talents of the century instead of as a promising dilettante. What made the difference between fame and obscurity had nothing to do with innate traits. It was that he succeeded in attracting the support of the field, was introduced to the latest developments in the domain, and was allowed to contribute to it.

So although traits that could potentially lead to eminence in a domain may be biologically constituted, their recognition as talents is socially constructed with reference to the particular needs and values of a culture. A child with the skills of a superior scientist cannot be recognized as talented except in a culture where scientific domains are well developed and where the gatekeepers to the field of science are actively looking for new talent. Among the Eskimos, who lack the tradition of painting, a child born with great sensitivity to color will not be recognized as having that talent. Athletic skills are considered to be a talent in the United States much more so than in Western Europe, and they were most highly prized in what used to be known as the Eastern Bloc countries, where the symbolic propaganda value of superior physical performance was of great importance.

At present, it is customary to call talented those children with an IQ in the top 3% or the top 5% of the IQ range. This assumes that a high IQ score signifies an all-purpose, abstract cognitive skill that can be applied to superior performance in any field, or at least in the more academic domains. Although there is no question that a general cognitive ability – something like Spearman's g factor – underlies accomplishment in many domains, it is also clear that in our culture we have exaggerated the importance of this abstract rational ability and enthroned it as some sort of superdomain that takes precedence over all others. Performance on IQ tests has become a domain in its own right, whether or not such performance has any consequences in other areas of life; and the testing industry has become a powerful field advocating its importance.

We are not interested in entering the argument over IQ testing, either pro or con. In this book we are going to explore talent almost exclusively as defined in terms of performance in some concrete domain – specifically mathematics, science, music, art, and athletics. In some of these domains, especially the first two, intelligence as measured by IQ tests is sure to play a major role. But intelligence per se does not interest us; the question we are looking to answer is what facilitates the development of individuals skills, of whatever kind, into talents that can be used in a meaningful sociocultural context.

WHY IS THE DEVELOPMENT OF TALENT IMPORTANT?

Folk wisdom holds that "talent will out"; in other words, we shouldn't worry about supporting individuals who show promise in certain domains, because if they are truly talented they will express their gifts regardless of help or hindrance. As we stated earlier, we take the opposite position, on both empirical and ontological grounds. In other words, we claim not only that potential talent often remains unexpressed, but also that the very concept of talent is meaningless except in a context of cultural forms and social recognition.

In terms of empirical evidence, Benjamin Bloom has shown how great an investment of resources is needed to nurture promising children until they are accepted by a field as talented.[2] The parents of a child with a musical gift, for instance, must spend great amounts of time and money finding tutors, teachers, and coaches; they must both provide transportation and chaperone the child through practices, rehearsals, competitions, and performances; and above all, they must find ways of sustaining disciplined involvement without alienating the child with too much pressure or too high expectations. Similar supports are involved in the development of any other talent. When the child's abilities are truly prodigious, parental and social investments need to be prodigious as well.[3]

Thus talent is best viewed as a *developmental* rather than as an all-or-nothing phenomenon. It is a process that unfolds over many years rather than a trait that one inherits and then keeps unchanged for the rest of life. Children are talented only in the sense of future potential; to fulfill that potential, they will have to learn to perform to state-of-the-art standards and will have to find opportunities for using their talent after their skills are developed. Historical conditions always affect the flowering of talent. Sometimes a given field will get social support and attract promising talent to it; a few years later that support may be withdrawn, and then even a prodigy will be unable to find a job and develop her or his talent to the fullest.

For example, these days many very able young physicists with PhDs from the best universities are underemployed because their talents, which a few decades ago would have been at a premium, are not absorbed by the laboratories that once would have given them an opportunity to do research and establish a reputation. In addition, there is a feeling abroad that theoretical physics is not as exciting as it was a few decades ago, and thus it may attract fewer potentially able students in the first place. Many bright young people who a generation earlier would have gone into medicine are now deterred by the high cost of medical insurance and by the dismal conditions in the urban hospitals that offer residencies. The simple point is that potential talent cannot be realized unless it is embedded in a cultural domain and unless it is socially nurtured until it is recognized as a genuine contribution by a field and permitted to unfold.

But why do we need to worry about nurturing talent in the first place? Is this a responsibility of society? Is there a collective benefit from the development of talent? These questions are difficult to answer, first, because they involve value-laden ideological issues, and, second, because the evidence required to answer them factually is lacking. We do not know, for example, whether the United States as a whole, or any of us individually, will actually be better off if all the children with mathematical gifts have the chance to develop them into full-blown talent.

Our position is that helping talents develop will result in long-term benefits both at the individual and at the societal level. At the individual level, it is difficult to argue that a person will be better off *not* developing her or his potentials to the fullest. It is true that a person with a great artistic talent may lead a quieter and more contented life as an average person than if he or she went on to develop those artistic skills and competed for scarce recognition. Yet from Aristotle to today, the consensus seems to be that even though the Muse may drive one to drink, drugs, and distraction, it is still better to listen to her voice than to ignore it. Not to hone skills we possess leads to regrets that can poison the rest of life.

At the societal level, the benefits of nurturing talent are even more evident. Occasionally the entire nation becomes aware of this. The importance of training in science and mathematics was much talked about in 1957 after the Soviets launched the first earth satellite, and again in the 1980s when Japanese technology appeared to have overtaken U.S. supremacy. Unfortunately, so far all the uproar has led to little actual improvement. Although at the very highest levels U.S. students perform as well as students of any other nation, and the nation still wins its share of Nobel prizes, average U.S. students, in comparative studies of math and science performance, consistently get mediocre to dismal scores when compared with average students from other nations.[4] The authors of a recent series of comparative studies of mathematical abilities conclude:

The deficiencies displayed by the American children were more serious than we expected. There was no area in which they were competitive with the children from Japan and Taiwan, whether in computation, speed, or the application of mathematical principles. . . . The situation did not improve between the first and fifth grades. Indeed, the status of the American children relative to the Chinese and Japanese children deteriorated.[5]

The urgency of nurturing athletic talent is usually recognized after each set of Olympic games when U.S. teams return with a disappointingly meager collection of medals compared with such countries as Germany and the former Soviet Union. To many, the development of traditional musical talent is seen as imperative because of the fact that so many of the great conductors and soloists employed in the United States are foreign-born. As for other artistic talent, its preservation rarely makes the list of national priorities; yet this too is occasionally seen as an important social goal, if for no other reason than to keep up with the niceties of other civilizations.

From a more general viewpoint based on an evolutionary perspective, it is a good strategy for any human group to develop fully as many of the skills of its individual members as possible – limited only by the bare necessities of survival. In other words, after a society takes care of what is needed to continue physical existence, the next most useful goal in which to invest resources is the development of individual gifts. A group that followed these priorities would be in the best position to evolve further, and it would face the future with the best chances for success.

It might be relatively easy to agree with this position as long as the gifts to be developed included mainly those we find currently useful, such as engineering or entrepreneurial skills. But the evolutionary perspective suggests a more radical conclusion: that every potential ability, no matter how esoteric it may appear at present, and as long as it is not clearly criminal or antisocial, should be nurtured in case it turns out to contribute to our future adaptation. In the next century the most important benefits to humankind may come from art, music, or philosophy rather than from technology. It would be short-sighted not to develop the talent of young people in these fields because right now these fields do not seem essential. One thing evolution teaches is that to take the present too seriously leaves one unprepared for the future.

THE DEVELOPMENT OF TALENT

Advancing the domain

If talent consists in an exceptional ability to perform by the rules of a recognized domain according to criteria set up by a relevant field, how can we encourage its development? There are at least three ways to do so. The first consists in changing some characteristics of the domain. For instance, as long as there was no accepted code for counting and for expressing quantities, even the potentially most talented mathematician could not be recognized as such. Only after numeracy rules were first formalized by the ancient Egyptians, Mesopotamians, and Greeks did it become possible for bright young people to demonstrate their skills in mathematics and to be recognized as talented in it. Architectural talent was not recognized in Europe until the 1400s, when Renaissance scholars rediscovered and formalized the rules for building in a systematic fashion. To take another example closer to us in time, before the invention of the motion picture camera there could not have been gifted film directors and cinematographers, because the entire domain of movies was yet to come.

Whenever a domain is rationalized, it becomes easier to measure performance in it and therefore to recognize promising talent. It is easier to tell talent in chess than in math, in math than in music, in music than in art, in art than in moral excellence – without for a moment implying that chess is somehow better or more important than moral excellence. It is just that the rules of chess deal with a very restricted domain; thus they are clearly structured, making it easier to recognize who performs best by them.

Academic domains are constantly being restructured by educators in the hope that the various subjects will become more easily accessible to students. Textbooks are revised, computers are enrolled in the teaching process, nationwide testing is instituted, the "new math" and its equivalents are painfully developed – all efforts to rationalize the content of domains for easier teaching. One of the consequences of such rationalization is that talent in such areas becomes easier to detect, nurture, and support.

Strengthening the fields

A second approach to the development of talent is to increase the field's ability to stimulate, recognize, and reward performance in a given domain. This strategy can be implemented in many different ways: by increasing the budget allocated to a given domain, by including the domain in the required curriculum, by creating more jobs in the field, and in general by increasing its visibility and prestige.

Whenever resources are funneled into a given domain, it will attract able young people who otherwise may choose a different career. For instance, the incredible flowering of the arts in 15th-century Florence occurred in large part because the wealthy bankers of the city decided to transform it into a "new Athens." The leading citizens sponsored competitions for works of art ranging from the enormous dome of the cathedral to the doors of the Baptistry, from statues to frescoes, from the building of palaces and churches to bridges. These competitions were taken very seriously by the entire community and were closely juried, and the winning artists were handsomely rewarded. This extraordinary focusing of attention on the arts attracted to artistic careers young men who otherwise would have become lawyers or bankers.[6] The Renaissance did not take place because central Italy by some genetic fluke suddenly produced a great number of biologically gifted artists. It happened because the field of art became infused with unprecedented resources.

Of course it is not only money and status that draw talent to a field. Certain fields at certain points in time develop a mystique that many young people find hard to resist. Marine biology, artificial intelligence, and environmental law are some current examples of glamorous fields. Whatever domain deals with state-of-the-art ideas or concerns becomes a door to the future and as such develops an almost magnetic attraction for young people eager to be in the forefront of progress. Finally, some domains provide more intrinsic rewards than others. Such a domain will not need much support from a field. For instance, the arts – painting, music, literature, dance, drama – will find talented young practitioners even when the external resources invested in them are minimal, simply because doing them is enjoyable and can provide a personally meaningful way of expressing deep emotions and of handling conflicts.

Therefore much can be done in the line of developing talent in a given area by altering the parameters of the field: by investing more social energies – money and attention – in it. Money alone is usually not sufficient. Just offering additional prizes and scholarships in math, for example, is not likely to attract more potentially talented young people. The critical attention of teachers, competition judges, journal editors, and other experts who monitor the performance of young mathematicians is also essential. There also has to be a realistic expectation that there will be attractive professional roles for mathematicians to fill once they finish their training.

The development of individual skills

Rationalizing the structure of a domain and increasing the resources of the field are important ways of developing the frequency and intensity of individual talent in a society. The third main way to affect this development is through the individuals themselves. After all, the importance of domains and fields notwithstanding, in the last analysis it is the people involved who must enact the superior performance we call talent.

There is not much at present that can be done to improve the biological substratum of talent. The possibility of breeding people for exceptional performance has often been considered, but no known society has had the nerve to implement a consistent eugenic policy directed at the improvement of talent – even though in many cultures various forms of endogamy may in fact have had this as a side effect. Whether we like it or not, with advances in genetic engineering it will soon be possible to change a person's physical and mental potential in the direction of superior skills in some specific domain. When that day comes, our descendants will be faced with some difficult choices we have been fortunate to be spared.

In the meantime, however, even though people can do little – and probably should do little even if they could – to improve the genetic stock, there are other ways to help the development of innate skills. Training is an obvious example. Entire nations – France in the 19th century, Germany before World War II, and currently Japan – have achieved outstanding success in science by taking primary and secondary education seriously and by supporting talented youth as if they were an important national resource. Even single high schools have become legendary for nurturing outstanding talent in a variety of domains. There is no question that schools can make a great difference in whether talent will flower or remain latent.

The family milieu is another crucial determinant. Potential talent can easily be sidetracked if the child experiences too much deprivation, conflict, or neglect on the part of parents. If the parental culture discourages abstract thought, it will be hard for a child to take an abstract domain seriously. Parents of children who show signs of talent in one of the arts generally discourage their offspring from entering a field that in our culture offers so few material rewards.

Even these few examples provide grounds for a generalization about what it takes to nurture individual traits into talent. The first is *information:* This is what supportive families and good schools provide. Without the knowledge-tools of the domain, potential cannot be actualized. The second is *motivation,* which is affected in part by the encouragement and support of the field and of the family. Unless a person wants to pursue the

difficult path that leads to the development of talent, neither innate potential nor all the knowledge in the world will suffice. The third requirement
is *discipline,* or the set of habits that allows a person to study and concentrate on a domain long enough to develop the skills required for superior
performance.

In the research that resulted in this volume, it is these last two dimensions that have been the central focus. We believe that little is known
about what makes a young person motivated enough to develop discipline
in an area of talent, and that, as a result, a great deal of potentially
valuable human talent is wasted in every generation. If we learn more,
perhaps we can slow down this brain drain that becomes more and more
dangerous as we move further into the age of information.

In dealing with the development of habits and motives alone, we are
forced to exclude from our purview essential questions of social equity.
There is no question that the development of talent on a national level
could be greatly accelerated and widened if access to domains were more
evenly distributed, and if fields were equipped to support the skills of
young people from a diversity of backgrounds. This book, however, will
ignore these issues and focus instead on how talent develops in a group of
relatively advantaged, mostly middle-class American teenagers, in the
hope of detecting general trends that will be applicable under other societal conditions as well. We are not neglecting social equity and the politi-
cal issues involved in the nurturing of talent because we think they are not
important. In fact, these issues are essential, and society must face up to
them sooner or later. But no single volume could do justice to all the
dimensions involved in the development of talent, and we opted for examining those we are trained to understand, namely, the more psychological
aspects of the problem.

But even though the external conditions of this sample are typical only
of a Midwestern semisuburban community and therefore cannot be generalized to apply to students from other cultures and social classes, it is
our contention that the psychological processes of these talented teenagers – the dynamics of attention and motivation – are panhuman and
will not vary greatly across time and space.[7]

We believe the main psychological process that leads from personal
skills to the mastering of a talent is not specific to domains, such as music

or mathematics; rather it is a mind-set necessary for the acquisition of talent in general. As such, it consists in a set of *metaskills* we expect must be present in order to realize one's talent. These metaskills include the development of complex attentional structures, or the ability to approach tasks with curiosity and concentration; the achievement of emotional autonomy, so that teenagers will tolerate the solitude necessary to cultivate their talent; and the ability to enjoy the activities relevant to their talent, so that intrinsic as well as extrinsic rewards will motivate teenagers to continue on their difficult quest.

One often hears in conversation with eminent people who know their field that talent is cheap. What they mean is that high intelligence and domain-related skills are much more common than one would think from the small number of people who actually succeed in developing them into a workable talent. Relatively few potentially talented musicians, artists, and mathematicians master these domains to the fullest extent of their capacity. When they grow to be adults, many of the musically gifted will still play some instrument as a hobby, having abandoned any ambition to perfect their skills; most individuals gifted in the visual arts will at best either teach art or work in advertising or industrial art; and the gifted mathematicians, if they are lucky, will find a job in some related field, working with computers, as actuarials, or in banking. Why does potential talent so seldom fulfill its promise?

In part the answer is simple and does not depend on personal traits but on the social realities that constrain fields. If there are not enough jobs and no opportunities to enact a role related to the domain, potential talent will often be insufficient to create viable careers. Each society has a limit to how many opportunities it can offer in any given area. According to census figures, close to a quarter million people in the United States claim to be artists, yet probably not one in a hundred among them can live exclusively on what can be earned from the sale of their work – not because they lack skills, originality, and determination, but simply because there is no market for their talent. There just aren't enough outlets where their work can be seen and appreciated, and there isn't a large enough audience to pay attention to what they do. Many successful painters ruefully admit that the difference between them and the hundreds of artistic "failures" is not greater talent but contacts and accidental events that created visibility for their work – in short, blind chance. In most domains, Saint Matthew's words "For many are called, but few are chosen" ring all too true.

Individual characteristics also help determine whether people will or will not develop their talent. Holding luck and other extraneous advantages constant, when a field can provide only a few openings they are likely to go to those who have the motivation and the discipline to take advantage of the opportunities. A young man or woman who really enjoys the domain and who has enough psychic energy disposable to invest in learning its rules is likely to persevere until an opening presents itself. In reporting an analysis of a longitudinal study of talented young artists, Jeanne Carney found that intrinsic motivation was an important trait for artistic success.[8] Art students who were primarily motivated by money or fame usually gave up trying to become artists unless they were immediately successful after graduation. If they did not start selling their paintings within a few years after leaving school, they found some more secure career, such as real estate, plumbing, or running a car dealership. The students who were primarily motivated by the creative experience itself, on the other hand, continued to paint or sculpt even if they received minimal recognition. After a time, some of them – but by no means all – began to be appreciated by critics, gallery owners, and collectors. In other domains of talent as well, luck favors those who are prepared, namely, those who are motivated and who have developed the disciplined habits of work that the domain requires.

FLOW AND THE DEVELOPMENT OF TALENT

In many previous studies we have found that when people experience flow, they will tend to repeat whatever it takes to produce the experience, for the sole reason that it is so enjoyable.[9] Such intrinsically rewarding flow experiences can be found in sports; games; religious practices and rituals; artistic activities like singing, dancing, and theater; and so forth. But almost any activity can produce flow and therefore be intrinsically rewarding. Work, caring for a child, or solving a mathematical problem can be so enjoyable that one keeps on doing it for as long as possible.[10] One of the essential conditions for flow to occur is that the opportunities for action in a situation match the person's capacity to act; that is, when challenges and skills are in balance, the activity becomes its own reward. Thus if a teenager succeeds in experiencing flow when involved in the domain of a talent, he or she will not only keep on learning and improving, but will enjoy doing so. The development of talent will have become intrinsically rewarding.

But the path toward the unfolding of talent is not an easy one. Instead of joyful development, what teenagers experience all too often is anxiety over excessive challenges or boredom when challenges are too few. Under such conditions of imbalance, they become increasingly alienated from their talent. It is no longer fun, and less and less time is devoted to it. New interests attract their psychic energy: some purposeful, some leading nowhere. Motivation and complexity decrease together; as the performance of talent becomes less enjoyable, the former challenges are no longer attractive, and skills deteriorate. The gifted teen loses interest, and the talent eventually is "wasted."

The talented students we interviewed varied greatly in terms of how much delight they found in the exercise of their gifts. Although their mental abilities were very similar, some felt pressured by parents and teachers to do what they were so good at doing, whereas others thought they were very fortunate to be able to use their gift. Some students were self-confident in their math ability, but others believed that they were not smart enough. A few put up with classes they thought were boring in order to get a useful degree; others could hardly wait to be in class. Each student had an individual perspective on her or his talent. Nevertheless a few basic differences cut across the great individual variety. Some examples might give a preliminary idea of how these teenagers thought about their talents.

A few quick sketches

Marla is an excellent student, nominated in science, math, and music. She likes biology and has future dreams about "going to Sea World and training porpoises," but her more realistic intention is to "hang around a hospital" so she can marry a doctor. She wants to have "a beautiful husband and kids, a home out in California, the easy life." The reason for taking science courses seems to be mainly extrinsic: praise from parents and teachers and a good ticket to the future. The only intrinsic reason for studying biology is that lab work can be fun when she can do things her own way and get them right.

Rachel is also a very talented young scientist, who wants to pursue a career in biology working with animals because "I always liked animals more than people. I thought they were better than people." She has always felt ostracized by the other children in school, and now she thinks of herself as a loner. The reason she liked seventh-grade chemistry was that she kept blowing things up and scaring the teacher. Rachel also does a lot of writing in order to relax and escape from a boring reality, but much of it is depressing and "death-oriented."

Like many other math-talented students, Sheila enjoys doing mathematics because of the challenge of figuring out problems, because "it has, like, definite answers." She would like to "be a biologist or something, or an archeologist," but her main goals are to make good friends and get married to a handsome guy ("It'd be nice if he's rich"). In describing how it feels when working on math is enjoyable, Sheila gives a good – if somewhat circular – description of the flow experience: "I feel like I'm being challenged. When it's too easy, you know, you don't really care for it. And when it's too hard, you don't care for it either. But if it's challenging, it's not too hard."

Greg is highly talented in music and math; his main concern is not to be too closely identified with the other math-talented students, who are all "weird," carry books with them everywhere, and act as if they know everything. He likes music because many of his friends also play in the orchestra, and they went on a tour of Europe last year. He started playing the French horn in fourth grade "because it looked so awkward, so interesting. Everything else looked very simple; the horn looked interesting." He is also taking advanced geometry in freshman year: "It's very easy. I like it; it's fun. I like all the rules. It's much more precise than music, which is imprecise."

Sal enjoys drawing and painting mainly because he is so good at it and many of his peers envy his talent. He hopes to have a successful career because he likes "nice cars and I love nice clothes." Emily likes to draw because "I always used to draw, like, everything. I did it probably 'cause I liked doing it. I just liked making people happy, I guess." Drawing "feels kinda like a magical kind of thing – when you draw something and you make it come out nice and everything. I enjoy doing that."

Susan was nominated in math, science, and music. Her scientific interest started in fifth grade with an archeological trip when she became fascinated with the scientists' ability to reconstruct the past from a few material clues. Now she enjoys doing lab experiments because "what gets me really interested is that you can predict what's going to happen," and she enjoys math because "I like the challenge of having to find the correct answer to something. What I also like about math is that you can relate other subjects to it. Even in an abstract way, everything at one point relates back to math." In music Susan particularly enjoys giving vocal concerts, "because it's something you have worked for, and you're giving to the audience, and you think it's very good." Susan plans to combine a career in science and business, because she would like to "have an impact on how things actually work." But at present her main goal is "to learn to like myself, because I'm always down on myself."

These 7 students are similar to the rest only in that each is so very different from the others. If we were to present excerpts from the interviews with the other 201 students, they would all seem in some sense unique. Yet even among these 7, it is possible to discern what might be important trends in the future development of talent. Some of these teenagers appear not to derive any particular joy from investing psychic energy in the domain. Doing math or art or music is for them not in itself rewarding. The reasons are all external ones: praise, pressure, expectation of future rewards. Other teenagers, however, like Sheila, Greg, Emily, and Susan in the sketches above, seem to derive a great deal of pleasure just from acting in the domain.

Our theory suggests that to keep young people involved in the difficult task of developing talent, it is essential for them to find rewards in what the domain requires. It is very hard for a teenager to keep studying physics if she cannot enjoy it, if she finds it boring or frustrating. The study that follows will pay particular attention to whether high school students can or cannot find flow in their studies, and why. From what we learn about this question, we hope to extract knowledge that will help us understand better how gifted young people negotiate the difficult years of adolescence, when so much promise is frittered away without a trace.

CONCLUSION

Whether a young person gifted with outstanding skills will grow into a talented performer in a domain depends on many unrelated factors. Some of them have to do with the culture: for instance, the availability and diffusion of knowledge and expertise. Other factors have to do with such societal variables as available resources and the amount of attention and encouragement the field can bestow. Much also depends on the social milieu into which the person happens to be born: the racial, ethnic, and economic class of origin. Luck also plays a large role: the kind of contacts one makes, the mentors one meets, and the unexpected opportunities that happen to come one's way.

There are also the personal qualities that contribute to the realization of talent. A person has no control over some of these: genetic contributions to intelligence, to special skills, and to temperament, for example. But there are also the traits where the individual can make some difference. These include the development of appropriate attentional structures, habits of concentration, and personality and motivational patterns.

We cannot increase the inborn gifts of our children, and as individuals we can do little to alter the cultural and societal parameters that affect the unfolding of talent. But if we understood better those elements of the equation over which we have some measure of control, we might be able to protect and nurture the unique human potentials that young people in our families, schools, and communities possess. This is the task we have set for the present volume: to chart the development of a group of gifted adolescents through high school in an effort to understand how personality, habit, and motivation help to retain their involvement in an area of talent.

NOTES

1 Bamberger, 1986; Benbow & Stanley, 1983.
2 Bloom, 1985.
3 David Feldman (1986), of Tufts University, is perhaps the only psychologist to have followed with repeated observations a group of "prodigies," i.e., children whose mental abilities are so far out of the ordinary as to challenge our generally accepted notions of cognitive development.

4 McKnight et al., 1987.

5 Stigler, Lee, & Stevenson, 1990, p. 25. A series of publications by the National Assessment of Educational Progress, based on extensive testing of 20,000 schoolchildren across the USA, keeps reporting unbelievable findings about what students don't know. For instance, the latest survey found that only 51% of eighth graders knew that the sun rises in the east and sets in the west (Jones et al., 1992).

6 Csikszentmihalyi, 1988a.

7 A good summary of the many studies on this topic is in Csikszentmihalyi & Csikszentmihalyi, 1988.

8 Carney, 1986.

9 The first complete description of the flow experience and its links to motivation was given in the volume *Beyond Boredom and Anxiety* (Csikszentmihalyi, 1975). For later developments in flow theory, see Csikszentmihalyi, 1982, 1985, 1990a; Csikszentmihalyi & Csikszentmihalyi, 1988; Inghilleri, 1986.

10 Csikszentmihalyi & Csikszentmihalyi, 1988; Csikszentmihalyi & LeFevre, 1989.

3

How the study was conducted: Methods and procedures

To anyone but the dedicated scholar, the methods sections of books and articles are not usually of pressing interest. Yet it is difficult to evaluate the conclusions of an empirical study unless the reader knows how the various abstractions that the authors mention were operationalized and measured. What do we mean by "talent" in this volume? How did we measure development? These and many other questions of a more technical nature are dealt with in this chapter, as briefly as possible yet in as much detail as necessary. We particularly invite readers to familiarize themselves with the basic workings of the study's primary data source, the Experience Sampling Method.

SELECTING THE TALENTED SAMPLES

Much has changed since the days when the IQ test was taken as the only "objective" measure of ability and academic achievement was for all practical purposes the sole focus of serious research. Recent theories increasingly view the expression of talent as a convergence of personal capacities with meaningful structures of accessible information (domain) and a social context (the field) that defines superior performance. In more dynamic terms, individuals may be born able, but they become talented only as their aptitudes are filtered through and socialized within the historically determined standards of particular fields. Adolescence is a period of life crucial to this passage from raw ability to socially mediated talent. Even more than gifted children, talented teenagers must face choices about how much time to invest in the development of their abilities, and about how much they will care about success in particular fields. Gone is the time when others could make such decisions for them.

The shift in research focus from raw aptitude and objective ability to a stance that recognizes and incorporates the social construction of talent has had a liberating influence on recent research into giftedness and creativity. On the one hand, this shift has broadened the intensive and systematic study of talent development into a number of previously neglected ability areas, such as dance, music, and art.[1] These arenas of action are studied increasingly on their own terms, with attention focused on the neurological and psychological propensities of the individuals involved, as well as the peculiar structures of the fields and domains within which individuals must learn to participate. On the other hand, this broadened research agenda has raised the possibility of a comparative science of individual talent development, informed by insights from a wide variety of areas.

But although these new departures pose exciting possibilities, they also raise vexing methodological questions. Primary among these are the questions that must be addressed at the outset of any study in this area: Who will be deemed talented? How will these individuals be identified? What sorts of evidence should be weighted most heavily – test scores, grades, expert judgments – when we search out the talented in specific fields?

In response to these questions, many investigators have proposed multidimensional models of talent identification. These models often incorporate a range of criteria, including indicators of personal motivation and attitudes and demonstrated accomplishments and potential creativity.[2] As research strategies, these models attempt wherever possible to synthesize judgments of informed members of the field, such as teachers and experienced practitioners, with "objective" evidence of superior performance and potential excellence.

A general strategy for identifying talent, however, can be suggested only after considering the broader research aims. Some studies may call for heavy dependence on standardized indexes of superior ability. Excellence in mathematical problem solving, for instance, may be best identified by standardized tests, independent of average school grades. Other talent areas may call for much closer attention to the patterns of interaction between learner and teacher, and thus rely more on the opinions of those adults who give young people their first taste of competent activity in specific domains.

A closely related problem in talent identification, which also depends upon the broader aims of the research at hand, is the question of where and when to study talent: that is, its social and psychological contexts. A number of studies of talent in mathematics and music, for example, have focused on specialized environments such as math camps or music camps, which limit nontalent-related distractions and allow complete concentration. Such contexts often provide invaluable opportunities to witness and chronicle the unfolding learning process under controlled conditions. But such contexts are less informative about the course that talent takes when faced with the distractions and pressures of everyday life. Perhaps because the schedules of preadolescent children are more amenable to control, the majority of talent studies also have tended to concentrate on these children, whose lives have yet to be complicated by the social and sexual transformations of puberty. For just this reason, fewer studies explore adolescent talent development in contexts in which all the diverse challenges facing the average teenager are in play. As greater emphasis is placed on the early identification of exceptional talent, adolescence has tended to become peripheral to the mainstream of interest in the literature of talent development.

As may be guessed, we do not subscribe to the belief that adolescence comes too late to alter the development of talent significantly. In our view, adolescence is the time when most persons first make critical decisions about how to allocate their own limited resources of attention and about what is most worth doing. No matter how thorough a child's training or how distinguished her or his performance, adolescence poses a fresh battery of social, psychological, and intellectual challenges to the smooth course of talent development.[3] It is the task of this book to throw light on the experience of talent in the context of the full range of adolescent life. In choosing a selection strategy, then, we searched for high schools and communities that offer rich opportunities for the exploration of a diverse range of interests yet also qualify as "normal" American adolescent settings.

The two suburban high schools chosen for this study were admirably suited to this purpose. Both possess statewide and, indeed, national reputations, with faculties that are often taken as models by other school systems. At the same time, both schools are quite large (more than 4,000 pupils) and located in communities with the full range of problems and pleasures that make up teenage life. Within each school, we pursued a mixed strategy of talent identification, balancing where possible standardized measures of student ability with teacher assessments of short- and long-term potential. In this way, we hoped to identify adolescents who possessed a superior grasp of their domains and who had impressed well-informed teachers as capable of full adult participation in their respective fields.

More specifically, in each talent area we first restricted the selection pool to 9th and 10th graders in accelerated or advanced classes. From this group, the teachers nominated subgroups of students who they felt possessed the potential to pursue talent development to superior levels of proficiency in their fields. Using this approach, a total of 394 students were nominated in the five areas of talent – mathematics, science, music, athletics, and art. Of these, 309 students (78%) were selected as talented in one talent area only, and 85 (22%) were nominated in two or more areas. This yielded a total of 505 talent nominations (including multiple nominations) from the two schools. Of this pool of nominees, 208 (53%) completed all aspects of the project's first phase of data collection in a reliable manner: 92 males and 116 females. All nominations in math, science, and athletics came from School 1. Musicians were drawn from both schools, and School 2 provided all the art nominees. Table 3.1 summarizes the distribution of the final sample across schools, sex, and high school year. Each talent area, of course, required some variation on this basic selection procedure, and we turn briefly to a discussion of these procedures.

Mathematics

Teachers in School 1 were asked to nominate those students who possessed the greatest natural ability and career potential in mathematics, from all freshman and sophomore math students in honors-level courses. From accelerated algebra, geometry, and trigonometry classes, 132 students were nominated: 68 girls and 64 boys. This group represented approximately the top 7% of all 9th and 10th graders in mathematics in School 1. Of this group, 68 students, 29 males and 39 females, agreed to

Table 3.1. *Summary of final talented teen sample across talent areas by sex, school, and year in high school (N = 208)*

	Grade 9		Grade 10		
	Male	Female	Male	Female	Total
No. of nominees					
Single talent	31	39	36	49	155
Multiple talents	9	8	16	20	53
	40	47	52	69	208
No. of nominations					
In mathematics (School 1)	12	14	17	25	68
In science (School 1)	10	7	11	19	47
In music (School 1)	9	17	14	21	61
In music (School 2)	6	4	4	4	18
In athletics (School 1)	12	9	17	20	58
In art (School 2)	6	3	9	10	28
	55	54	72	99	280

join the project and completed its initial phase. Of these, 26 were nominated in mathematics only, and 43 were nominated in other talent areas as well. All nominated students were working at a level at least 1 year ahead of their average classmates' introductory (freshman) algebra or (sophomore) geometry classes. Placement in these advanced classes was based upon demonstrated mastery of advanced junior high school algebra, along with superior standardized test performances. In addition, a large number of those nominated had attended the high school's introductory algebra classes as junior high school students and were well known to the nominating instructors. Within this group, a subgroup was also involved in mathematics competitions with other regional high schools.

Science

The selection process closely resembled the one for mathematics. Teachers in the science faculty of School 1 were asked to nominate, from a pool of freshman and sophomore honors-level science students, those students who possessed the greatest academic ability and career potential in science.

From accelerated biology and chemistry classes, 76 students were nominated: 40 boys and 36 girls. These students represented approximately the top 8% of the 9th and 10th graders in science from School 1. Of this group, 47 students, 21 boys and 26 girls, joined the project and completed the initial phase of the study. Of these, 11 were nominated in science only, and 36 were nominated in other talent areas as well. All science nominees were working at a level at least 1 year ahead of average freshmen in introductory science or average sophomores in biology classes.

Music

Teachers in the award-winning music departments of both high schools were asked to nominate those freshmen and sophomores who in their opinion possessed sufficient ability to pursue music as part of a career. Subjects had to be full-time performers in one or more of the school's auditioned vocal or instrumental ensembles. There were 123 nominees, 51 boys and 72 girls. Of these, 79 (33 males and 46 females) joined the project and completed the first phase of the study. Many of these students had participated in the highly regarded pre-high-school dramatics and music programs of both schools, and a number had remained active in music and drama as well as doing ensemble work. A strong subgroup within the sample was already engaged in professional performance outside of school hours.

Athletics

The school that provided the sample of student athletes has a regional and statewide reputation as an athletic powerhouse. During the period when our sample was enrolled (1984–9), this school competed in the final rounds of state championship tournaments no fewer than 20 times and won state and regional championships in such highly competitive sports as swimming, baseball, football, soccer, volleyball, basketball, tennis, and wrestling. Every year a high percentage of its athletes are sought by colleges with nationally competitive athletics programs, and these students have gone on to be very successful.

Coaches were requested to nominate those student athletes who in their opinion possessed the talent to compete successfully in their sport on the collegiate or professional level. The coaches nominated 127 athletes, 72 males and 55 females. Of these, 58 (29 males and 29 females) representing excellence in a wide range of sports available through the school completed the first phase of the study. Many of these athletes had participated in pre-high-school athletic programs offered by the high school and the surrounding community and were already well known to the coaching staff. Of the final 58 students, 38 were nominated in athletics only, and 20 were nominated in other talent areas too.

Art

Of the five domains examined in this study, the criteria for identifying talent in art are the most subjective by nature and the most difficult to define operationally. Adolescent artists, even the best, typically have yet to exhibit their work in public and submit it to expert judgment. High school art courses often are tailored to the pace of individual development and do not provide a ready measure of natural ability. In finding superior art students, then, we were particularly dependent on the informed judgment of instructors familiar with the work of their students. The art department that provided our sample is considered to be among the finest and most innovative in Illinois. The high school maintains a large full-time fine arts staff to take care of the broad student participation, and has made a long-term commitment to providing resources for talent development. The art department provides regular opportunities for the exhibition of student pieces in the school, and it encourages student participation in regional exhibits and competitions, where the students are consistently successful.

Instructors nominated those freshmen and sophomores who in their opinion possessed career potential in some area of the fine arts. They nominated 47 fine arts students, 23 males and 24 females. All 28 students in the final sample of artists, 15 males and 13 females, were enrolled in art courses for academic credit. Many of these students had enrolled in pre-high-school talent development programs offered by the high school and were known to the teaching staff.

We realize, of course, that the general selection strategy outlined above is not without drawbacks. Our approach probably ensured that all members of the final sample were talented (and this avoided what statisticians call Type I error).[4] But dependence on teacher nominations does not exclude the possibility that capable teens who are either underachieving or achieving in venues outside the school will be missed (Type II error). This latter possibility is a particular concern in arts and athletics. In these talent areas, many opportunities for the instruction and expression of talent at a high level are available to teenagers outside of school hours. Indeed, parents of gifted teens often find that their children exhaust curricular offerings so quickly that they must seek new resources beyond those available in the schools. Would excluding such students limit the validity and utility of the present study's findings?

While we take these potential sources of sampling error seriously, we think it likely that other features of the study's overall design work to limit bias. The danger of overlooking low achievers was mitigated to some degree by collecting nominations at the outset of the school year. Nominating teachers based their judgments on students' prior performance in courses taught by someone else. In any case, since it was one of the primary purposes of this study to track the career of demonstrated talent through high school, it was necessary to begin with students whose abilities had already been noticed by knowledgeable adults. We leave it to future research to study the careers of students whose unsuspected or underutilized abilities bloom late in the high school years.

The danger of underrepresenting students on alternate talent tracks was mitigated somewhat by the unusually comprehensive offerings of the two high schools. As chapter 4 will bear out, the students in our final sample were engaged in an impressive variety of musical, artistic, and athletic activities, often at a very high level of performance. It is inevitable that some talented performers were not identified, but we are confident that the results derived from this sample are broadly relevant to the experience of most comparable talented teens.

METHODS FOR THE STUDY OF TALENT: A TWO-PART STRATEGY

Just as our primary interest in the experience of talent shaped the approach to sample selection, so it also guided what research strategies and methods were used. In particular, we wanted to understand how teen-agers' daily experiences and self-perceptions influenced their eventual decisions about talent development. This focus seemed to dictate a dual-phase longitudinal research design. The first phase of data collection would concentrate primarily on each teenager's experience of talent, with central emphasis on the day-to-day perception of talent. This phase took place during the first half of the high school career, when the subjects were in either Grade 9 or 10. Many measures were collected during this period, but the central focus of research was the Experience Sampling Method (ESM), a naturalistic approach to the study of subjective states.

The second phase of data collection, two years later, would concentrate primarily on the development of talent. This phase centered on the growth of interest as well as on accomplishments in the domain. By adopting this approach, we hoped to discover those aspects of talent-related experience and activity that most contribute to the cultivation of talent over time. In the remainder of this chapter we briefly outline the major procedures and measures that were administered during the two phases of the study.

FIRST PHASE: STUDYING THE EXPERIENCE OF TALENT THROUGH THE ESM

After the initial pool of eligible teenagers had been identified, letters were sent out explaining the project and inviting participation. We also arranged meetings with parents and students in which the project was described and questions answered. More than half of the nominated students agreed to participate.

Among the sample characteristics examined, only the year in high school affected participation patterns to any significant degree. Subjects who were nominated as 10th graders were significantly more likely to participate than were 9th graders ($\chi^2 = 10.04$, $p < .002$).[5] This bias probably reflects the general set of difficulties that freshmen face in adjusting to high school life. The impact of these difficulties may have been exacerbated by the nominating schedule, which delayed the selection of freshmen until 3 months after the beginning of the school year. (The delay in contacting 9th graders was unavoidable: The new students had to have time to adjust, and teachers needed time to revise the rosters of the advanced academic classes.)

Some interaction between gender and high school year was also apparent, with sophomore girls somewhat more likely to participate. Freshman boys were less inclined to participate and more likely to drop out of the study in its initial and most demanding phase (see discussion of ESM below). Gender in itself, though, did not make an appreciable difference. Finally, a trend toward higher participation among multiply talented students was also evident. Although not statistically significant, this trend does lend some assurance that the selection procedures were biased, if anything, toward the inclusion of greater levels of talent. It should be noted that the combined impact of gender, grade, and number of talent nominations accounted for less than 5% of the final participation pattern. These groupings may not be represented in perfect proportion in the final sample, but they are all well represented.

The extraordinary nature of our primary research technique, Experience Sampling, made thorough preparation of our student subjects and their parents an especially high priority. Beeper studies, as they are now sometimes called, use electronic pagers to chart the course of daily life and experience. In response to ESM signals, subjects fill out a detailed report of their current activities, thoughts, companions, and feelings. It is a demanding method that requires a substantial commitment from researchers and participants alike. Fifteen years of ESM research, though, have more than done justice to the efforts of those involved. As a methodological innovation, ESM bridges the precision of paper-and-pencil measurement and the ecological validity of on-site observational techniques. Its contextual immediacy avoids the biases and distortions to which more global self-report measures are sometimes prone. As a research tool, it has already entered the methodologies of numerous fields, from life span development to cross-cultural investigations to the study of such clinical disorders as anorexia, bulimia, and schizophrenia.[6]

The particular ESM procedures adopted for this study followed those that had worked well with adolescents in studies conducted at the University of Chicago.[7] Each teenager was briefed on the procedure before beginning the week of signals. During the initial meeting with researchers, students filled out a sample Experience Sampling Form (ESF) to ensure that they understood all instructions. The ESM pagers were

designed with two signaling modes, beeping and vibration. The participants were instructed to set the pagers on the vibrate mode as often as
possible in order to minimize disturbance to their surroundings, and they
were shown how to wear the devices.

Each teenager was to carry the pager for 7 consecutive days, including
one weekend. Daily, 7 to 9 signals were broadcast to the pagers between
the hours of 7:00 a.m. and 10:00 p.m. on weekdays and 7:00 a.m. and
midnight during the weekend, for an average total of 60 potential responses. All paging occurred between October 1985 and May 1986,
during periods when regular classes were in session. Only respondents
who completed at least 15 ESFs within 30 minutes of the signal were
included in the final sample. Of the teens who started, 208 (91%) met
this criterion, with an average of 36 valid responses each.

After completing the week of ESM, each participant returned for a
second meeting with a member of the research staff. During this debriefing session, the students were asked how the week had gone and if they
had experienced any problems completing the ESF booklets. In most
cases, failures to respond to the signal were related to random forget-
fulness, signal failure, or the temporary movement of subjects out of
signaling range. Under some circumstances germane to the study of
talent, such as athletic competition, response proved difficult. The majority of teens felt that their ESM weeks were representative of their usual
experience and did not feel that the pager had altered their feelings or
patterns of behavior in appreciable ways. This is confirmed by the structure of the data we eventually collected, in which all the major settings
and situations common to American adolescence are well represented.

The experience sampling form

The greatest challenges in ESM research are posed not by logistical
headaches but rather by selection of the questions to ask. Should the
limited space available on each ESF be devoted to physical well-being or
to emotional states or details about thoughts and activities? Many emphases are possible, and the ESM has been employed by now to explore a
number of widely divergent research interests.[8] The ESF format that we
selected was originally developed to test the theory of flow and optimal
experience. In fact, use of the ESM and understanding of optimal experi-

ence have developed together over the past 15 years, leading to a number of revisions in both theory and method. The contribution of flow theory to the ESF used here (Fig. 3.1) is its phenomenological orientation. The self-report form reflects the view that experience consists of more than the "inner life" of the individual. Rather it embodies the convergence of the perceiver with the world, a transaction of external and internal dimensions. Both must be measured if we are to understand what is constant and what is variable in everyday experience.

Measuring the external dimensions of experience

By "external dimensions" we mean the conditions, settings, and situations of everyday life that help to shape how people think and feel. The ESF included four major categories of daily experience: time (when), location (where), activity (what), and companionship (who). The fifth *w*, why, was also well represented, but it is considered below as an internal dimension. A team of researchers coded the open-ended categories (location and activity), based upon coding schemes developed during an earlier study of average adolescents. After an initial period of training, the reliability among these coders remained at a level of 95% agreement. Most disagreements were resolved easily through group comparison and discussion, leading in turn to minor adjustments in the schemes.

Temporal factors do not figure large in our present discussion of talent, but they were important in ascertaining the reliability of each individual's ESM sampling. The ESF elicited the data and time of each signal as well as the time of response. Only those signals that were responded to within 30 minutes were considered valid; the ones remaining were excluded from further analysis.

Location, the second external dimension, was elicited with the open-ended question "Where were you?" at the beginning of the ESF. Participants were asked to respond as specifically as possible. Responses were coded into five major categories – home, school, job, public places, and in transit – divided into a total of 86 subcodings. A summary of location by major category headings is to be found in Appendix 3.1.

Two questions related to the third external dimension: the type of activity in which the student was engaged. Teens were asked to describe specifically the "main thing" they were doing, as well as "other things,"

Date:_____ Time Beeped:_____ am/pm Time Filled Out_____ am/pm

As you were beeped...

What were you thinking about?_____

_____

Where were you?_____

What was the MAIN thing you were doing?_____

_____

What other things were you doing?_____

_____

WHY were you doing this particular activity?
    ( ) I had to   ( ) I wanted to do it   ( ) I had nothing else to do

	not at all			some what			quite			very
How well were you concentrating?	0	1	2	3	4	5	6	7	8	9
Was it hard to concentrate?	0	1	2	3	4	5	6	7	8	9
How self-conscious were you?	0	1	2	3	4	5	6	7	8	9
Did you feel good about yourself?	0	1	2	3	4	5	6	7	8	9
Were you in control of the situation?	0	1	2	3	4	5	6	7	8	9
Were you living up to your own expectations?	0	1	2	3	4	5	6	7	8	9
Were you living up to expectations of others?	0	1	2	3	4	5	6	7	8	9

Describe your mood as you were beeped:

	very	quite	some	neither	some	quite	very	
alert	0	o	.	-	.	o	0	drowsy
happy	0	o	.	-	.	o	0	sad
irritable	0	o	.	-	.	o	0	cheerful
strong	0	o	.	-	.	o	0	weak
active	0	o	.	-	.	o	0	passive
lonely	0	o	.	-	.	o	0	sociable
ashamed	0	o	.	-	.	o	0	proud
involved	0	o	.	-	.	o	0	detached
excited	0	o	.	-	.	o	0	bored
closed	0	o	.	-	.	o	0	open
clear	0	o	.	-	.	o	0	confused
tense	0	o	.	-	.	o	0	relaxed
competitive	0	o	.	-	.	o	0	cooperative

Figure 3.1. Standard Experience Sampling Method (ESM) Form (ESF) (side 1).

Did you feel any physical discomfort as you were beeped:

Overall pain or   none   slight   bothersome   severe
discomfort   0   1   2   3   4   5   6   7   8   9

Please specify: _____

Who were you with?

( ) alone   ( ) friend(s)   How many?_____
( ) mother   female ( )   male ( )
( ) father   ( ) strangers
( ) sister(s) or brother(s)   ( ) other_____

Indicate how you felt about your activity:

	low								high	
Challenges of the activity	0	1	2	3	4	5	6	7	8	9
Your skills in the activity	0	1	2	3	4	5	6	7	8	9
	not at all								very much	
Was this activity important to you?	0	1	2	3	4	5	6	7	8	9
Was this activity important to others?	0	1	2	3	4	5	6	7	8	9
Were you succeeding at what you were doing?	0	1	2	3	4	5	6	7	8	9
Do you wish you had been doing something else?	0	1	2	3	4	5	6	7	8	9
Were you satisfied with how you were doing?	0	1	2	3	4	5	6	7	8	9
How important was this activity in relation to your overall goals	0	1	2	3	4	5	6	7	8	9

If you had a choice. . .

Who would you be with? _____

What would you be doing?_____

Since you were last beeped has anything happened or have you done anything which could have affected the way you feel?

Nasty cracks, comments, etc: ***

Figure 3.1 (*cont.*). Standard ESF (side 2).

on separate lines of the ESF. They were instructed to be thoughtful in making a distinction between primary and secondary activities, particularly in designating the main activity. Primary and secondary activities were coded into three major categories – productive (e.g., homework), leisure (e.g., television), and maintenance (e.g., showering) – and then

divided further into 10 subcategories (e.g., school-related) and 155 specific codings. A sample-wide breakdown of activity by major subcategory
appears in Appendix 3.2.

The fourth external dimension, companionship, was elicited through
the question "Who were you with?" This was followed by a choice of
seven major categories, including an open-ended "other" option. The
category of friends included two further codings, for number and sex.
These categories are not, of course, mutually exclusive, and the students
were instructed to indicate as many categories as necessary to describe
their social situation. This resulted in a total of 91 combinations of companions, including those specified in the "other" category. A sample-wide
breakdown of percentage of time spent in major companionship categories appears in Appendix 3.3.

Measuring the internal dimensions of experience

Internal dimensions refer to subjective responses – physical, cognitive,
emotional, and motivational. The ESF assessed two general features of
subjective response: the content of consciousness (thought) and the quality of experience. In choosing what feelings and perceptions to measure,
we tried to sample equally from the traditional triad of psychic dimensions: the emotional, cognitive, and motivational aspects of consciousness.
We focused special attention, though, on the intensity of those states most
centrally implicated in the flow experience.

The content of thought was the subject of the first open-ended question on the ESF, "What were you thinking about?" Students were instructed to respond as specifically and thoroughly as space would allow.
Codings were arranged to correspond as closely as possible to the major
activity categories discussed previously, with a final total of 210 possible
codings. After reliability training, the team of coders reached a reliability
level above 95% for the major categories and above 90% for the individual categories. Disagreements were discussed among the group, and
new codes were added when necessary.

A large number of scaled measures were included on the ESF to
measure the intensity of five general features of experience: affective tone,
activation or potency, self-esteem, intrinsic motivation, and cognitive efficiency. In addition, questions regarding the perceived degree of challenge

of the activity and the student's perceived skills in meeting the challenge were included. The relationship between the challenge and skill measures is the linchpin of the ESM assessment of the flow state. Finally, three features of the activity's perceived importance – to the subject, to others, and to overall goals – were assessed. Three types of scales contributed to these measures: Likert, or summary, scales, on a continuum from 0 (low) to 9 (high); 7-point semantic differential scales (e.g., *sad* v. *happy*); and categorical scales (e.g., Why were you doing the activity?).

Two aspects of the student's emotional response to her or his current activity were explored on the ESF: affective tone and the level of potency or activation. Previous ESM research has shown these two aspects of emotional well-being to be closely related but nonetheless statistically distinct.[9] To represent these two dimensions, we drew from a battery of "semantic differential" scales that force choices between opposing feelings, such as *happy–sad*, or *closed–open*. These 7-point scales required the respondents to fit themselves along a fixed continuum between each opposition.[10] Following earlier ESM research with teens, three scales were summed to approximate affective tone: *happy–sad*, *cheerful–angry*, and *lonely–sociable* ($\alpha = .78$). Four scales were summed to approximate potency: *passive–active*, *drowsy–alert*, *weak–strong*, and *bored–excited* ($\alpha = .80$). These scales rather than individual ESF items are used throughout much of this study to summarize and compare the emotional well-being of groups and individuals.

Self-esteem has become increasingly important in recent years as a distinct focus of ESM research.[11] Although closely linked to emotional tone and potency, ESF self-esteem refers to the respondent's perception of how well he or she is faring in the present activity. ESF self-esteem is measured by adding the scores of the following five closely related Likert scale items: feeling good about oneself, living up to one's own expectations, living up to others' expectations, the sense of succeeding, and the sense of satisfaction with performance ($\alpha = .86$).

Among the perceptual characteristics most associated with optimal experience is a well-focused, integrated attentional field. Cognitive efficiency represents the extent to which the respondent can control the allocation of attentional resources. Four items were included to represent facets of optimal cognitive functioning: the level of concentration, the perceived ease of concentration, perceived clarity rather than confusion, and a lack of self-consciousness. Unlike daily affect and self-esteem, which are relatively stable across situations and within individuals,[12] cognitive efficiency is very sensitive to situational factors. For this reason, the four aspects of attention included on the ESF rarely converge in everyday consciousness and do not constitute a statistically reliable scale. The items, therefore, are reported separately in those portions of our research involving the cognitive aspects of talent and optimal experience.

A similar situation holds for another vital dimension of experience associated closely with flow: the sense of intrinsic motivation. Two ESF items inquired into the intrinsic versus extrinsic nature of the respondent's motivation in pursuing the primary activity. The question "Why were you doing this particular activity?" explored the extent to which the main activity was undertaken voluntarily. Three responses were listed – "had to," "wanted to," "nothing else to do" – and combinations of these responses were permitted. A variable representing the percentage of time that each individual pursued a voluntary activity was derived from these data. A second question, "Do you wish you had been doing something else?," tapped the respondent's intrinsic interest in the activity, using a 9-point scale. In addition, two semantic differential scales assessed the respondent's degree of engagement with the activity: *involved–detached* and *open–closed*. Because of differences in the form of assessment used, no single intrinsic motivation scale was created.

Other ESF scales are also significant to the present study. The theory of flow posits that the perceived ratio between challenge and skill is the primary condition for the optimization of experience in any activity. When the actor feels that the challenges of the activity and the level of skill are both above the weekly average, then the concomitants of flow – intrinsic interest, focused attention, ease of concentration, and so on – are also likely to be present. In addition to their use as individual scales, the ESF measures of challenge ("Challenges of the activity") and skill ("Your skills in the activity") were employed to derive a measure of the challenge–skill ratio. Challenge and skill scores were standardized, and each ESF was coded as belonging to one of four challenge–skill quadrants: high challenge/high skill, high challenge/low skill, low challenge/high skill, and low challenge/low skill. These quadrants correspond to the four major experiential situations predicted by the flow theory: flow, anxiety, boredom, and apathy. Two versions of the quadrant variable were derived, the first standardized within the challenge and skill scores of each individual, and the second standardized on the level of the entire group. Further details of this procedure are supplied in chapter 11.

Two other ESF variables are of theoretical interest to the present study: the sense of control and the importance of the current activity to overall goals. Both variables were assessed using 9-point Likert scales. Although the perception of control is somewhat ambiguously related to deep flow,[13] it is nonetheless considered an essential component of effective psychological coping. The question used in this study was oriented toward situational coping: "Were you in control of the situation?" The feeling that what one is doing is related to long-range goals figures importantly in this study as one aspect of a balanced, or autotelic, approach to talent development. In other words, a student's undivided attention to talent development is felt to require the synergistic relation of short- and long-term interests. Long-term goals were assessed with the question "How important was this activity in relation to your overall goals?"

Other first phase measures and procedures

Administration of the ESM formed the basis of the study's first phase, but students also completed a number of other important measures. Since these measures are described at greater length in chapter 4, here we need only touch on their administration. During the initial meeting with researchers, and in addition to their introduction to the ESM, students were given a number of forms and questionnaires. These included a general biographical questionnaire and two personality inventories: the Personality Research Form (PRF) and the Offer Self-Image Questionnaire for Adolescents (OSIQ).[14] In addition to biographical and demographic information, the general questionnaire emphasized talent-related preferences and accomplishments, family functioning, stressful events, and physical maturation. The PRF and OSIQ measures tap dimensions of personality and self-image of special importance to the study of adolescent development. The students were instructed to complete these forms during the ESM week and return them to researchers during the following week's debriefing session. Most complied; those who could not were provided time to complete the forms after the ESM debriefing.

The final meeting with researchers was an open-ended interview of each student. In most cases, two 40-minute sessions were required to tape-record the interview. The protocol of the interview consisted of three parts (see Appendix 3.4.). Part 1 focused on the personal development of the teenager, with particular emphasis on general self-image, interpersonal influences, and the content and motivation of major goals. Part 2 focused specifically on the history and current status of individual talent development, including the teenager's talent-related experience and plans. Given the limits of time, multiply talented students were asked to discuss their preferred talent first and then their other talent(s) if the schedule allowed. Part 3 asked the student to rate the applicability of 12 possible reasons for pursuing training in their talent area(s). These statements were grouped into intrinsic, extrinsic, and interpersonal motivations for sustaining talent development.

Finally, a questionnaire dealing with parental experiences, expectations, and styles of child rearing was mailed to each parent (see Appendix 3.5). The form asked for demographic information but also correlated closely with the family sections of the student's questionnaire. We hoped that the combined questionnaires would throw light on the contribution of the family as an integrated system to the development of adolescent talent. A moderately high response rate from at least one parent of each child was obtained (65%).

SECOND PHASE: CHARTING THE DEVELOPMENT OF TALENT

During the project's second phase, the emphasis shifted to the development of a wide range of ways to measure talent development. These measures would include both "hard," or objective, indexes of achievement, such as grades, and so-called soft, or subjective, ratings of accomplishment and engagement, and be drawn from teachers and from the students themselves. The hope was to develop as varied and textured a portrait as possible of the unfolding involvement of the student with her or his talent through the high school years.

Examining the record of achievement

Our study benefited from access to all athletic records, academic transcripts, and related material maintained by the two high schools. The individual departments of each school kept, in addition to official transcripts, detailed records of those who involved themselves in such departmental activities as sports teams, math competitions, and art showings. From these records it was possible to develop a number of ability and achievement measures, both general and talent-specific.

Two measures of general intellectual achievement are employed throughout most analyses in the study, the Preliminary Scholastic Aptitude Test (PSAT) and the percentile class rank. Both measures were available for the great majority of students: PSAT, 80%; percentile rank, 95%. A percentile measure of class rank (class rank/class size) was developed to neutralize small but significant differences in class size between the two high schools. We did not use general grade point averages because of differences between the grading systems employed by the two high schools. However, the same weighting system for grades had been employed by both schools to adjust class rank for the effects of course difficulty. In most cases, these measures were used in this study to control for the mediating impact of intellectual ability on relationships between talent-associated experience and talent outcomes. For instance, if we found that freshmen who enjoyed mathematics continued to develop their talent as seniors, we would not be sure whether it was enjoyment that caused continuing development unless we also controlled for mathematical aptitude. Keeping track of scholastic achievement allowed us to determine that it wasn't simply the case that the more gifted the students, the more they continued to perfect their talent – which would have been a rather obvious conclusion.

Academic and athletic achievement records were used to develop two measures of talent-specific accomplishment: annual grade point average (GPA) in the talent area and annual level of course difficulty. Annual GPA was coded from letter grades using the following scale: $F = 0$, $D = 1$, $C = 2$, $B = 3$, $A = 4$. Neither school used plus or minus qualifications of grades. Semester grades for each year were averaged to produce the annual GPAs in the talent area, which were averaged, in turn, to yield the mean talent GPAs. No analog to a GPA was available for athletic performance.

In order to gauge the level of difficulty of courses on the academic transcript, we first analyzed the curricula in each talent area. These analyses resulted in a system of course difficulty rankings for math, science, music, and art. A similar system was developed for athletics, beginning with the athletic awards of the school and continuing upward to the highest levels of regional and statewide athletic attainment. These systems, each defining a measure of course attainment, were then reviewed, amended, and approved by high school faculty in the relevant departments. The final "course level" variables are included in Appendix 3.6.

Examining the ratings of instructors

Two formal assessments of student characteristics, performance and potential, were completed by teachers. The first assessment was collected at the end of year 1, but was utilized only in preliminary phases of the study. The second teacher assessment was collected at the end of year 3 as students concluded either Grade 11 or 12. This rating focused on attributes and behaviors that evidenced high performance and promise in talent-related activities. Examples of items include the student's enjoyment of challenge, capacity for concentration, and realization of potential (see Appendix 3.7). Factor analysis indicated that all the items belonged to a single dimension, and the seven highest-loading items were added (α = .96) to obtain the Teachers' Rating score. This score is used as one criterion in determining student involvement and development (see chapter 10).

Measuring subjective involvement with talent

The major task of the second phase of the study focused on the determination of just how involved with talent development the students remained as they approached the end of high school. In order to explore these issues, we devised an extended questionnaire centered on two primary issues: the quality of experience while engaged in talent-related activities and the degree of commitment to further investment in talent. Its format was modeled closely on previous self-report measures of flow experience, most notably that used by Mayers in 1978 for a sample of average adolescents. This questionnaire was delivered in homeroom classes to each of the 208 students who had completed the ESM reliably 2 years earlier. Of these, 165 (79%) returned the form completed. Of the remaining students, 30 provided responses to the "Personal Interests

Survey" portion of the questionnaire over the telephone, raising the partial response rate to 93%. This section was most crucial to the follow-up effort, for it provided direct self-reports of continued interest and time investment in the talent area. A summary of the questionnaire sections used in the chapters that follow is included in Appendix 3.8.

Three general measures were derived from the information in these sections of the questionnaire. Part A, the "Flow Descriptions," posed questions concerning experiences closely associated with flow: concentration (1), effortless confidence (2), intrinsic motivation (3), and memorable moments (4). It was hoped that each statement would evoke in the students the intensity of experience that is typical of flow moments. Students were to indicate if they ever had such experiences, their frequency, and the activities that produced them. The responses were later coded for whether or not students mentioned talent-related activities in reply to any of the three questions. This yielded two possible outcomes: (a) The student mentions that her or his talent area had been a source of flow experience; (b) the student does not mention talent as a source of flow.

Further flow scales were created from responses to the items in Part B. Students were asked to list the activity with which they were most intensely involved, the one that required the most work in school, and the one that was their favorite. These three activities, in addition to being with family, watching television, and doing homework, were then rated according to the frequency of 11 brief statements associated with optimal experience. A 5-point scale was used (1 = *almost never;* 5 = *almost always*). The 11 items included a broad range of flow-related feelings, such as "I get involved," "I clearly know what I am supposed to do," and "I would do it even if I didn't have to." The 11 responses were summed across each activity to create six flow scales evidencing moderate to high reliability (alpha indexes range between .71 and .92; mean α = .82).

In addition, two questions from the "Personal Interests Survey" (Part C) were used to identify a subgroup of highly committed students. Students who reported that they pursued talent-related activities every day (item 1), and felt sure that they would select their talent as a college major (item 6b), were categorized as committed and the others as noncommitted. We shall have more to say about these groupings and their meaning in chapter 11.

Finally, the "Complex Family Questionnaire" (CFQ)[15] was included as a supplement to the follow-up questionnaire. Twenty-four items explored family conditions thought to facilitate the experience of flow, both in and beyond the home environment, using a 4-point response scale (1 = *definitely no;* 4 = *definitely yes*). More detailed discussion of this and other family-related measures is included in chapter 8, where family influences on talent development are considered.

CONCLUSION

In formulating a research design for this study, the main goal was to explore the ecology of talent development during adolescence. Because growth proceeds so quickly and along so many diverse fronts during these years, we wanted to know how teenagers learn to balance talent with other developmental tasks. Further, we sought to discover the kinds of balance – in personality, in goals, and in daily living – that best integrate talent into a future that a teenager can pursue wholeheartedly.

With these motives in mind, we decided early not to seek out teenage subjects in specialized gifted and talented programs. It was possible and even tempting to assemble "superkids" in math or music. But it was essential that the final sample be one in which all the forces that normally compete for the attention of teens were present and in play. These are exactly the distractions, of course, that specialized programs are intended to minimize. At the same time, it was equally important for the sample to be significantly above average across the talent fields. Otherwise we would not be confident that the interactions of talent with other aspects of teenage life would reveal themselves clearly.

The group that emerged from the mixed selection strategy outlined at the beginning of this chapter met all requirements reasonably well. As will become clearer in the next chapter, students in each talent area, though not uniformly gifted, are by all relevant standards unusually bright and talented. The ESM data provide very rich and detailed descriptions of everyday teenage settings and situations. Together with the other measures assembled here, these data should offer insights of interest both to talent development specialists and to all those who face the challenge of helping teens realize their unique gifts and potentials.

NOTES

1 Feldman, 1986; Gardner, 1983.
2 Csikszentmihalyi & Robinson, 1986; Newland, 1976; Roth & Sussman, 1974; Tidwell, 1980.
3 Bamberger, 1982; Janos, 1990; Robinson & Robinson, 1982.
4 A Type I error in statistics refers to an overly liberal conclusion, where a false result is admitted as being true. A Type II error is an overly cautious conclusion, where a true result is rejected as being false. These errors are inevitable outcomes of statistical conclusions, which can never lead to certainty but deal only with probabilities.
5 Of the various simple statistical notations, the reader unversed in statistics needs to be familiar only with the so-called p, or probability value. The p-value indicates the probability that a certain statistical test or relationship is due to chance. The smaller the p-value, the less likelihood of chance and hence the greater probability that the difference is real. A p-value of .05, or 5% probability of chance, is usually accepted as the upper limit of statistical significance. A smaller value is more significant. In the case in question, the difference between 9th and 10th graders is significant at the .002 level of probability, meaning that only twice in a thousand tries could such a difference have come about by chance. Hence the odds are 998 to 2 that 10th graders in this school were more willing to participate in the study than 9th graders.
6 For an extensive review, see Csikszentmihalyi & Csikszentmihalyi, 1988, and the recent applications to psychopathology reported in deVries, 1992.
7 Csikszentmihalyi & Larson, 1984; Csikszentmihalyi & Nakamura, 1986.
8 For a review, see Csikszentmihalyi & Larson, 1984, 1987.
9 See Csikszentmihalyi & Larson, 1987; Kubey, 1984.
10 Osgood, Suci, & Tannenbaum, 1957.
11 Csikszentmihalyi & Csikszentmihalyi, 1988.
12 Csikszentmihalyi & Wong, 1991.
13 Csikszentmihalyi, 1975, pp. 44–46.
14 Jackson, 1984; Offer, Ostrov, & Howard, 1978.
15 Rathunde, 1989a.

4

What are talented
teenagers like?

The development of talent is an ongoing process that has emotional and motivational components in addition to the obvious cognitive ones. To nurture a gift to fruition, one must have discipline as well as skills, and one must have access to social supports and cultural opportunities. It would be expected therefore that talented young people differ from their "average" peers not only in the quality of their gifts but also in a number of other dimensions.

From our perspective it seems clear that the development of talent involves more than the careful cultivation of an isolated academic skill or a disembodied aptitude measured by tests. At its best, it involves the development of a mature personality that can cope with the many opportunities and obstacles of the field. In this chapter we begin to explore the kind of people talented teenagers are by comparing them with available statistical norms in three broad areas: ability and achievements; the social and economic circumstances of their families; and finally, patterns of personality. The next chapter will extend the comparisons of average and talented teens to describe what they do and how they feel in various daily activities.

SIGNS OF TALENT

When selecting a strategy for choosing the talented sample, we decided to place considerable emphasis on the evaluations of teachers and coaches – in other words, on the judgment of the relevant field. We hoped in doing so to gather a sample composed not of just superachievers but of teens who gave signs of unusual promise, even if they had yet to "catch fire." Still, it is fair to ask, just how talented were these teens? Did their actual performance live up to their billing as bright and exceptional individuals? Although the answers to these questions may seem obvious, it is important at the outset to understand just where the talented stand academically, athletically, artistically, or musically in relation to their peers. It is very likely that such ranking plays a critical role in how talented teenagers think about themselves, their future, and their relationships with others.

Mathematics and science students

Appendix 4.1 (Tables A and B) provides a close look at the talent-related academic accomplishments of the mathematics and science students. By any standard, the record for both groups, and especially that subgroup of students nominated in both math and science, is an impressive one. According to the California Achievement Tests, which the students took before entering high school, all three groups approach or exceed the 90th percentile nationally. The most impressive scores are found among the combined-talent students, who show a long record of academic superiority throughout the elementary grades. This level of performance on standardized tests remains true throughout high school, including the crucial Preliminary Scholastic Aptitude Test (PSAT), which determines the selection of National Merit Scholars. Of the 87 students in the combined sample, 19 were nominated as semifinalists for National Merit Scholarships, and 74 qualified as Illinois State Scholars, reflecting excellence on the Academic Competence Test (ACT). Clearly the majority of these math and science students far exceed the national adolescent norms for academic ability.

A second distinguishing aspect of the academic record of this group is the level of performance attained across the curriculum over the high school career (Table B). Again, the record of the 28 students nominated in both math and science is particularly impressive. Their location in the top 5% of their high school classes indicates strength throughout the curriculum and evident superiority in all subject areas. The 40 students nominated only in math were on the average in the top 15% of their class in Grades 9 and 10, and the 19 students nominated only in science were on the average among the top 10%.

It is interesting to note certain differences in the overall academic performances of the mathematics and science students. Whereas mathematics students demonstrate high mathematical and verbal skills on standard tests, their overall academic performance lags somewhat behind their talented peers in the sciences. Why this is true is not immediately clear. It is possible, of course, that the severity of grading in advanced math courses deflates the grades of mathematically talented teens. But this difference may also reflect differences in the patterns of interest and attention typical of teens talented in math and the sciences. Science involves the blending of verbal and mathematical modes of inquiry. Young scientists are encouraged to develop and exercise these skills in tandem. Young talented mathematicians, even verbally fluent ones, do not need verbal skills in order to enjoy the rewards of their talent. They may come to see the study of language or history as secondary to their real strengths and interests. Confident as quantitative thinkers and aware of the tangible rewards that mathematical ability can afford, they may focus less attention on achievement in nonmathematical areas of study. In any case, although math and science students will often be treated in this book as closely allied, there are also differences between them that are intriguing to consider.

Athletes, musicians, and artists

Excellence in the three remaining talent areas is not as easily identified. With its passion for recognition and statistics, athletics presents the easiest problem in this regard. Even varsity letters, however, are awarded on the basis of many factors, including participation and sportsmanship, and the relative quality of performance from year to year is difficult to track. The arts place considerably less emphasis on competitive distinction and more on cooperative skills and individual improvement. Also, the range of individual prizes is very wide, and their criteria are often idiosyncratic and hard to compare. Nonetheless, the measures that are available do indicate consistent excellence among the students in all three talent areas.

The high school that supplied the sample of student athletes kept detailed records of the athletic accomplishments of all enrolled pupils. Appendix 4.1C compares the athletic achievements of the student athletes selected for this study with the accomplishments of their classmates who were not selected. Specifically, the numbers represent the percentage of those in each group who attained high levels of performance in at least one sport relatively early in their high school careers – by the end of the sophomore year.

Two aspects of this sample's athletic achievements are especially notable. First, the athletics program of the high school we studied is very competitive, especially among male students. During the study more than one third of the school's males competed seriously as freshmen and went on to fill junior varsity positions by their sophomore year. This caused intense competition for the few varsity positions available, and only a small percentage of males managed to break into the varsity ranks as underclassmen. Among the female students, overall participation was lower, which accounts for the greater number of varsity positions available to younger female athletes. Nonetheless competition among female students for the top spots on their teams was almost as fierce as for males.

Second, the comparison confirms that the talented teens as underclassmen were already in the vanguard of leading athletes at this very competitive high school. Given the selection procedure, of course, it is not surprising that all of the talented teens had taken their class numerals as freshmen. More notably, though, the talented teens were much more successful than their peers at advancing into junior varsity and varsity positions during sophomore year. By the end of senior year, 82% of the talented males and 83% of the females had achieved varsity status, well above the schoolwide percentage of 18 for males and 11 for females. For a high percentage of the talented athletes of both sexes, their achievements by the end of their high school careers were considerably more impressive. Of the 58 talented athletes, for example, 70% remained involved over all 4 high school years. More than half (31) competed in the final round of a regional championship contest as starting players at some point in their high school careers. Of these championship players, 21 were honored as Most Valuable Players, were recognized by area newspapers, or qualified and competed in state-level championships. And 7 achieved state championships or were honored as All-State designates.

It is worth noting that these high-performance athletes represent a very wide spectrum of backgrounds and accomplishments. They include students from all of the major ethnic and religious groups in the community, and they range widely in academic ability. The group's mean PSAT scores

of 44 Verbal (79th percentile) and 50 Mathematical (82nd percentile), for
example, exceed the national averages for high school juniors, but the
scores also include a large percentage below the national mean. A mean
composite ACT score of 21.9 locates them at the 70th national percentile
for academic achievement; their grades place them on average in the top
30% of their high school class. High standard deviations for both PSAT
scores and class ranks indicate that these athletes vary academically from
the very brightest to the most severely limited students in their school.
Individual diversity, then, rather than "jock" uniformity, would appear to
characterize this sample of able teenage athletes.

When we turn to the sample of talented musicians, we encounter a
somewhat higher level of overall academic performance. Their PSAT
scores (47.8 Verbal, 87th percentile; 52 Math, 83rd percentile) locate
them within the 85th percentile among juniors nationally, and their mean
ACT composite score (25.4) places them within the 90th percentile in
academic achievement. As a group the musicians average in the top 20%
of their high school class. The solid academic performance of the musicians no doubt reflects the broad academic background of the sample,
33% of whom were also nominated as talented in math or science.

In the music curricula of both schools, the students who participated in
the study were clearly among the top performers. All of the music students were music readers, and most of them sight readers. Almost all
(95%) maintained a music grade point average (GPA) of 3.5 or better
during their first 2 years of high school, and on the average they had
completed more than nine graded music courses by the end of high
school. Among the group of participants were 10 who eventually won
scholarships to colleges of music and 26 others who received regional
recognition for excellence in music competitions.

Among the talent groups, the sample of 28 artists evinced the lowest
commitment to general academic achievement. The average composite
score of the 20 artists who took the ACT (mean ACT composite = 22)
locates them at about the 70th percentile among high school juniors, but
the group's mean class rank locates them at about the 60th percentile of
their high school class. Less than half elected to take the PSAT or SAT
examinations, which are usually considered important for admission to
the more competitive colleges and universities.

The artists' attainments within the art curriculum, however, more than bear out their considerable commitment to achievement in their talent area. During their first 2 years of high school, 85% of the artists maintained art-related grades of B or better. Whereas only 2 students failed to progress beyond the introductory level, over two thirds had advanced into the school's difficult advanced art courses by their junior year. Art scholarships eventually were offered to 10 students, and 3 others received formal recognition for their exhibitions at regional art competitions. To some degree, then, the artists' apparent lack of interest in overall academic achievement probably reflects an early focus on the art curriculum as their primary career path. This exclusive focus on art at the expense of academic subjects is typical of gifted young artists.[1]

FAMILY BACKGROUND

Another way to compare talented teens with their average counterparts involves material, social, and psychological resources. Foremost among the advantages that might help teenagers develop their talent are the material resources of the family and the kind of psychological support parents are able or willing to give them.

Social and economic resources

All the dimensions of socioeconomic status, or SES – high level of parental education, high income, high occupational status – provide obvious academic advantages to children who are lucky enough to be born into the right families. For example, a 1985 report on education in Chicago claimed that of all the African-Americans and Hispanics enrolled in inner city high schools, only 38% graduated, and only 8% read at or above the national average.[2] Social class and ethnic background predispose some children more than others to an early exposure to the domains of literacy. For instance, use of elaborate language in the family context,[3] parental reading,[4] and generalized cultural attitudes toward education[5] all influence strongly the ease with which a child will fit into and prosper in the school environment.

If socioeconomic status is an important factor in achieving literacy, it is even more essential for the development of talent. A number of recent studies, most notably that of Benjamin Bloom in 1985, have documented the demands that full development of talent place on time and resources within the family. Parents who value talent development must often absorb heavy costs, not only financially but also in terms of privacy and of availability to other family members. It makes sense that parents with better access to resources – more disposable income, more education, and better social contacts – should enjoy definite advantages in supporting their children's talent development and in mitigating its costs.

The talented students in our study do indeed appear to belong to the more advantaged families in their community. Using 1980 census information, Appendix 4.2 compares the families of the talented teens with the community at large in terms of three measures of potential family advantage: parental income, level of education, and occupational status. Information about family income and parental education was provided directly by parents; occupational status was determined from both parental and student reports.

All three sets of data appear to tell the same story. The families of talented teens have higher gross incomes and are twice as likely to have incomes above \$40,000 ($\chi^2 = 50, p < .001$). Both mothers and fathers are more highly educated than their average counterparts (mother's $\chi^2 = 94.3, p < .001$; father's $\chi^2 = 38, p < .001$). Talented teens also tend to have fathers with higher occupational status ($\chi^2 = 59, p < .001$). Average teens were 2.5 times as likely to have a father in a low-status (usually blue collar) occupation. None of the parents in the talented sample had less than a high school education, and over 80% had at least a bachelor's degree. Especially noteworthy is the educational difference among the mothers. Whereas only 34% of mothers in the community at large have a college degree, a full 82% of the mothers of the talented sample are college graduates or better.

Material resources, then, do indeed distinguish talented teenagers from their peers in the community. It is probable, though by no means inevitable, that these resources have opened doors to challenging opportunities for many of them, from private lessons to championship competitions to stimulating conversation around the dinner table. It is also likely that these advantages have freed the talented group from constraints, such as after-school jobs, that sap the time and enthusiasm of less fortunate teens. This in itself is not that surprising. But are there factors beyond income or status, involving the sorts of psychological support family members provide one another, that also distinguish talented and average teens?

The complexity of family contexts

To investigate this possibility, we administered the Family Adaptability and Cohesion Evaluation Scales (FACES II) questionnaire[6] during the initial phase of our study. FACES II provides its users with recent data from a nationwide sample of adolescents, making it ideal for our purposes. This scale is organized theoretically around two central dimensions of family interaction: *cohesion* and *adaptability.* Family cohesion is defined as the extent of emotional bonding that members have established among themselves. Family adaptability is understood as the ability of the system to change in response to situational and developmental stress. Four levels are identified for each dimension. A family's cohesion is characterized as either disengaged, separated, connected, or enmeshed.[7] For the sake of simplicity, however, test scores may be summarized into four combinations of high and low cohesion and adaptability. For example, a family may be characterized by high cohesion but low adaptability (HI/LO).

As Table 4.1 indicates, talented and average teens do differ in their perceptions of family functioning. The two groups are similar in their sense of family cohesion ($\chi^2 = 0.99$, NS)[8] but see the levels of adaptability in their families as significantly different ($\chi^2 = 24.1, p < .001$). In particular, talented teens are more likely to view their families as more flexible and less often as structured. When level of cohesion and adaptability are considered in tandem, producing the four groupings outlined above, talented and average respondents show significantly diverging proportions ($\chi^2 = 19, p < .001$). A z-test of the proportions of the two groups in the HI/HI combination confirmed the expectation that talented teens would be more likely to see their families as high in both cohesion and adaptability (44% vs. 35%; $z = 2.51, p < .006$). As confirmed by other studies, these findings suggest that moderate to high family cohesiveness coupled with high adaptability seems to provide the best context for adolescent development.[9]

The families of talented adolescents appear to provide solid advantages

Table 4.1. *Family adaptability and cohesion evaluation (FACES II):*
Comparison of talented and average students

	Talented (%) (N = 190)	Average (%) (N = 416)	χ^2	$p <$
Cohesion factor			0.99	NS
Enmeshed	22.2	20.2		
Connected	31.3	31.1		
Separated	28.3	31.1		
Disengaged	18.2	17.6		
Adaptability factor			24.07	.001
Chaotic	19.5	20.0		
Flexible	44.1	29.2		
Structured	22.6	36.1		
Rigid	13.8	14.7		
Cohesion/Adaptability quadrants			19.0	.001
LO/HI	20.0	13.8		
HI/HI	44.2	35.4		
LO/LO	26.8	34.9		
HI/LO	8.9	15.9		

in terms of both material and psychological support. Unfortunately, there
is no SES information available on the normative FACES II sample, making it impossible to determine whether or not SES relates significantly to
family functioning. The income levels in the talented sample are too
homogeneous to pursue this interesting question here. We have, however,
by no means said the last word about the family and its crucial role in the
support and cultivation of talent among teenagers. In chapter 8 we shall
return to a more refined theoretical understanding of just how family
structure affects the realization of teenage abilities.

TALENT AND PERSONALITY

The results concerning the material and psychological resources in the
family suggest that the context in which average and talented teens live

differs a great deal. The advantages a more affluent, educated, and supportive family can provide a teen are certainly important. But do these advantages actually translate into different personal characteristics? Do talented and average teenagers differ in terms of self-concept and personality traits? Adolescence has long been seen as a time when feelings about self and others, and about efficacy and effectiveness, take enduring shape.[10] It makes sense to expect, for instance, that in order to develop their gifts, talented teens would be likely to cultivate traits conducive to achievement and discipline.

In order to explore this hypothesis, we turned to two questionnaires often used by researchers who study teenage personality – the Offer Self-Image Questionnaire (OSIQ) and the Jackson's Personality Research Form (PRF). Both of these instruments provide recent data concerning average adolescent populations. The OSIQ focuses on the self-experience of adolescents in specific psychosocial situations, both as they understand themselves and as they think they are seen by others or by the self as me.[11] The PRF concentrates on 20 attributes, spanning a wide range of attitudes and psychological characteristics, such as achievement motivation, exhibitionism, and playfulness. In this section we present the results of the OSIQ comparison of talented and average teens. Then we consider the PRF comparison, starting with an overall review of the 20 attribute scales. Finally, we take a closer look at a subset of scales that provides a measure of each person's ability to derive intrinsic rewards from highly challenging activities – what we have come to call the autotelic personality.

The situational self: A look at self-image

Adolescence is a time when emerging concerns about social and sexual competence begin to place increased demands on a young person's time and attention.[12] At the same time, it is a period for redefining previous roles as a family and community member and for seriously attending to personal interests that may blossom as adult commitments. In the case of the talented, many of these new developments may provide opportunities to explore further their exceptional abilities. Other emerging concerns, however, compete for time that was formerly the exclusive domain of talent development. For example, peer pressure and the new sexual interests brought about by puberty are likely to interfere with exclusive dedication to music or to mathematics. But just how concerned most talented teens are about the conflicts of adolescence is not yet well understood.

To investigate this question, we made use of the OSIQ, which uses 12 subscales that measure distinct dimensions of self-image. Four subscales – impulse control, emotional tone, body and self-image, and level of psychopathology – assess overall psychological well-being. Two others – moral attitudes and idealism – assess commitment to socially responsible behavior. The remaining 6 scales measure feelings of competence in interpersonal and achievement-oriented contexts. Of our talented 9th and 10th graders, 177 (76 males and 101 females) completed the OSIQ in a reliable manner: 31 math students, 55 music students, 25 science students, 44 athletes, and 22 art students. Their scores were compared within gender groups with a sample of average adolescents gathered during the early 1980s.[13]

For both males and females, only one measure differentiates the talented and average groups at a statistically significant level, the Sexual Attitudes subscale. This suggests that talented teens are more conservative in their sexual attitudes and less confident of their sexual attractiveness than their same-sex average peers. This difference is corroborated further by factor analytic evidence that, among the talented, sexual attitudes are a separate dimension of self-image and are relatively uncorrelated with other OSIQ subscales. Among the average teens, factor analysis located open and confident sexual attitudes more centrally among the other OSIQ indicators of emotional and interpersonal well-being. Otherwise, the talented group exhibits a pattern of self-image at the lower end of the normal range for their age group.

There is some variation in the self-image of students in different talent areas. Perhaps the most striking contrast for males is a marked difference between students who prefer science and those who prefer music. The self-image of male science students is very positive. It includes high confidence in academic and intellectual capacities (Goal Orientation, Mastery, and Superior Adjustment), less anger and impulsivity (Impulse Control), and greater satisfaction with family life. Male musicians, on the other hand, express less confidence about their abilities and seem to be anxious about personal attractiveness and peer relations. Male art and math students tend toward the musicians' pattern; the athletes most closely parallel the average teens.

Among talented females, self-image is on the whole more uniformly close to the average norms. Unlike their male peers, the female scientists exhibit a mixed self-image profile, usually toward the low end of the normal range. The tendency toward conservative sexual attitudes among the females reaches statistical significance only among the math students. It is interesting that among all females except the artists, the Family Relationships subscale approximates or exceeds the average mean, and Sexual Attitudes appears low. The female artists reverse this pattern. This may suggest some general link between the two subscales for females and a correlation between poor family relations and more open attitudes toward sexuality among female artists in particular. In any case, it makes sense that part of the female artist's struggle to assert a personal style likely involves some conscious rejection of conventional values, including an assertion of sexual liberation. That no such pattern was evident among the male artists probably reflects the continued (if implicit) differentiation in U.S. culture between the gender roles and attitudes thought to be appropriate for each sex.

Personality attributes

Another approach to understanding personality focuses on overall attitudes, motives, and values that apply to behavior across many situations. The PRF was designed to take just such an approach to adolescent personality, supplying average adolescent data for purposes of comparison. In this analysis, we compare the talented males and females with data on a sample of U.S. 9th and 10th graders collected in the mid 1970s.[14]

Tables 4.2 and 4.3 summarize this comparison by sex. What is most immediately striking is the strong core of attributes that distinguishes the talented males and females from their average counterparts. Together these attributes are relevant to both the mastery of a domain and performance within it as specified by the standards established by particular fields. The talented are intellectually curious (Understanding) and actively receptive to information from the world around them (Sentient). At the same time, they express an unusually strong desire to excel (Achievement), are willing to persevere in order to attain their goals (Endurance),

Table 4.2. *Comparison of PRF personality profiles of talented 9th- and 10th-grade males and average male adolescents (scale means and standard deviations)*

	Average (N = 316)	Talented (N = 69)
Abasement	7.42 (2.62)	4.99 (2.70)**
Achievement	9.09 (3.08)	10.62 (3.43)**
Affiliation	9.62 (2.92)	10.20 (3.02)
Aggression	9.02 (2.94)	10.01 (3.03)*
Autonomy	7.36 (3.17)	7.33 (3.12)
Change	9.06 (2.39)	7.75 (2.39)**
Cognitive structure	8.89 (2.92)	9.19 (3.24)
Defendence	7.95 (3.17)	8.77 (3.08)
Dominance	8.15 (3.61)	10.22 (3.71)**
Endurance	8.79 (3.11)	10.10 (3.25)**
Exhibition	7.95 (3.27)	9.28 (4.06)**
Harm avoidance	6.00 (3.61)	7.54 (3.92)**
Impulsivity	7.70 (3.21)	7.14 (3.88)
Nurturance	8.98 (3.11)	9.54 (3.32)
Order	7.21 (3.64)	7.07 (4.81)
Play	9.80 (2.63)	10.03 (2.93)
Sentience	7.41 (2.71)	8.41 (2.57)**
Social recognition	9.51 (2.82)	10.55 (2.95)**
Succorance	7.10 (3.07)	6.83 (3.18)
Understanding	7.19 (2.53)	7.88 (3.15)*

$*p < .05.$ $**p < .01,$ both two-tailed.

and prefer to lead others and control rather than react to events (Dominance). They possess a great desire to display their accomplishments and gain the attention of others (Exhibition) and are less prone than average teens to question their own worth or judgment (Abasement). This core of attributes would seem to be well suited to the cognitive and motivational as well as social, field-specific challenges of talent development.

Some attributes are prominent among one sex only. The talented males show a certain conservatism in their attitudes, valuing stability and predictability over rapid change (Change), and preferring to avoid unusual

Table 4.3. *Comparison of PRF personality profiles of talented*
9th- and 10th-grade females and average female adolescents
(scale means and standard deviations)

	Average (N = 313)	Talented (N = 105)
Abasement	8.36 (2.61)	6.29 (2.70)**
Achievement	8.82 (2.97)	9.88 (3.40)**
Affiliation	11.00 (2.77)	11.27 (3.06)
Aggression	7.96 (3.24)	8.52 (2.85)
Autonomy	5.46 (2.70)	6.05 (2.79)
Change	9.50 (2.53)	8.95 (2.97)
Cognitive structure	9.10 (2.68)	8.75 (2.55)
Defendence	6.85 (2.99)	7.97 (3.01)**
Dominance	6.31 (3.49)	9.03 (3.88)**
Endurance	8.13 (3.10)	8.92 (3.58)*
Exhibition	8.25 (3.77)	9.44 (4.31)**
Harm avoidance	8.88 (4.15)	9.31 (3.75)
Impulsivity	8.11 (3.36)	8.04 (3.41)
Nurturance	12.26 (2.58)	12.36 (2.28)
Order	8.06 (3.83)	7.04 (4.40)*
Play	10.25 (2.62)	10.62 (2.80)
Sentience	8.71 (2.85)	10.79 (2.62)**
Social recognition	10.46 (2.46)	10.47 (2.71)
Succorance	9.43 (3.02)	9.81 (3.17)
Understanding	6.70 (2.43)	7.93 (3.55)**

$*p < .05. **p < .01$, both two-tailed.

physical risks (Harm Avoidance). Heightened stability may be important
to the conservation of energy that cultivation of superior talent requires;
risk avoidance may reflect a subordination of sensationalism in favor of
commitment to long-term goals. It is possible, on the other hand, that a
precocious goal orientation among the males leaves them prone to a
certain rigidity and lack of spontaneity. The theme of dominance is extended by the males to include a proactive attitude toward external threats
and an enjoyment of argument (Aggression). Similar themes are involved
in the females' tendency toward "Defendence" as well as a tendency to

reject criticism. The males also possess an unusual need for social recognition, a desire that may parallel the tendency toward exhibitionism but could also reflect concerns about social competence that we saw earlier in the OSIQ.

Some patterns in the PRF results also suggest certain androgynous traits, especially among the talented females. In the first place, they are strong in such traditionally male attributes as Dominance and need for Achievement. They are also less inclined than average teenage girls to identify with traditional "feminine" values, such as orderliness, neatness, and predictability. For their part, the males are more than normally ready to take an aesthetic, sentient perspective on experience, less likely to identify themselves with physical bravado, and less inclined to dislike routine and predictability. These attributes have all been identified as highly gender-specific characteristics among average male and female teenage populations.[15]

TALENT AND THE AUTOTELIC PERSONALITY

A growing body of research argues for close links between androgynous personality patterns, talent utilization, and creativity during adulthood. Many of these studies have drawn on recent biosocial evidence suggesting gender differences in the hemispheric organization of the brain associated with hormonal changes prior to birth. Specifically, women appear to show a greater facility with concrete/spontaneous information, and males enjoy advantages in processing abstract/symbolic information.[16] This has led some researchers to postulate that individuals who cultivate both "male" and "female" modes of information processing should favor behavioral patterns that exploit talent more effectively. In an interesting application of this hypothesis, Spence and Helmreich in a 1978 study used masculinity and femininity scales to study the productivity of established scientists. Productivity was measured by the number of references to their subjects' publications in the Science Citation Index. True to their hypothesis, the most productive scientists scored high on both the masculinity and femininity scales.

Of course, the notion that "optimal" personality development involves a dynamic, dialectical tension between opposing traits or psychological processes is perennial to philosophy and modern psychology. It runs through Aristotle's description of the golden mean and is central to Nietzsche's perspective on greatness of personal character. John Dewey saw aesthetic experience as the outcome of an interplay between moments of openness and closure in consciousness, leading to optimally complex organizations of psychic energy – what he called a state of active receptivity.[17] Among psychologists, Piaget identified the progressive equilibration of accommodative (modifying) and assimilative (receptive) adaptations with cognitive development among children. His "genetic epistemology" drew heavily, in turn, on biological models of organic development. It explained the emergence of intelligence as the integration of two complementary processes – "accommodation" to outside reality and "assimilation" of what one learned from outside reality to mental schemes. Both Rogers's "fully-functioning person" and Maslow's "self-actualizer" represent personalities that are at once spontaneous, ideographic, and open to the moment while also capable of working hard, of doing abstract synthesis, and of planning for the long term. In 1983 Tetlock referred to those who can differentiate and integrate novel information as possessing a "complex" cognitive style.[18]

One important aspect of this productive tension between traits or processes that has yet to receive thorough and explicit attention is motivation. What enables some people to summon the energy required to keep these otherwise opposing tendencies in dynamic play? What characteristics enhance the individual's enjoyment of this tension? We think that an essential part of the answer lies in an understanding of optimal experiences. As we stated in our introduction to this volume, flow in consciousness emerges when one perceives a well-calibrated balance between the challenges that an activity poses and the skills with which one can immediately respond. These conditions correspond to an experience of optimal balance in which just enough information is present to occupy attention fully without overloading it. People in such situations report an effortless sense of unity with what they are doing, an altered perception of time, and a desire to sustain the state of deep involvement, even to the point of missing meals and losing sleep.[19]

We can all think of a time when we have been immersed in an activity that evoked these feelings, sometimes without our seeking them out. Yet it appears to be equally true that individuals differ widely in their capacities to initiate, sustain, and enjoy such optimal experiences. There are many reasons why this might be true. The pleasures associated with flow are highly desirable, but they are also intensive and energy demanding. They require a willingness to summon energy to meet a potential challenge and to risk learning the limits of one's present capacity. They also require a level of control over attention that permits both the opening of consciousness to new information – the formulation of challenges – and the focus, or fastening of consciousness, on those units of information most relevant to the building of skill. Without both sides of this dynamic equation – challenge and skill, novelty and familiarity, opening and fastening – individuals find themselves either chronically bored because they are unable to find challenges or anxious because they are unable to control them.

The term "autotelic," meaning self-directing or self-rewarding, describes the set of personal characteristics that enables a person to sustain and enjoy the intensive dialectic that results in the experience of flow. The mark of the autotelic personality is the ability to manage a rewarding balance between the "play" of challenge finding and the "work" of skill building. Over time, as a young person learns to master this balanced tension, there will emerge an enduring personal project or life theme as well as a distinctive style of engagement with the world.[20] Thus autotelic individuals should enjoy clear advantages in realizing the development of their talents to the fullest extent. On the day-to-day level, where others see only difficulty, their deep sense of interest aids them in recognizing new challenges, with new opportunities pitched just far enough ahead of current skills to mobilize but not overwhelm psychic resources. In the long run, the emerging sense of a life theme acts as an organizing agent in consciousness, authorizing the devotion of extensive time to projects that reflect deep personal interests.

It seems to be an unfortunate fact that most people lack this interest in discovering challenges and developing skills. Adults in our culture tend to prefer relaxing situations of low challenge, even though they feel better when the challenges are higher.[21] Both adolescents and adults spend most of their free time in undemanding leisure, such as watching television, even though they claim to feel passive, dissatisfied, and unskilled when doing so.[22] Given these general trends, one would expect that autotelic personality traits might be a necessity for young people who are trying to excel.

But does the possession of unusual talent enhance the prominence of autotelic patterns in personality? This certainly seems to be a reasonable proposition. To be naturally gifted in music, to take only one example, does not simply involve perfect pitch and a good memory for melodies. It also means to be so attuned to the domain of sounds that opportunities for interest and action are relatively easy to identify – indeed, almost impossible to resist. But without the motivation and endurance for cultivating these native skills, the talent will remain only an unfulfilled promise. Similar dynamics apply in all the talent areas considered here. Although natural endowment may not be a guarantor of personal happiness, it undoubtedly promotes early and relatively effortless experiences of flow at relatively complex levels of performance.

The cluster of PRF attributes that distinguishes talented from average teens clearly suggests the autotelic pattern we have just described. The performance of the talented on the Sentience and Understanding subscales indicates an unusual curiosity and openness to experience as well as spontaneous attunement to the information provided by the senses. The superiority of the talented teens on the Achievement and Endurance subscales attests to the value they place on industriousness, perseverance, and the attainment of personal goals. The results of the PRF analysis strongly indicate that the talented begin adolescence prepared to experience flow in activities with high potential for personal growth.

CONCLUSIONS

It is clear from the results summarized in this chapter that those adolescents who had impressed their teachers as being talented not only possessed natural gifts but were also fortunate in having the family background and personality traits that are conducive to success in their respective fields. Their scores on standard tests of academic achievement, their scholastic performance, and their accomplishments in their fields clearly show superior promise. There is no question that these young people are indeed talented in one of the five domains.

But in addition their families have educational and economic resources considerably above what is typical of the community in which they live. Furthermore their families are unusually flexible and yet cohesive, thus providing a context that facilitates the cultivation of talent. Finally, despite a somewhat negative self-image and perhaps extreme sensitivity that might make them more than usually vulnerable to criticism and self-criticism, the talented teenagers entered adolescence with personality attributes well suited to the difficult struggle of establishing their mastery over a domain: a desire to achieve, persistence, and a curiosity and openness to experience. These traits add up to an autotelic personality.

But will these advantages also help in keeping talent alive through the crucial and troublesome years of high school? In part III of this volume, we shall return to the question of whether family background, parental support, and autotelic patterns of personality continue to help the development of talents. We now turn, in chapter 5, to a comparison of gifted and average adolescents based on the data collected with the Experience Sampling Method. This will enable us to find out in more detail whether talented teens experience the various aspects of their everyday life like average adolescents – in terms of both what they do all day and how they feel about what they do.

NOTES

1 More than any other occupational group, young artists rate high the value appropriate to their vocation, to the exclusion of all others (Getzels & Csikszentmihalyi, 1976). In other words, they value aesthetics more than clergymen value religion. The same singleness of purpose shows in their lack of interest in academic subjects in school.
2 Wilson, 1987, pp. 57, 58.
3 Miller, 1982.
4 Beattie & Csikszentmihalyi, 1981.
5 Cole, Gay, Glick, & Sharp, 1971; Ogbu, 1978, 1990; Snow, Barnes, Chandler, Goodman, & Hemphill, 1991.
6 Olson, Bell, & Porter, 1982.
7 Olson, Sprenkle, & Russell, 1979.
8 "NS" indicates that a given statistical test is not significant.
9 Beavers & Voeller, 1983.

10 Csikszentmihalyi & Larson, 1984; Erikson, 1968; Offer & Offer, 1975.
11 Offer, Ostrov, & Howard, 1981.
12 Csikszentmihalyi & Larson, 1984; Griffin, Chassin, & Young, 1981; Offer, Ostrov, & Howard, 1982.
13 Whalen & Csikszentmihalyi, 1989.
14 Nesselroade & Baltes, 1974.
15 Gilligan, 1982; Spence & Helmreich, 1978.
16 Rossi, 1987.
17 Dewey, 1934/1980.
18 Maslow, 1971; Piaget, 1977; Rogers, 1961; Tetlock, 1983.
19 Csikszentmihalyi, 1975; Csikszentmihalyi & Csikszentmihalyi, 1988.
20 Csikszentmihalyi & Larson, 1984.
21 For instance, U.S. adults were found to have much more frequent flow experiences at work than in free time, yet their motivation at work was uniformly lower than in leisure (Csikszentmihalyi & LeFevre, 1989).
22 Most of the free time of both children and adults is now spent watching television, yet the quality of experience is reported to be generally worse when watching TV than when doing almost anything else (Kubey & Csikszentmihalyi, 1990). This finding is certainly one of the more mysterious facts of human nature.

5
How talented teenagers live

We have seen that teens with special talents also have unusually effective social supports and a distinctive profile of personality traits. Compared with their average peers of the same age, they have developed better control over impulses, are less stereotyped by gender, and are better able to enjoy experiences, because they are highly focused on achievement and endurance yet at the same time are sensitive and open to the environment. The only discordant note in this generally favorable picture is provided by some of the findings from the Offer Self-Image Questionnaire (OSIQ). According to this measure, talented teenagers see themselves in somewhat less positive terms than their average peers do, and they are especially dissatisfied with their sexuality. These results suggest two aspects of the downside of talent: excessive expectations about self and some frustration about the repression of normal instinctual interests – or rechanneling of attention – that the development of talent requires.

But to get a better idea of how these abstract personality traits actually affect talented adolescents, we need to get a better idea of what they do all day and how they feel about what they do. In this chapter, therefore, we compare talented and average students in terms of time use and quality of experience. How do talented students spend their time? Do they work harder and play less than average students? When compared with average students, are they more likely to be alone or with family and friends? Are talented students happier and more motivated than average teens when studying? These are some of the questions we shall now try to answer.

In order to do so, we have first to find a comparison group of average students to contrast with the talented sample. For this purpose, we selected 41 freshmen and sophomores from a previous Experience Sampling Method (ESM) study.[1] This "average" sample matched our talented sample as closely as possible in age and approximate socioeconomic background. The average sample had attended the same high school. The one difference between it and the talented groups was that data concerning the former was collected 8 years before the present study.

Several kinds of comparison were made. First, we examined possible differences in how talented and average students use their time. The proportions of time spent in different activities (i.e., productive, leisure, and maintenance) and with different companions (i.e., family, friends, and alone) were compared. Second, we tried to find out whether the experience of talented and average students is different across different activities and companions. Four experiential variables were used in the analysis: affect (a composite score of how happy, cheerful, and sociable students reported being); activation (a composite score of alert, active, strong, and excited); concentration; and the wish to be doing the activity. Third, the kinds of activities that talented and average adolescents engaged in were compared when they were alone, when they were with their friends, and when they were with their family. Of special interest was whether talented students did more productive work and engaged more often in structured leisure activities than average students.

THE USE OF TIME

When trying to understand how one person differs from another, perhaps the most important fact to know is how the two are spending their time. The pattern of time use is one of the most revealing characteristics of a person or a group. It indicates where attention is focused and where psychic energy is invested. A person who spends long periods watching television will have different information stored in her or his mind than – and will develop different habits of action from – one who spends more time with friends or reading or playing a musical instrument. Patterns of time use are important, because time is limited and because a person cannot do more than one thing well at the same time. Given a total of 16 or so waking hours each day, or 112 hours a week, each of us must decide how to fill those hours, and the choices we make determine what our lives will consist of. These choices are especially crucial in adolescence, when the pattern for the future course of one's life is being set.

To find out whether talented and average students spend their time differently, we counted the number of responses in different activities and with different companions based on the data from the ESM questionnaire, and then computed them as a percentage score for each person. For instance, if a student gave 40 responses through the week and 10 indicated that she was doing productive work, her percentage score of productive activities would be 25. The same information can be interpreted as suggesting that this student spent approximately 25 hours a week studying or working, because the pagers sampled randomly from approximately 100 waking hours through the week.

The comparison of time use in different activities is summarized in Table 5.1. As the table shows, when both groups were in school the talented students were significantly more likely to be involved in classwork. In other words, when compared with average students, they tended to be in class more often and spent more time listening to the teacher, engaging in class discussion, presenting a project, taking notes, and so forth. This may be partly because many of them took more advanced courses and more courses related to their talents.

Outside school, however, talented students did not seem to study more than average students. Both groups spent about 11–12% of their time doing homework and studying. Because talented students tended to take more classes yet spent the same amount of time studying outside class, they were probably able to work more efficiently. They also spent significantly less time working at paid jobs outside school. Whereas the average teen worked at a job about 5% of the time, the talented did so only 1.6% of the time. In fact, less than one fourth of talented students even had a job. In contrast, about half of the average students worked outside school.

The two groups differed considerably also with respect to leisure activities. First, the average adolescents spent significantly more time in such socializing activities as parties, going out with friends, and talking to peers. Second, students in the talented group were more often involved in art activities and hobbies that require concentrated, skilled performance. Third, talented students watched more television than average students. The amount of time the two groups spent in sports and games, reading,

Table 5.1. *Percentage of time spent in different activities*

Activity	Talented (N = 208)	Average (N = 41)
Productive		
Classwork	16.32	10.38***
Studying	12.19	10.90
Job	1.60	4.94**
Leisure		
Socializing	13.43	18.08**
Sports & games	2.70	3.96
Television	11.67	6.17***
Listening to music	1.70	1.76
Art & hobbies	4.25	1.22***
Reading	3.43	3.22
Thinking	3.51	2.52
Other	1.11	3.08***
Maintenance		
Eating	5.05	5.88
Personal care	7.06	7.18
Chores & errands	4.73	11.86***
Rest & napping	3.23	3.05
Others	3.15	2.19

Note: These percentages are based on approximately 7,000 self-reports for the talented group and 1,500 for the average group.

Significance of t-tests between the two groups: **$p <$ .01. ***$p <$ .001.

and thinking were about the same. Although average students appeared to engage in informal social interactions more often than talented students, the latter were more frequently engaged in more structured leisure activities.

When talented students were free, they tended to be involved in activities related to art and hobbies more often than average students. These hobbies included working on computers, collecting stamps, singing, drawing, and so on. To enjoy these activities requires skill and knowledge. Ability and interest in such areas as math, music, and art might have allowed these students to develop the kind of expertise needed to enjoy structured leisure activities. Students in the average group may either not have seen the challenges in these activities or lacked the skills and knowledge to pursue them, and thus were less often involved in leisure requiring complex and disciplined behavior.

Talent and television

These findings are consistent with expectations. But talented students were also more likely to watch television when they had free time. This finding could be due partly to a cohort difference. The data on the average group were collected in the late 1970s, whereas the data on the talented group were obtained in the mid 1980s. Children and teenagers of the 1980s presumably watch more television than those of the past, especially since VCRs have become widely available. But the difference – approximately $5\frac{1}{2}$ hours per week – is too large to be accounted for by technologically induced cultural changes in viewing habits.[2]

One interesting issue to consider is whether talented students watched more television than average students because of a more intense or stressful life style. For instance, many students spent several hours every day working on activities related to their talent. Does this mean that they have a greater need for relaxation? We did not find any support for this proposition. The amount of time spent studying was not correlated with the amount of time spent watching television, nor with the amount of time spent in talent-related activities.

To examine further the reason why talented students watched more television than average students, we tried to find out what kinds of television programs students watched. Unfortunately, students did not often provide such information on their ESM response forms. Only about half of the television responses mentioned specific programs. The largest category was sports programs. The large number of talented athletes in the sample may explain this finding. These students had a keen interest in sports, and TV sports programs might be both entertaining and educational for them. Hence they might have watched more sports programs than other students.

Watching videotapes, which has definitely increased in the past 5 years, might also explain the difference. Additionally, cable television, which has become more popular in the last decade, provides more choices of programs and may also increase the frequency of television watching. It is also possible that for 13- and 14-year-olds watching television is more stimulating than interacting with peers, and for this reason talented teens spent more time doing it. If this is the right explanation, as they grow older they may gradually outgrow the medium and end up watching less TV than average adolescents. At this point all we know is that, contrary to expectations, talented teens watched more TV in early adolescence than comparable average teenagers.

The proportion of time spent in routine maintenance activities was similar for both groups in our study. One interesting difference was that average adolescents appeared to do chores around the house twice as often as the talented. It is unlikely that the average adolescents did so voluntarily. It is more likely that they were required by their families to do so, whereas the parents of the talented group were more willing to exempt them from routine chores.

THE CHOICE OF COMPANIONS

It is not only what we do that determines the pattern of our lives, but also whom we choose to associate with. There are individuals who cannot tolerate solitude and must always surround themselves with other people. Such persons have a hard time acquiring complex skills or concentrating on difficult problems. But for adolescents, it also matters how much time they spend with friends versus family. Too much involvement with the family might retard the process of individuation, whereas too little might interfere with the gradual process of maturation.

Table 5.2 compares the two groups in terms of the amount of time spent alone and with various companions. Contrary to expectations, talented and average adolescents did not differ significantly in the amount of time they spent with friends. However, the former were more often in the

Table 5.2. *Percentage of time spent alone and with various companions*

Companions	Talented (N = 208)	Average (N = 41)
None (time alone)	30.79	25.56*
Family		
Parents only	8.28	3.88***
Siblings only	7.71	4.09**
Parents & siblings	3.02	8.29***
Friends		
Friends only	27.29	31.50
Friends & parents	.70	2.76**
Classmates	20.61	18.85
Others	1.60	5.07

Significance of *t*-tests between the two groups: $*p < .05$. $**p < .01$. $***p < .001$.

company of either their parents or their siblings, whereas the latter were more often with parents and siblings at the same time. Perhaps these strong differences mean that talented adolescents were involved in more intimate, one-on-one interactions with members of their families, whereas average teens were involved in more diffuse and less personal interactions. Overall, talented students spent slightly more time with their families, but the difference was only marginally significant ($p = .06$).

The most interesting difference concerns the amount of time spent in solitude. Talented teenagers appear to spend about 5 more hours a week alone than do average teenagers. Several studies have shown that being alone is usually not an enjoyable experience.[3] It is possible that talented students are more able to tolerate solitude and are therefore alone more often. It is also likely that the motivation to develop talent-related skills requires that they be alone.

In conclusion, the time use analysis suggests that each week talented teens spent about 6 hours more doing classwork, $5\frac{1}{2}$ hours more watching

TV, 3 hours more involved in art and hobbies, and $3\frac{1}{2}$ hours more in personal care. Average teens, on the other hand, spent 3 hours a week more working at jobs, 7 hours more doing chores and errands, and $4\frac{1}{2}$ hours more socializing with peers. In terms of companions, talented teens spent 5 hours more each week alone, 4 hours more alone with parents, and $3\frac{1}{2}$ hours more with siblings only. Average teens, on the other hand, spent 5 hours more a week with both parents and siblings and 2 hours more with parents and friends.

These patterns, in turn, suggest that the talented adolescents were in the process of forging for themselves patterns of life that would make it possible for them to develop the gifts with which they were endowed. They invested more psychic energy in activities that require skills and discipline, spent more time in solitude, and when they were with other people were more likely to be with one person at a time. In other contexts, we have remarked on how difficult it must be for American adolescents to learn how to become mature adults, given how little time they spend alone with their parents.[4] Talented teens are fortunate in being able to be twice as often in that presumably secure socializing context.

In the next section we shall see more closely, by crossing activity and companionship categories, how the two groups differed in their use of time. This analysis will reveal what students did while they were with different types of companions.

ACTIVITIES IN DIFFERENT SOCIAL CONTEXTS

Table 5.3 summarizes the differences between how the students in the two groups spent their time when they were either alone or with different kinds of people. When they were by themselves, talented teens spent much more time socializing – talking on the phone, writing letters, or doing something else related to people or social interaction. So although they were physically alone more, they were likely to be less lonely because their attention tended to be focused more on interaction with other people. Each talented teen spent on the average almost 3 hours a week in such solitary socializing, whereas their average counterparts did it for less than $\frac{1}{2}$ hour a week.

Whereas talented adolescents, when they were alone, tended to watch

Table 5.3. *What do talented teens do when they are . . .*

... *alone? Compared with average teens, they*
Make more phone calls and write letters more often ($p < .001$)
Work less ($p < .01$)
Watch TV more ($p < .05$)
Do fewer chores & errands ($p < .001$)
Are involved in more self-care ($p < .001$)

... *with friends? Compared with average teens, they*
Study more ($p < .01$)
Play fewer sports & games ($p < .05$)
Watch TV more ($p < .05$)
Do fewer chores & errands ($p < .001$)
Do more art & hobbies ($p < .001$)
Work less ($p < .05$)
Do more thinking ($p < .01$)
Do less socializing ($p < .05$)
Do more self-care ($p < .001$)

... *with family? Compared with average teens, they*
Watch TV more ($p < .05$)
Play fewer sports & games ($p < .05$)
Listen to music more ($p < .05$)
Do fewer chores & errands ($p < .001$)
Do more self-care ($p < .01$)
Spend more time in transportation ($p < .05$)

Note: p values refer to *t*-tests comparing talented and average students.

TV more often, spent more time on personal care, did fewer chores around the house, and worked less at outside jobs, the difference between the two groups was even more pronounced in the company of peers. When they were with friends, talented teens studied more, did more arts and hobbies, listed "thinking" as their main activity more often, and engaged in more TV viewing. On the other hand, the average teens did more socializing and playing sports with their friends and also tended to work more and do more chores. A similar pattern of activities distinguished the two groups of teens when they spent time with their families, with the talented spending more time watching TV, listening to music, and involved in personal care and transportation, and less time playing sports and doing chores.

One large difference between the two groups needs mentioning, because it is puzzling and unexpected. In every social context, talented teens spent significantly more time in self-care and grooming than average teens did. A typical 12–13-year-old spent about $3\frac{1}{2}$ hours a week washing, combing hair, dressing up, and so forth. A talented teen spent exactly twice as much time – approximately 1 hour a day. Is this a sign of greater concern for socially sanctioned appearance? Could it be, as the OSIQ data in chapter 4 suggested, that talented adolescents feel less secure about the image they present to the world? Or is it an indication of a latent narcissism, a preoccupation with the self flagged by the high score on the Exhibition factor of the PRF? We do not know the answer, but these questions are worth pursuing.

The differences in time use suggest a rather clear and consistent picture of the life environment of talented adolescents. They were more protected from the routine exigencies of life than their average peers: They had to work less and did not need to do as many household chores. These findings tally with the demographic results concerning family support reported in the preceding chapter. On the other hand, talented teens seemed to be missing some of the more active and interactive opportunities typical of adolescence, such as sports, games, and socializing – although when they were alone their attention was more focused on other people. Even when they were with friends they tended to study, think, and become involved in structured leisure more than average teens. Perhaps this pattern of time use with peers was a reflection of their "immature" sexual attitudes. They also seemed to be more dependent on their parents. They spent more time with them driving in cars and engaged in the more passive joint leisure activities, such as watching TV and listening to music.

According to the facile stereotypes of our era, it would be easy to label the talented teens' behavior pattern as "nerdish," and to think of them as coddled children. But perhaps the disciplined seriousness of their lifestyle is the only possible adaptation to the talents they possess. The development of a mathematical ability or a musical gift requires precisely this kind of sharpened focus; the more pleasant and easygoing lifestyle typical of U.S. adolescence would diffuse and eventually dilute such talent.

How a person invests the limited time at her or his disposal is an important question. But equally important is how a person experiences the events of daily life. How happy one is or how much one concentrates at any given moment will add up slowly to a determination of the quality of life. The next section examines how talented and average teenagers feel in general and how they feel when involved in different activities and in the company of various people.

HOW THE TALENTED EXPERIENCE DIFFERENT ASPECTS OF LIFE

The first question to be addressed is: Do the two groups differ in the overall quality of experience? Do talented teens generally describe themselves as more happy, active, cheerful, and strong than their average peers? To answer this question, we compared the mean scores of the two groups on the nine dimensions of experience reported in Table 5.4.

Both groups filled out the Experience Sampling Forms for 1 week. As seen in Table 5.4, talented students rated themselves as having significantly lower moods than average students on all but one of the nine dimensions of experience. The variability of mood was about the same for both groups. What do these somewhat disturbing results mean? They may be simply due to response biases – that is, average students, who are somewhat less self-critical than the talented, could be rating themselves more favorably than they actually feel. This explanation is supported by the higher self-criticism of the talented shown by the negative OSIQ self-image. It is also possible that the talented group actually felt less positive than their average counterparts. Being regarded as having special gifts might bring excessive pressure. Parents and teachers have higher expectations of what they can achieve. Such students might also set higher standards for themselves and might feel more depressed when they fail to meet them.

Finally, it is possible that the very lifestyle necessary for developing talent also depressed the quality of experience, at least in the short run. People generally feel worse when they are alone and much better when they are socializing with friends. The fact that the talented teens spent more time alone and less time socializing would automatically result in

Table 5.4. *Mean level of moods over the course of a week*

Mood	Talented (N = 208)	Average (N = 41)
Affect		
Happy	4.87	5.15**
Cheerful	4.51	4.89***
Sociable	4.59	5.06***
Potency		
Alert	4.68	5.04**
Active	4.25	4.46
Strong	4.41	4.69**
Excited	4.10	4.43**
Concentration (How much were you concentrating.)	4.39	4.82*
Motivation (Wish to be doing activity)	4.29	5.26***

Note: The figures above are group means based on individual means. The actual number of observations that contributed to them was over 7,000 for the talented group and over 1,500 for the average group.

Significance of *t*-tests between the two groups: *$p < .05$. **$p < .01$. ***$p < .001$.

their overall moods being worse. The 6 more hours a week the talented spend focusing on classwork probably also depressed their moods somewhat. Feeling less happy, cheerful, sociable, alert, excited, and so on might be the price they have to pay for the kind of life they must lead in order to develop their talent.

But is the relative quality of experience different for the two groups? For example, do talented students feel relatively happier when studying than average students? This is an important question, because here response bias can be ruled out by comparing each student's average response in an activity or companionship setting with the same student's overall average for the week. We compared talented and average students' responses while engaged in different activities and while being with various companions, using z scores for the same nine experiential variables: Affect (a composite score of happy, cheerful, and sociable), Potency (a composite score of active, alert, strong, and excited), Concentration, and Motivation (a wish to do the activity), calculated from individual raw scores. Mean z scores in each situation were then computed for each student.

The comparison of the two groups' experience of different activities revealed very strong similarities. For instance, both groups reported lower affect, potency, and motivation but higher concentration in classwork compared with their respective baselines for the week. Their experience in leisure activities was the opposite. Both groups tended to report higher affect, potency, and motivation but lower concentration than the averages of the week. This experience while engaging in everyday maintenance activities was usually neither positive nor negative. These results are consistent with past findings.[5]

Similarly, as expected, both groups felt most positive with friends, least positive alone, and more or less average with the family. Despite the great similarities in how the two sets of teenagers experienced the different facets of their lives, there were some noteworthy exceptions. These can be summarized by considering each of the four main dimensions of experience.

Affect. First, talented teens tended to feel relatively more happy and cheerful in productive activities, such as classwork and studying, and especially when working. Their experience in such activities was usually not positive, but it was significantly less negative than for average teens. And when they were alone, talented teens were significantly less unhappy than average teens – presumably in part because solitude for the talented is more social; that is, it involves more writing and more phone conversations.

Potency. The two groups were remarkably similar in how active, alert, strong, and excited they felt in different activities. Their z scores were almost identical in each context, except for one significant difference: The talented reported higher potency when working (but then, it should be remembered that they worked much less than average teens). They also felt relatively more potent when reading and thinking. In terms of companionship, the only significant difference between the two groups was when students were alone. In that context, talented teens felt less passive and weak than did their average peers.

Concentration. Talented students reported relatively higher levels of concentration than their average peers when involved in classwork, studying, reading, and sports and games. But in less demanding activities, such as household chores, socializing, and watching TV, their concentration levels dropped well below those of average students. Apparently the attentional structures of talented teens are more efficient in that their concentration varies with the complexity of the task, rising when it is needed and dropping when it is not. There were no differences between the two groups in terms of how level of concentration varied with companionship.

Motivation. Talented students reported significantly higher levels of "wishing to do" when reading and thinking, but they were even with average students when doing classwork and studying. The average motivation of talented students when alone was slightly positive, whereas the motivation level of average students when alone was quite negative, resulting in a sizable relative difference ($p < .001$). When compared with average students, talented students seemed to enjoy solitude more, which is usually an unpleasant experience for teenagers.[6]

Overall, the quality of experience of the two groups of students in various situations was more similar than different. There were some exceptions, however. The most important ones concern the experience of solitude and of those activities, such as reading, thinking, and studying, that require a certain amount of quiet and reflection. Although both groups reported feeling worse while alone than when they were with friends or family members, the experience of talented students was less negative than that of average students.

The ability to make use of time in solitude is an important asset, especially for adolescents. Much productive work can only be done when one is alone. Being alone also allows an individual to turn attention inward, thus becoming more sensitive to one's needs and goals. In other words, solitary time, if used appropriately, is a time when skills can be developed and challenges identified.

CONCLUSIONS

The comparison of time use and quality of experience between talented and average teens begins to suggest the difficult compromises the development of talent entails. To a certain extent, talented adolescents had to trade off immediate enjoyment for nurture of their special gifts. They could not afford as much time just socializing with friends, and they had to spend more time alone, thus depriving themselves of the spontaneous good times that teenagers usually thrive on. They were helped in this respect by their families and by their autotelic personality traits, especially the strong need for achievement and endurance that they possessed. The downside, however, is that the moment-to-moment quality of their moods suffered.

But talented teens seemed to have developed two ways of coping with their rather isolated and regimented situation. First, the activities they did when alone or with their families tended to involve more leisure (e.g., television watching, art, and hobbies) and less work (e.g., outside jobs and household chores), thus providing a certain level of immediate enjoyment. Second – and perhaps not coincidentally – they had learned to enjoy solitary activities; for instance, they were more motivated than average students when alone and when reading or thinking. And when they were alone they tended to be less lonely because their attention was more focused on interactions with other people.

In general, it seems that talented students had a tendency to engage in activities that would help them maintain a positive experience *in the long run*. Both when alone and when with friends, they were more often involved in challenging activities (e.g., art and hobbies while alone and doing homework with friends). Talented adolescents also appeared to use time more effectively. When alone, they maintained contact with others by talking on the phone or writing letters, which would make them feel less lonely. Their concentration was more closely responsive to the demands of the situation. While with friends, they studied or did arts and hobbies. Hence being with friends involved more than immediate enjoyment.

In many ways these conclusions are reminiscent of ancient wisdom – for instance, Aesop's fable of the grasshopper and the ant. In that story the ant works hard all summer, rushing about to gather seeds and store them in his burrow. The grasshopper spends the summer jumping from party to party, playing his music and telling everyone how much smarter he is than the poor ant, who is wasting this tremendous opportunity for a good time. Of course when winter comes the ant is snug at home while the hungry grasshopper goes begging for food.

But the results of our study show that reality is much more complicated than the fable. In some respects, the talented teens acted more like the grasshopper; in other respects, they acted more like the ant. For example, they worked and did chores less often than their peers – clearly grasshopperish characteristics. On the other hand, they spent less time socializing and more time involved in complex activities like classwork – antlike traits, for sure.

No human teenager – no matter how talented – could spend all of her or his time preparing for the future. Even the most gifted need to waste a few hours relaxing with friends or watching television. Yet the scarcity of time is an issue even for 12-year-olds. The talented have many advantages, but having more than 24 hours a day is not one of them. If they want to make something of the gifts they have, they must learn to manage that most precious of all resources, time. They must also learn to enjoy the kind of solitary, disciplined activity that leads to the development of talent.

Of course the argument concerning talented teens applies as well to all adolescents. Even though in these chapters we contrast talented with average teenagers, the purpose of these contrasts is to understand what it takes to develop any kind of talent, not only the exceptional kind. Our interest in talented students arises mainly because they exhibit more clearly the processes that every student displays to a lesser or a greater extent. By studying talented teens we can understand more easily what is true for every student. The choices that talented students must make between immediate gratification and long-term development, and between solitude and companionship, are the same choices every young person must make, regardless of her or his level of talent.

All of us have gifts that are potentially useful and worthy of being appreciated. But to develop these latent talents we must cultivate them, and this takes time and the investment of psychic energy. The lifestyle that talented adolescents develop can show us some of the choices all of us must make in order to cultivate our gifts.

NOTES

1 Csikszentmihalyi & Larson, 1984.
2 Robert Kubey, personal communication, 1990.
3 Csikszentmihalyi & Larson, 1984; Larson & Csikszentmihalyi, 1978; Larson, Mannell, & Zuzanek, 1986.
4 For example, average teenagers in one of our previous studies spent no more than 5 minutes a day alone with their fathers (Csikszentmihalyi, 1990a, p. 274; Csikszentmihalyi and Larson, 1984, p. 73).
5 Some of the most complete normative data for how adolescents feel in the different activities that make up their lives can be found in Csikszentmihalyi & Csikszentmihalyi, 1988; Csikszentmihalyi & Larson, 1984; Csikszentmihalyi & Wong, 1991.
6 Csikszentmihalyi & Larson, 1984. Actually, at every age people report lower moods when they are alone: Larson & Csikszentmihalyi, 1978; Larson, Mannell, & Zuzanek, 1986.

PART II

The development of talent

6

Fields and domains of talent in adolescence

The preceding chapters have begun to show the traits that distinguish talented adolescents from their more average peers. In general, they have supportive families with above-average income, they are developing personality characteristics appropriate to the cultivation of talent, and they are learning behavioral habits and personal reward systems that are consistent with the focused use of time and attention. The downside of this pattern is a perhaps excessive self-criticism and a paradoxical combination of early maturity with prolonged sexual latency. Together these add up to a less positive quality of experience overall.

These findings, based on the comparison of talented students with their "average" counterparts, is expanded in the chapters of part II by a more detailed focus on the traits and processes that are most closely related to the development of talent itself. This chapter reviews the opportunities for expressing talent that are open to high school students in their domains and fields and how they are likely to affect the experience of the students involved with them. The next chapter deals with how students actually experience their work in the various talent areas. Chapters 8 and 9 explore how the family and the school contribute to the cultivation of talent in adolescence.

THE CONTEXT OF FIELDS AND DOMAINS

Each of the special domains of talent – art, mathematics, and so on – is represented during the high school years by an organized setting that allows gifted young persons to develop their talents in that area. Without an institutional network of people and activities to support the domain, it would be next to impossible for a teenager to learn and to practice the necessary skills.

In the domain of athletics, for example, the field includes coaches, clinics, and competitions, ranging from the local to the international level, that make it possible for physically gifted youngsters to perfect their skills in a public arena. Without a regular series of games or meets, which often require expensive and painstaking organization, an athlete is literally unable to assess her or his competence, and is certainly unable to demonstrate it. Superior athletic performance also attracts the attention of the media, and young stars become used to seeing their names in the school paper or in the sports pages of the local papers. Some of the athletes become involved in the management of teams, help obtain the financial sponsorship of local merchants, and take offices in the national amateur and professional sports associations. All of these apparently marginal activities constitute the field in which athletic talent manifests itself. In their absence, young people might develop their muscles and stamina just as well, but they could not develop their *talent*, because talent involves public evaluation and recognition. For these to be present, it is necessary to have a field.

The same argument holds for the other domains covered in this study – art, math, music, and science. For each domain, there must be recognized ways of selecting, training, coaching, evaluating, and rewarding promising candidates. The school is the institution primarily responsible for providing the fields relevant for talented youngsters. But many other individuals and institutions are also involved: first and foremost parents, then churches, youth groups, businesses that provide prizes, national organizations, government agencies, private patrons, the media, and probably several more. To understand how talent develops in adolescence, we must consider how these fields are constituted, because they have an important effect on whether teenagers will continue to use their gifts or give them up.

Understanding the development of talent also requires that, in addition to considering how the field is constituted, we consider the type of information in each domain and how it is organized. The process of learning the skills associated with the arts is likely to be different from learning those connected with the sciences.

There are many similarities in the way teenagers learn to develop their talent, regardless of the domain in which they are gifted. For instance, as we have just said, most talent-related activity tends to take place in the school or to be sponsored by the school. But there are also important differences among domains in terms of where, how, and with whom they are encountered, and these differences, in turn, have an impact on the way the activity is experienced and therefore on the rewards it provides the performer.

For example, gifted young artists mostly work in a studio class at school. There they work by themselves but are surrounded by peers engaged in similar activities. The drawing or sculpture of one student is accessible to the others and therefore can be shared as it progresses. The work itself can perhaps be best characterized as an *expressive performance;* that is, although the teacher often provides a common theme or task, the students are free to execute it in accordance with their own tastes and concerns.

The way science is practiced is in some ways similar, in some ways different. Young science students spend most of their time working on experiments in a school lab, which in some ways resembles the art studio. But in the lab there is less opportunity to follow the progress of peers, and therefore the lab experience tends to be more solitary. A great deal of preparation also goes into science: Students must spend many hours alone poring over books. Perhaps most important, working in a lab is seldom experienced as an expressive performance. The point of most high school lab experiments is to replicate, as meticulously and accurately as possible, some standard procedure. Thus goals are typically more *instrumental* and less personal.

The practice of mathematics takes place in a substantially different environment. It does not require studios or laboratories; most of the action takes place with textbooks, notepads, and computers. Thus it tends to be a more individual, lonelier activity than the other two. Yet strong high school math programs have added an important social dimension to this essentially solitary activity. High school math teams are often very gregarious: Members spend much of their free time in the math club discussing advanced topics in the domain. The constant competition both within the team for top positions and between teams from different schools makes high school mathematics more similar in this respect to athletics than to art or to science.

From the point of view of competition, music as practiced in high school does not lag far behind. After one of the students in our sample was selected for the 19th flute chair in the statewide orchestra, whereas her friend was given the 12th chair, she said, "That was like a bullet through my head." In some schools, orchestra positions are reassigned every week, keeping up a relentless pressure on young instrumentalists. Music resembles art because it involves an expressive performance, but it also resembles science in that, before becoming expressive, the performance must conform to the strict impersonal standards of the domain. In terms of where the activity takes place, music again is similar to art in that it tends to be rehearsed and performed in a studiolike space within the school and in company with many other peers. But music also involves much solitary practice at home or in a private teacher's studio.

In addition to field differences, students must learn to adjust to and work within the confines of the particular domain itself. Each domain requires the assimilation of a specialized body of knowledge that is important for manipulating and interpreting relevant information in the domain. For instance, young musicians must learn to read music as a prerequisite to expert performance. Young scientists must learn the rudiments of the scientific method in order to understand the significance of experimental design. Vast differences exist in the type of information dealt with in each domain, in its ultimate purpose, and thus in the rules for interacting with it. As a result, just as field differences are likely to affect a student's learning experiences, differences among domains will also.

Although it would be easy to exaggerate stereotypic differences that are associated with the arts and sciences in Western culture, and although it is our ultimate intention to bridge the chasm that usually lies between them, it is useful to first draw some clear distinctions before assessing any common ground. It is likely that there are some basic differences between these general domains that fuel the cultural stereotypes and thus impact the way they are perceived by teenagers in high school. Understanding these differences may be helpful in avoiding any simplistic dichotomies that restrict the range of teenage enjoyment and involvement in the arts or sciences.

One basic distinction often made between the arts and sciences concerns their ultimate aims: The symbols of the former (tones, colors, movements) are evaluated in terms of intrinsic aesthetic criteria; those in the latter (words, ideas, numbers) are judged by their contribution to systems of rational truth. Both provide goals that encourage individuals to grow, but each attempts to do this in a different way. Aesthetic judgments rely heavily on the emotional appeal of a work of art and on the training of the senses and the body (new ways of seeing, hearing, moving, and so forth); rational judgments rest upon conceptions of truth and upon continued cognitive growth (new ways of thinking, discussing, measuring, and so forth). Although under closer scrutiny it is apparent that nonrational modes of thinking, with little basis in empirical evidence, are important to even "positivistic" scientists[1] and that rational planning characterizes segments of the artistic process, the aesthetic–rational (or emotional–cognitive) distinction is a good place to draw a line in a preliminary comparison between the arts and the sciences.

Because artistic symbols tend to be more immediate and concrete and scientific ones more cumulative and abstract, individuals working in each domain proceed differently. John Dewey comments, for instance:

Those who are called artists have for their subject-matter the qualities of things of direct experience; "intellectual" inquirers deal with these qualities at one remove, through the medium of symbols that stand for qualities but are not significant in their immediate presence. . . . Thinking in terms of colors, tones, images, is a different operation technically from thinking in words.[2]

Suzanne Langer suggests that forms, colors, lines, and tones are also symbols, but she distinguishes them as *presentational* symbols; that is, things that provide a more sensuous "presentation" of the world.[3] Science, on the other hand, according to Langer, deals with *discursive* symbols that represent objects abstracted from their original context, thus allowing them to be studied and compared rationally.

These different emphases in the arts and sciences tend to be exaggerated in high school for didactic purposes. For instance, from the earliest grades, education in the arts is often more sensitive to the child's immediate interests, emotions, and *motivations*. It sees in the child's self-centeredness and impulsivity the seeds of future character and individuality, development of which is the educational ideal. Instruction is thus child-centered, and parents, teachers, mentors, and so on tend to "get behind" the child/student and encourage the free expression of feelings. In contrast, an emphasis on *disciplined work* is more characteristic of science, particularly in high school. Because facts are classified in relation to general principles, lessons can be well ordered and arranged to progress in measured and logical steps. Parents, teachers, and the wider community of scientific scholars encourage less the playful exploration of the student and more the pursuit of long-range goals.

FIELD, DOMAIN, AND EXPERIENCE

Having briefly discussed some of the differences associated with contexts of talent development, we may now consider how these differences impact the subjective experience of those who operate in different domains. Our perspective suggests that the type of domain and how it is enacted in a particular field determines in part how teenagers will experience using their skills, and that, in turn, will impact on how motivated they will be to continue developing those skills. For instance, because people in general, and teenagers especially, tend to feel sad and anxious when they are alone and thus try to avoid solitude as much as possible,[4] it is very hard for them to tolerate the long hours alone that serious study in science and mathematics requires. Gifted young persons might give up not because they lack the cognitive capacity to process the relevant information but because they cannot stand working alone.

The introduction of competitive math tournaments to a certain extent mitigates the loneliness of this pursuit, but at a price: The cut-throat pressure of math teams tends to alienate those young men and women who prefer a more supportive environment. It has been our impression that many promising young mathematicians – and especially many young women – become disengaged from math not because they are unable to keep up with the cognitive challenges but because they cannot bear the supercharged atmosphere of the math clubs, where the topic of conversation always includes each member's latest standing on the team. There are a great deal of envy, barely veiled hostility, and jockeying for power and sympathy in these conversations, and some people just don't wish to put up with the stress involved. Unfortunately, when a student drops out of the *field* of mathematics in high school, he or she is also likely to drop out of the *domain* altogether.

The same observations hold for any of the other domains. Competition, for example, is a major stumbling block for some adolescents in athletics and the arts. The requirement to perform or display one's work in public is an obstacle for some students in music and art while being an incentive for others. The environment in which all the teens enact their talent – the school building with its usual symbolic associations of constraint – leaves its own mark on the students' quality of experience.

The types of symbols the domain uses and the way they are taught – whether didactically or spontaneously – add yet another dimension to how the use of talent is experienced. Of course this situation is to a certain extent unavoidable. There is no way to practice art, music, or mathematics in some pure, abstract state; the practitioner must necessarily become immersed in the domain and involved with such requirements of the field as curricula, teaching styles, tests, and competitions. Therefore, if we want to understand why some young people continue to perfect their gifts while others do not, it is important to consider the different kinds of rewards made available by the domains and fields for those who develop their talent.

THE REWARDS OF TALENT DEVELOPMENT

There are two fundamental reasons why a young person might devote large amounts of psychic energy to developing a talent. The first class of reasons includes *intrinsic rewards*, that is, the fun, enjoyment, and curiosity one feels as one performs in the domain. For instance, children will spontaneously draw or make sounds on an instrument for the sheer "pleasure of being a cause." Many artists, musicians, and scientists claim that what keeps them working in their domains in later life is a continuation of the same experience.[5] It doesn't matter in this context whether the joy is conscious or not or whether it is something like a sublimated expression of a repressed desire, a defense against anxiety, or a form of escape. What does matter is that the person finds in doing the activity a reward sufficient for doing it.

The second set of reasons for doing something consists in *extrinsic rewards*. These include grades in school, prizes in competition, money, status, or any other incentive for performing actions that is external to the action itself. When a student plays the violin less because she derives joy from the sounds she makes and more in order to please her mother or her teacher or to get a place in the school orchestra or to have a chance to be accepted at Juilliard or to become famous, we say that her behavior is motivated primarily by extrinsic rewards.

No one is always and exclusively motivated by only one of these sources of reward. Both extrinsic and intrinsic considerations are generally present in most of our actions. Even a great genius like Leonardo da Vinci, who was constantly driven by curiosity and the sheer pleasure of discovery, always computed carefully the money due him from patrons for his works, and he moved from Florence to Milan to Rome to France, depending on which prince wanted to finance his work. But some artists spend more time thinking about fame and money than others.

The distinction between intrinsic and extrinsic rewards does not apply only to individuals; it applies to activities as well. Some activities, like sports, are primarily motivated by intrinsic rewards; others would not take place unless there were strong extrinsic rewards to motivate them. For instance, very few teenagers would go to school if the extrinsic rewards for attending were lifted. Only a small percentage would attend classes just for the sake of acquiring knowledge.

A simple rule of thumb suggests that if performance in the domain is not enjoyable in itself, then the field must provide extrinsic rewards to attract gifted young people to it, whereas if the activity is intrinsically enjoyable, then fewer extrinsic rewards are needed. It is important to understand what rewards are involved in any given situation, because that will go a long way toward explaining why some young people will keep practicing a gift and others will not. We focus first on the extrinsic rewards that the five fields and domains of talent under consideration typically provide, and then turn to intrinsic rewards.

Long-range extrinsic rewards

The five talent areas differ most dramatically in terms of the kinds of future incentives they are able to offer those students who become involved in them. The science curriculum of the school points to careers in engineering, medicine, and other prestigious and financially rewarding jobs. The instrumental attitude of many students gifted in science and math toward their courses is well summarized by the young man who told us, "Well, the only reason they'd be important is if I was going to get a job using the knowledge from the classes." The importance of science and technology is reinforced by the media, science clubs and prizes, scientific journals, visits to museums, and so forth. A young person entering a career in this field can feel reasonably assured of adequate financial and social rewards.

Teenagers with athletic promise have a much murkier future. Despite the enormous media coverage of athletes and athletic events and despite the great symbolic importance of sports in our culture,[6] the field does not have many career rewards to offer, and what it does offer is severely limited to an athlete's early years. Although star football and basketball players earn astronomical salaries, an athletic career is more like playing the lottery, where a very few extravagant winners are balanced by a great many losers. More realistic careers might involve coaching or other teaching, managerial, or administrative jobs related to sports and physical education. For middle-class youth, athletic talent does not translate into an attractive adult occupation. For them, athletics is more a matter of intrinsic rewards and of lifestyle than a viable occupational option. On the other hand, for those from depressed economic backgrounds, athletics may represent one of the few ways to escape from long-term poverty.

The "fine" arts are also notorious for providing high extrinsic rewards to a few individuals and almost none to the overwhelming majority. For every Picasso, there are at least a thousand obscure artists who spend their lives painting without selling a canvas. But a visually gifted young person has other options that offer more steady careers: teaching art in elementary school, high school, or college; doing commercial art for an advertising firm; doing industrial or interior design.[7] Such jobs rarely provide the opportunity for great talent to manifest itself, but many artists teach or do commercial work hoping that in their free time they will be able to create a masterpiece.

When all is said and done, artistic talent, like athletic talent, is presumably motivated more by intrinsic than by extrinsic rewards. Still, many students see a career in which they can use their visual gifts as a definite option. One of our students expressed well the combination of present enjoyment and future expectations that keeps him interested in art:

My major goal, my ultimate goal, I'd love to design cars. . . . It would be something that I would like to do because I love cars and I like working with my hands. To me, a new car is like a work of art. . . . Although it has got to be uniform and conform to structure, you can still give it your artistic signature.

Music, like art and athletics, cannot accommodate all the youthful talent with commensurate adult jobs. Some gifted young people will become teachers of music, fewer still may make their living as instrumentalists, and 1 or 2 in 10,000 might become professional composers. For these few, music absorbs all their disposable psychic energy. A gifted cellist in our sample was already as a high school sophomore preparing for the entrance exams at the music school of her choice: "I am really centering my whole life around [the exams] because it's that time; it's getting close to college. I have to give up everything else just so I can make it my life." But for the great majority, music will become only a part of their lifestyle, an activity to which they will turn in their free time because it is enjoyable, not because it has any extrinsic rewards for them.

Immediate extrinsic rewards

It is not only the long-range rewards offered by the various fields that are quite different; the kind of support available to teenagers for each field also varies widely. Math and science, for instance, are recognized as socially important, and high schools often require courses in these subjects for graduation. Parents encourage their children to develop talent in these areas, and teenagers extend grudging respect to their peers who are good in these subjects.

Support of athletics by the community is tinged with a certain degree of ambivalence. On the one hand, athletics is the least "serious" domain, with the least academic legitimacy, of the ones considered here. On the other hand, a good athlete can get more attention and recognition in high school than a person with any other kind of talent. At least in the short run, physical performance brings students many obvious extrinsic rewards, such as traveling to meets, getting their pictures in the paper, and being promised athletic scholarships. Young persons who are good at a sport may feel that they are wasting an opportunity if they do not get seriously involved with it, whether or not they like it.

Music also has its own ambivalences as a potential career. It is certainly considered by many to be an important domain; a young child who can play the violin or the piano well is considered accomplished, and the child's parents can bask in reflected glory. Therefore parents are often glad to see signs of musical talent in their children and are willing to encourage and develop those talents, sometimes at great expense. Yet few consider a musical career appropriate, especially for males. Thus the encouragement of a musical talent is often qualified; it is something worth cultivating, but one should not take it too seriously. Also there is nowadays – and perhaps there has always been – a generational split in attitudes toward what type of music really counts. Parents and teachers endorse classical music, whereas the peer group usually prefers whatever happens to be the latest musical style. These contradictions concerning the value of musical talents are not lost on gifted teenagers and must raise serious questions in their minds about the future.

Despite its cultural importance, the domain of art arguably benefits the least from external rewards in high school. A student who draws well gets a certain amount of attention from classmates, but typically neither parents nor teachers outside the art department feel very enthusiastic at the prospect of an adolescent considering a career as an artist. More than in any other area of talent, a young artist is on her or his own, generally lacking the external supports that the admiration of peers, the encouragement of parents, the curricula of schools, and the prestige of the media bestow on those who have special gifts.

But external rewards – whether the long-term expectations tied to a career or short-term support and encouragement – are not the only ones that motivate a young person to persevere in the difficult path that leads to the development of talent. Each domain provides a set of intrinsic rewards that are just as important as the extrinsic ones – and perhaps more so.

The intrinsic rewards of talent

When we look at the rewards intrinsic to the various domains, the picture looks quite different. Intrinsic and extrinsic rewards present almost a mirror image of each other. Math and science, which are strongly supported by both present and future external incentives, are not as obviously enjoyable as playing music, painting, or running a race. Therefore we might expect that in the absence of extrinsic rewards gifted adolescents may still continue to develop their talents in art, athletics, and music, whereas they may not in science and math.

The lack of momentary and direct involvement of the senses is one reason why the domains of math and science are often experienced as less intrinsically enjoyable. In the expressive performance of the arts, for instance, meaningful goals are near at hand: The artist sees the painting take shape moment by moment, and the musician can enjoy the song as it is played. Involvement with the abstract symbols of science is less likely to evoke pleasurable emotional responses; important goals are apt to be more abstract and off in the future. Meaningful feedback in the arts is also more instantaneous, and the control of one's actions often requires a momentary physical reaction (e.g., the movement of a brush or a finger on an instrument). In contrast, feedback for a young (or mature) scientist's or mathematician's work may come from teachers or colleagues weeks later, and even then the appropriate response may not be clear and may require further deliberation. These conditions in math and science are likely to make intense concentration harder, thus detracting from the merging of self-awareness with action that is typical of flow experiences.

This is not to say that the pursuit of the hard sciences cannot be enjoyable. In fact, if we read the testimonials of famous scientists, we get the impression that there is nothing as rewarding as the pursuit of abstract mathematics or theoretical science. When someone asked Albert Michelson, the first U.S. Nobel prizewinner in physics, why he devoted so much of his life to the esoteric task of measuring the speed of light, he answered, "Because it was so much fun."[8] Many other scientists compare their work to an "interesting game,"[9] to the excitement of discovering a new land,[10] or to the pleasure of solving puzzles.[11] In fact, many scientists describe their work in terms of the flow experience. In 1990 George Klein, the world-famous tumor biologist, edited a collection of essays by scientists from around the world entitled *Creativity and Flow*.

There is no question that at the higher levels of physics, chemistry, biology, and math, these domains provide the joy of giving order to chaos and of creating beauty, which is very similar to what the artist or the composer of music experiences. But in the early years, when students are exposed to the subject in high school, these intrinsic rewards are rarely available. Instead most students, even the gifted ones, tend to view science and math as difficult, arcane subjects that must be faced with great fortitude. Teachers all too often discount the importance of intrinsic motivation and help perpetuate the belief that mastering the sciences is not only difficult but needs to be unpleasant as well.

Fortunately, most students with a scientific inclination are able to feel at least some of the sense of enjoyment and wonder that science at its best has to offer. Teenagers respond more intensely to concrete evidence, to events that have direct implications for their lives, and to issues that they care about. Thus, an interest in biology often has its roots in love for one's pets, and the pursuit of chemistry may start with an interest in building firecrackers. Sometimes the experience of wonder is triggered during a visit to a science museum or by an experiment in a biology lab. A 14-year-old relates his enthusiasm for a course in geology:

I'm glad I'm taking it, I really am 'cause there's so much that goes on in the world, things like rocks changing. And when you think about it, this world is 4.5 billion years old, and to think of all that time that you don't know about. You are a dot, you are a fraction of a fraction, and there is everything out there and you don't know about it yet.

It is harder for a teenager to experience the same sort of tangible excitement when involved with mathematics. Several gifted students complained about math being too abstract and too removed from "real life." However, for young people for whom the abstract beauty of math is not sufficient, there is one means by which they may be able to experience its intrinsic rewards: computers. Almost all gifted math students spend vast amounts of time learning program languages, inventing new ones, and designing games and useful programs. The computer allows students to set goals appropriate to their skills and provides clear feedback for their attempts at mastery, thereby making it possible for them to enter the intrinsically rewarding flow experience while working with numerical algorithms. It may not be the highest form of mathematical reasoning, but it is certainly a convenient gateway for entering the realm of numbers.

In contrast with the "hard" sciences, music, athletics, and art are flow activities par excellence. They can provide the kind of concentrated involvement that most people find intrinsically rewarding. When one plays a piece of music, the goals are usually quite clear: The score spells out what needs to be done in the finest detail. The feedback is instantaneous – a note not well played is immediately detected. The player can choose to play pieces that are well matched to her or his skills or can reach for new challenges. A gradient of increasingly complex challenges is available, ranging from "Three Blind Mice" to Beethoven's late quartets. Because of these elements in the constitution of the domain, even a beginner can be captivated by its beauty and can enjoy performing for its own sake.

The visual arts, like music, easily provide immediate rewards. The effects of drawing or sculpting are immediately visible. A child does not need any training to enjoy fingerpainting. If the child's efforts are pleasing, the reinforcement is immediate. Both the young artist and her or his peers can tell right away if the lines of the developing drawing are realistic, neat, and detailed, which are the aesthetic criteria young children spontaneously use.[12] Here, too, as in music, the challenges a person can take on in a lifetime are potentially infinite, and so are the skills one can learn. But what is important in this context is that from the earliest stages of performance the arts can be highly enjoyable.

For those who are physically gifted, the domain of athletics provides even more concrete and immediate satisfaction. First, bodily exercise is pleasurable in itself, offering biologically programmed rewards similar to the pleasures of eating, drinking, resting, and sex.[13] Second, performing well with one's body is a source of pride and self-esteem. Finally, there is a universal clarity and concreteness to physical performance that perhaps no other domain can match. In athletic competition there is usually no doubt about how well one is doing and who is doing the best. A girl who jumps higher than her friends and a boy who runs faster than the others get clear and immediate information concerning their abilities.

If acting out a talent were only boring or stressful, it is unlikely that young people would ever develop their gifts. The reason we do have mathematics, music, and other similar domains is that, hard as it is to develop mastery in them, the process itself can be very gratifying. Yet the adults who are in charge of the various fields of learning often forget that joy is the best teacher.[14] In trying to interest teenagers in a subject, we tend to stress the future usefulness of knowledge or to resort to threats and bribes rather than using wonder and enjoyment as leverage for learning.

THE COMPLEXITY OF FIELDS AND DOMAINS

This chapter has thus far described some general differences in the fields and domains of talent and how such differences are likely to affect the subjective rewards available to students. Now it is time to consider these differences in light of the theory of complexity and optimal experience.

According to this perspective, optimal growth is the result of the interaction between two processes: integration, associated with stabilizing trends, and differentiation, associated with change. These general characteristics can be operationalized in different ways, depending upon what system one is studying and the perspective and needs of the researcher. Our approach looks at their effect on subjective experience: Integration should manifest itself as momentary positive feelings of satisfaction; and differentiation, as feelings of dissonance or challenge that require future action and change.

The logic of integration and differentiation can also be applied to what happens in school (e.g., to teacher–student relations in class). For instance, an integrated classroom is cohesive, stable, and supportive of its members (in this case, students); a differentiated one is more individualistic, specialized, and perhaps even competitive. In terms of talent domains, integrated ones harmonize bits of information into an overall gestalt, whereas in differentiated domains facts may take precedence over theories, and specialized information has priority. As mentioned earlier, integrated fields and domains are likely to enhance immediate experience: People are warm and supportive, and information is clear and meaningful. Differentiated fields and domains, on the other hand, present obstacles that have to be contended with and sometimes struggled against. For instance, one might have to evaluate and incorporate another's point of view, change one's mind, or argue for one's position.

Our theory suggests that complex systems promote optimal experience and the growth of talent. An integrated system is likely to be beneficial for growth in the short term because it allows an individual to be comfortable and secure enough to be receptive to the immediate environment. But such a system would lead to stagnation if it were closed and did not allow for future change (i.e., differentiation). Thus a differentiated system may facilitate growth in the long term because it obliges an individual to think ahead and consider changes that alter the status quo.[15] The rest of this chapter explores whether these ideas can shed further light on the arts–sciences distinctions discussed earlier. For instance, what opportunities for integration and differentiation do the various fields and domains of talent in high school afford high school students? What imbalances are present that may impede talent development?

Integration and differentiation in fields and domains

The arts and the sciences are both potentially complex social and informational systems. Both arts and sciences provide opportunities for cooperation and individuality and for synthetic thinking and the analysis of novel detail; thus each can stimulate harmonious experiences as well as challenging ones. However, it may be the case that high school students talented in different disciplines are confronted with lopsided opportunities for integration and differentiation.

Teens in our study suggested that high school science instruction places a greater emphasis on external control through authoritarian teachers; on processes of abstraction and rationality; on specialization, facts, and progress; on solitary work; and on long-term instrumental goals. These observations seem consistent with what many students say, regardless of whether or not they are talented, and they make sense when we consider the nature of the scientific process. In other words, it is perhaps characteristic of science – through measurement, objectification, quantification, and so on – to abstract parts of some phenomenon from their natural context, often for purposes of description and future control. Whereas there is little doubt about the positive value of this approach, science as it has matured has generated a bewildering amount of information that must be learned in order to stay current. It is thus little wonder that students tend to view science as difficult and as high on the dimension of differentiation.

Many students go further and imply fragmentation. Thus the familiar lament "What good is it going to do me to memorize all these facts?" Such students feel they are showered with decontextualized dates, names, discoveries, and ideas that make little immediate sense to them. Some students understand the importance of this work and its relation to their future scholastic goals, so they are challenged to learn it. But they seldom understand the "joy of insight" that real scientists feel when a new way of looking at the world is uncovered.[16] Students do little more than memorize information that "everyone is supposed to know" and forget the real men and women who generated it, for whom science was a comprehensive, and often enjoyable, way of life.

In contrast, high school classes in art and music have a different ethos – and present a different danger. Teachers are typically more nurturing and supportive of their students, and the work is more often communal, at least in class. The directly experienced tonal and visual symbols of music and art classes create an immediate world that is often experienced as complete in itself. Students are more expressively, rather than instrumentally, involved and thus seldom feel alienated from their work. These qualities enhance harmonious feelings. But students also said that they often felt unchallenged by such classes (see also chapter 9).

Although there are many exceptions to these generalizations, especially when they describe adult artists and scientists working professionally, such stark contrasts are indeed present in the high school. When these differences are exaggerated, a young scientist runs a greater risk of differentiation without integration or of having to accommodate challenge without feeling a sense of joy. The young artist, on the other hand, faces the opposite impasse: integration without differentiation, or feeling momentary enjoyment without any pressure to plan for future challenges. In terms of our theory of complexity, neither of these extreme alternatives is desirable.

DIVIDED INTEREST IN THE ARTS
AND SCIENCES

If the observations above are valid, we might expect to find differences in the ways in which students in the arts and sciences work with their talents, differences that will reflect the problems of overintegration and overdifferentiation just described. Specifically we looked to see whether each area was characterized by a divided interest, or an inability to bring together feelings of momentary enjoyment with the feeling of facing important challenges. A divided interest pertains when an experience is exciting in itself but is not linked to future growth and change (i.e., the problem we expect to see among students in the arts), or conversely, when an experience is felt to be important to future growth but is uninvolving at the moment (i.e., presumably the problem of the science students).[17]

The ESM was used to measure these differing modes of experience. Momentary interest or involvement was operationalized by summing the items "involved," "open," and "excited." The feeling that an activity mattered for the future was measured by the single ESM item "How important is this activity to your overall goals?" The distributions for these two variables were divided at their medians, and the pager signals to which teens responded while working in their talent areas were classified into one of four quadrants: high momentary involvement/high importance to goals; high involvement/low importance; low involvement/high importance; low involvement/low importance. Each student's signals were then aggregated, resulting in a percentage score for each quadrant. For instance, if a math student responded to four talent-related signals while in math class and one fell in each quadrant, then the corresponding percentage in each would equal 25.

For purposes of this chapter, only the percentages for the low involvement/high importance quadrant and the high involvement/low importance quadrant for students working in the sciences ($n = 94$) and the arts ($n = 84$) were compared. Figure 6.1 confirms the expectation that each area has a unique profile, one that is almost the mirror image of the other. The science students were more likely to be in a state of low momentary involvement while feeling that what they were doing was important to their future goals. Those in music, athletics, and art were more likely to be feeling open, excited, and involved in what they were doing but that it was unimportant to their long-term goals. This reversal between modes of engagement resulted in a significant interaction effect ($p = .001$).

This finding adds some detail to the preceding theoretical argument. It supports the notion that the way the arts and sciences are constituted in high school creates specific obstacles for students. Those in the sciences may have trouble feeling connected to what they do at the moment. On the other hand, students in the arts face the opposite hurdle. They are more likely to have their eyes on the scenery, as it were, instead of paying attention to the road signs that provide an indication of where they are heading.

Undivided interest, and thus genuine education, maintains a bridge that allows going back and forth between these two foci of attention. "In an educational scheme," Dewey comments, "the occurrence of a desire is not the final end. It is an occasion and a demand for the formation of a plan and method of activity."[18] This statement, which few would find reason to quibble with, is difficult to implement because of its abstract nature and the obscurity of its practical implications. The finding summarized in Figure 6.1 begins to flesh out those implications, and it suggests

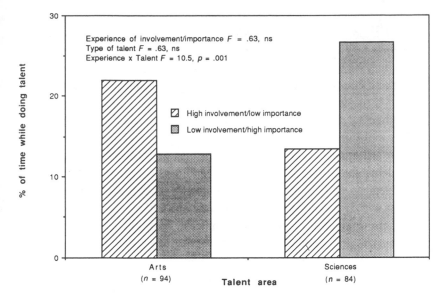

Figure 6.1. Comparison of students talented in arts and sciences on frequency of momentary involvement and importance to future goals.

others. For instance, if the development of talent in the sciences must overcome the obstacle of low momentary interest, we would expect that those students who were able to enjoy the task at hand would more often succeed, whereas those who keep to the typical pattern would tend to become disengaged. Conversely, arts students who can relate what they are enjoying now to some future plan of action would be more likely to stay committed to their talents, whereas the involved but undirected ones would eventually lose interest. These hypotheses will be tested in chapter 11.

Correcting the balance

As opportunities for integration and differentiation drift farther apart in the daily school experience, it becomes progressively easier for teenagers to adopt an either–or attitude toward their subjects. In other words, many students may take for granted that math and science will be dry and abstract, with little chance for enjoyment. This will reinforce the pattern already observed, namely, that they will see the importance of studying without really getting involved. Conversely, many students will perceive art as needing little disciplined thought. They will be content to enjoy themselves without making connections to past or future aspirations.

In these circumstances, one of the best things educators and parents can do is to play devil's advocate and build up the position that needs strengthening. Real-life examples of individuals who do not fit the stereotypic mold are readily available, especially in the biographies of eminent creative artists and scientists. Perhaps the best way to raise the awareness of students about the complexity of their future is to introduce them to real scientists and artists. They may quickly shed their image of the faceless and dry scientist if an enthusiastic one is put before them. Likewise there would be less illusory romanticism about the arts if successful musicians, athletes, and artists were asked to give realistic accounts of the discipline needed to succeed in their professions.

A historical awareness also provides important information. For example, the study of the cosmos in classical times was thought to afford the best opportunity for integrating scientific knowledge with aesthetic experience.[19] Nowadays a synthetic approach to understanding the ecosystem could provide a similar chance for unification. After all, until recently artists in many civilizations, like that of ancient Egypt or medieval Europe, were primarily technicians. They were absorbed in practical tasks, and personal expression was subordinated to functional demands. Even master artists were relatively anonymous craftworkers who did not sign their works.[20]

It is often overlooked today that the master–apprentice relationship, which characterizes training in music and art, has also been characteristic of scientific mentorship. A mentor–learner link enhances a student's feeling of support and membership in the field in several ways. It brings greater sensitivity to the personal needs of the student. Closer contact with a teacher, particularly if he or she is a professional working in the field, provides a real-life model for personal commitment and enjoyment. In the high school setting, this master–apprentice relationship can be translated into the opportunity for a few students to share ideas within a cohesive, guided group. Such an approach may be impossible to accomplish on a schoolwide scale, but perhaps in the case of a few bright students more opportunities might be created for them to form groups and spend time with teachers or other professionals involved in actual research. It is, after all, in the day-to-day joys and puzzles, adjustments, flashes of insight, and hands-on research that the scientist's feelings of expressive performance manifest themselves.

Your musicians, artists, and athletes, on the other hand, can be made more aware of the long-term demands and challenges of their prospective careers. For instance, a serious attempt could be made to demonstrate the importance of the hard work, social recognition and contacts, material rewards, and so on that are involved in applying artistic talent in the real world. In this way, the young artists, musicians, and athletes may perhaps acquire some practical insights to better equip them in planning their careers.

In summary, our perspective suggests that opportunities for achieving complexity and for finding optimal experience may be somewhat limited by the constitution of the fields and domains of talent in high school. Our findings show that students in the sciences were more likely to feel that what they were doing was important to their future but were unable to feel involved or excited about it. Musicians, athletes, and artists, on the other hand, were involved but did not see how today's activities were related to the future. The chapter closes with suggestions about how parents and teachers might help students correct these imbalances. The next chapter uses the ESM and individual case studies to provide more detail on the experience of talent in these crucial years of life.

NOTES

1 Holton, 1973/1988. A classic treatment of the subjective assumptions underlying the thinking of scientists is that of Michael Polanyi (1958).
2 Dewey, 1934/1980, pp. 73–74.
3 Langer, 1957.
4 Csikszentmihalyi & Larson, 1984.
5 Weisskopf, 1991.
6 Coleman, 1961; Henry, 1965.
7 Getzels & Csikszentmihalyi, 1976.
8 Cited in Chandrasekhar, 1987, p. 25. This Nobel prizewinning astrophysicist

has also expressed himself often concerning the importance of aesthetic considerations in science, notably in his volume *Truth and Beauty.*

9 Dirac, 1978, p. 7.

10 Schlick, 1934.

11 Kuhn, 1970, p. 36. Kuhn implies that scientific paradigms more often change because young scientists get bored by them than because they are disproven.

12 Hart and Goldin-Meadow, 1984.

13 A good summary of the evolutionary origins and functions of pleasure can be found in the recent book by Lionel Tiger (1992).

14 Csikszentmihalyi, 1990b.

15 See also Rathunde, 1991a,b.

16 Weisskopf, 1991.

17 Rathunde, 1991a, in press.

18 Dewey, 1938, p. 71.

19 Gadamer, 1986.

20 Hauser, 1951. Even such artistic geniuses as Botticelli, Verrocchio, and Leonardo spent a great deal of their time designing furniture, decorations, and other useful objects without feeling that they were compromising their integrity. The notion that the fine arts must stay aloof from practical needs is a recent conceit based on Romantic ideology.

7
The experience of talent

Intellectual and artistic gifts do not grow by themselves or in a vacuum. They must be constantly nurtured in the context of a social field, and they have to grow within the rules of a complex symbolic domain, or they will not flourish. If students do not enjoy operating in the field and the domain – if they fail to derive intrinsic rewards from using their talent – the likelihood of their continuing to develop their gifts is greatly reduced.

Therefore it is important to know more precisely how these adolescents feel about their talent. What is the content of their minds when they do math or music or science, and how is it different from experiences not involving their areas of talent? How often do talented teens encounter the intrinsically rewarding flow state as they work in their domain?

These questions deal with vital issues if one believes, as we do, that the quality of experience will to a large extent determine whether an activity will be repeated or not. In other words, teenagers who enjoy doing science will be more likely to continue scientific training than those who are bored or feel threatened by it. In chapter 6 we developed some theoretical and descriptive arguments about these issues. But in order to understand how talent develops, it is essential to collect some empirical facts about how gifted students actually perceive the rewards available in their domains.

PORTRAITS OF TALENTED TEENS

Before turning to a statistical investigation of these issues, we shall present case studies that describe in depth the attitudes of three rather typical students. Josh is a gifted math student who loves programming

125

computers, Sheila centers her life on singing, and Ben has set his sights on a career as a product designer. In their early teens, these young persons have already fashioned rather concrete life themes based on skills that set them apart from most other adolescents, a set of skills that they deeply enjoy using. Their stories provide some of the flavor of what it means to be talented and will serve as an introduction to the sample as a whole.

Josh

In most respects Josh's preferences and interests resemble those of other males his age. A freshman at his school, he participates in a broad range of sports and looks forward to his first taste of high school athletic competition. His conversation turns easily to cars, rock groups, and his favorite foods. He can't wait until he is old enough to get a driver's license. But in at least one way Josh is quite an extraordinary 14-year-old. For Josh possesses a truly exceptional gift for mathematics. He combines this gift with formidable abilities in language and science as well as in most other academic subjects he has attempted thus far.

Meeting Josh in person, one would not suspect him of being a gifted type, an impression that would please him. Describing himself as shy and easygoing, Josh seems determined not to come across as brainy, or anything other than a average teenager. Like most adolescents, he does not want to be recognized as outstanding by adult standards, lest he alienate his peers. "I try not to let things like school take over my whole life," he says, adding that in general he tries "not to take everything too seriously."

Math, he admits, has always been easy and natural for him and has never demanded much hard work. Accelerated into advanced mathematics classes since the second grade, he was more than a year ahead of his peers by sixth grade and successfully competed in regional math tournaments. He began freshman year in high school in an advanced junior section, studying college algebra and trigonometry. By sophomore year he had exhausted the school's considerable offerings in mathematics.

Although he is aware of the magnitude of his talent, Josh's goals reflect a conventional pattern of "good grades, college, preferably in California, and a high-paying job." Asked why he wants a good job, he replies, "I want not to have to worry about where everything is coming from – have enough to be comfortable." When confronted with a hypothetical choice between a job that was enjoyable, and one that paid a lot of money, Josh answered, "I'd like to think I'd choose to do what I'd like to do, but you never know."

He knows that in these plans for a comfortable future, math figures as his "strongest suit." But rarely does Josh show enthusiasm for mathematics in itself. In his interview answers, math is a part of the generally uninteresting province of school, a typically boring place that nonetheless provides occasional opportunities for recognition and display. Of the things he admits enjoying about math, competition with the school's math team stands out because it provides a sense that he "knows what he is doing," that he is in control of a problem. He especially enjoys the satisfaction of cracking a problem for the first time, particularly one that is complex and interesting.

Compared with the guarded enthusiasm of the interview, the record of responses to the Experience Sampling Method (ESM) shows a different picture. Despite his blasé protestations, there is no question that mathematics takes up a great deal of Josh's attention and that it provides some of the most rewarding experiences of his young life. Over 25% of his pager responses during the week of ESM experimentation involve mathematics in some form. Most of these instances involve computers: playing chess against a PC, reading an article about computer poetry, trying to write a program that will play a rock song, watching a program "completely blow up." The highest moods he reported all week were on a Monday afternoon working hard on a problem with the math team. It was a session that combined enjoyment of the company of his friends with real interest in the elusive solution to the problem. When he is thinking about math Josh always reports a level of skills above the average, sometimes much above. He also tends to report high challenges when working with math, and these are usually matched to the level of reported skills. Generally his moods when working with the computer are also appreciably above the mean – in other words, for Josh doing mathematics is usually a flow experience.

So even though Josh wishes to appear "cool" about his talent and does not want to seem too serious about it, the domain of mathematics has succeeded in providing sufficient intrinsic reward to sustain his investing attention over extended periods of time. This exclusive investment of psychic energy, which is very rare in adolescence – or, for that matter, in adulthood – is necessary to reach the higher levels of proficiency in any domain. As Newton replied when asked how he developed the universal theory of gravitation, he did it "by thinking about it constantly." One cannot think all the time productively about something one does not enjoy.

But the task of cultivating talent does not rest on Josh's shoulders alone. As is the case with most of the other teenagers we studied, Josh's entire family acts as a support system to help him concentrate. His mother, especially, clearly expresses high hopes for her gifted son. Seeing him as a potential "astronaut, physicist, or astronomer," she is emphatic that he "should use his extraordinary gifts . . . to make the world a better place." She expects that he will earn a "doctorate in something that interests him" and hopes that "he'll be driven more by his interests than by large amounts of money."

The only cloud on the horizon, as far as Josh's mother is concerned, is the potentially harmful effect of peers. She worries that Josh is too sensitive and therefore emotionally fragile, and that his friends are more callous and superficial. On this issue Josh disagrees. Intent on becoming more friendly and outgoing, he has chosen these friends precisely because they "aren't really the smart, smart type," thus helping him avoid acting like "a complete weird person." Recently he joined one of these friends on the water polo team, a sport he finds enjoyable but that conflicts with the practice schedule of the math team.

Josh's case illustrates several of the dilemmas confronting young people with exceptional intellectual gifts. On the one hand, there is the attraction of the peer group with its "normal" interests and values; on the other hand, there are parents who expect ascetic dedication to the cultivation of talent. There is the attraction of making a lot of money in the future, counterbalanced by the possibility of helping make the world a better place. There is the enjoyment of being with friends and of doing sports, counterbalanced by the solitary enjoyment of solving difficult problems on the computer. To a certain extent these options are not mutually exclusive, and Josh does a good job of trying to do justice to them all. But attention is a limited resource, and in a 24-hour day he can concentrate on only so many things. How Josh allocates his attention in the 4 years of high school will determine to a large extent whether his outstanding mathematical talent will be realized or not.

Sheila

A 15-year-old 10th grader when she began the study, Sheila was nominated as talented by the school faculty in three domains: mathematics, science, and music. Although her ability in math is clear (90th percentile on the PSAT) and she is doing work in advanced geometry, she claims no special enthusiasm for it. She finds much more cause for curiosity and intellectual excitement in science. Although the rigors of the chemistry lab sometimes cause her competitive anxiety, Sheila claims to enjoy the intellectual challenges involved and is seriously considering a scientific career. But by far the greatest passion in Sheila's young life is vocal music. At the beginning of sophomore year, she is part of two choral groups that have daily rehearsals and is also rehearsing for the school's fall musical. Her vocal parts include demanding solo roles.

The record of Sheila's ESM week attests to the role of music and performance-related activities in her daily experience. During the week she carried the pager, in addition to various rehearsals she appeared in an afternoon play and attended a recital at a different school. Of the 54 responses she provided, one third involve either thinking about or playing music. In many additional instances she reports that she would rather be singing than doing whatever she happens to be doing at the time. Music and performance give shape to Sheila's day and provide rewards more intense and memorable than any other activity of everyday life.

But what are these rewards exactly? Sheila often refers in her interview to the immediate intensity and excitement of performance situations. In moments of peak performance, she reports being able to feel her "imagination take over" through her singing as the surrounding reality grows "cloudy" and indistinct. The day-to-day satisfaction of singing includes the challenge of unusual harmonies; the immediate grasp of what made those harmonies either "right" or "wrong"; the chance to work with people excited about and committed to excellence; and the many opportunities to go back and get a passage "just right." The ability to control the pitch and timbre of her voice is one of the reasons she prefers singing to playing the violin, which she gave up in third grade because she could not tune the instrument properly.

The rewards Sheila mentions spontaneously in the interview correspond point by point to the dimensions of the flow experience: high challenges, clear goals, immediate feedback, and a sense of control, all leading to a concentration that excludes any distraction and creates a sense of participation in an almost other-worldly reality.

What is impressive about her moments of solo performance, as documented by Sheila's ESM record, is that while concentration and the sense of challenge are far above her weekly average, self-esteem is also unusually high, even higher than the level of skills. Singing with the choir also produces a similar effect, although not with the intensity of solo performance. Of course music and acting do not always lead to enjoyable involvement. Sometimes Sheila becomes angry with other choir members who "act obnoxious," and she is sometimes ensnared in webs of jealousy that are distracting and depressing. But overall, music clearly provides the high points of her life, and the intensity of enjoyment suggests that she will continue developing this talent as far as she can.

Sheila is quick to acknowledge the influence of her family on her desire to achieve her best. Both parents have PhDs in chemistry and are happily engaged in teaching and research careers. It is after their model that Sheila is considering a career in science. Sheila's mother, who did not have the chance to develop her own musical interests, has always encouraged Sheila to develop hers. In fact, she may have put too much pressure on her daughter; Sheila abandoned the piano early, in part because she felt excessive maternal insistence.

In terms of vocal talent, Sheila has followed more in the footsteps of her older sister, whom she has always idolized. When her sister began to perform in high school musicals, Sheila sought out child roles in those productions. Part of her excitement over an upcoming musical performance stems from the fact that her sister had sung the same role 10 years earlier.

When Sheila began formal vocal training at age 12, her parents and grandparents faithfully attended concerts and recitals and provided transportation to rehearsals and events. Her current family life includes the usual tensions over independence and privacy, but Sheila continues to feel a bedrock confidence in her parents' commitment to her personal happiness and talent development.

At the same time, though, these feelings of basic security do not entirely insulate Sheila from worries about the future, and especially from the ambiguities of a career as a professional musician. She wonders about how good she really is and is concerned about being able to decide wisely. Because she has been brought up in such a supportive family environment, she is worried about whether she will be able to endure the loneliness of a performing musician's transient life. The deaths of two grandparents to whom she was very close have heightened her awareness of how fragile life is. In considering all this, a career in science seems a safer option; it would allow for the stable family life her parents have enjoyed, as well as for the rewards of curiosity, inquiry, and material benefits, even though science may not provide the exhilarating passion that music engenders in Sheila.

Sheila's story, like Josh's, again illustrates some of the constant themes in the lives of gifted adolescents. In this case, the dialectical process of differentiation and integration with respect to the family is clearly shown in Sheila's resistance to parental pressure on the one hand and her dependence on parental modeling and support on the other. The tension between the relative safety of science and the greater intensity of her experience in music reflects in part the conflict between extrinsic and intrinsic rewards. The need to navigate a safe course through the tensions and jealousies of the peer group also emerges in her story. How Sheila will resolve all these conflicting demands on her attention is going to determine how much psychic energy she will have left to devote to the cultivation of her talent.

Ben

Generally it is difficult to find a 15-year-old with a clearly developed sense of identity: a "life theme" that integrates into an original pattern a sense of the past with that of the present and the future.[1] Most teenagers tend to have a fragmentary sense of self made up of conventional role expectations like being a good student or being popular or being "cool" (or "intense," "intimidating," or "bad," depending on the jargon of the moment). For average teens the future is similarly stereotyped; they expect to have a well-paying job, a happy marriage, a house in a good neighborhood with two or three cars in the garage, and so on.[2]

Teenagers with special gifts tend to have a more finely articulated sense of who they have been, who they are, and who they want to become. Ben is a good example of a young man with a life theme that is taking an unusual direction. Ben's interest in art began in third grade when his colorful and imaginative pictures captured the attention of teachers. Several teachers after that were impressed by his talent and established "pretty close" supportive relationships. He enjoyed both their praise and the activity of drawing: "It was something that came easy to me and that I liked to do."

The intrinsic rewards of art clearly became more intense with time as Ben perceived increasingly difficult challenges and developed the skills to match them. One significant event in eighth grade that affected his artistic development involved building – from his own design – a Viking ship out of balsa wood, with all the oars and shields. "I started working with balsa wood and saw that I could create things, not just draw them. I had so much fun doing that." Another project that gave him unusual satisfaction was construction of a replica of an ancient Chinese grain grinder after he saw a traveling exhibit of Chinese technology. "To me, seeing that it came out and actually worked – that's great, I love it."

According to Erik Erikson's model of psychosocial development, identity in adolescence develops after a person gains a sense of competence by overcoming a sense of inferiority through industrious application to concrete tasks. In Ben's case, this seems to have occurred in eighth grade. "That was about the best year because that was when I coordinated not only drawing but also construction into one. That is when it *all came together.*" Ben's evolving life theme combines a love of drawing with a love of working with his hands. "I work well with my hands and drawing and everything. Architecture and design would be something I could do with . . . my talent." One way Ben hopes to express this potential is by designing houses and cars.

Ben senses a continuity in his life theme that reaches back to childhood and extends through the present into the future. "I always like drawing and I always liked cars. Ever since I was little I had cars – Matchbox cars.

Right now my room has all car posters and models. I just like cars, that's all." Such a life theme, or consistent "narrative,"[3] enables Ben to make sense of his past experience while simultaneously providing a selective frame for the present and future investment of attention. Thus experiences related to his talent become more integrated, relevant, and enjoyable.

The feedback Ben has received from the successful use of his skills has given him self-confidence and a strong autonomous orientation: "I'm competitive in what I do, and I like to see myself succeed; when I don't succeed at what I do I get pretty angry at myself." But Ben defines success not in the usual extrinsic terms – as fame or riches – but rather in terms of self-generated criteria: "To me being my own boss would be successful, to others making a lot of money would be successful. Just knowing that you have accomplished this yourself . . . that's successful." Ben believes that the goal of combining art and automotive design has been his own discovery, and that is important to him. He doesn't feel influenced by any particular person or by public opinion at large: "It is something that *I* want to do."

But Ben's autonomy and self-confidence are not at the expense of being isolated or insensitive to others. Perhaps this is the difference between individuality nourished by intrinsic rewards and individualism secured through extrinsic recognition. Extrinsic rewards like money, fame, prizes, grades, and other forms of recognition tend to be always in limited supply, distributed according to a J-shaped curve; they are zero-sum in that they inevitably create invidious distinctions between the haves and the have-nots. A person who succeeds in accumulating extrinsic rewards is likely to develop a sense of privilege and smugness. Ben, on the other hand, shows a remarkable awareness of the necessity of coordinating his goals with the goals of significant others: "I'm helpful to others and still think of myself when doing things. When I do badly I feel bad because I try to live up to my expectations, while I'm living up to the expectations of others."

First and foremost among the significant others whose expectations are important to Ben are his parents. "I love my parents very much and I like to see them happy in what I do. Pretty much anything I do I consult them, *even if I don't need to.*" This last comment illustrates nicely the degree of differentiation and integration Ben has achieved with respect to his family: He is open to their input while retaining a sense of competence and independence.

His parents reciprocate this respect. Ben says they give him the help he needs when he asks for it, but they won't make decisions for him: "A lot of things they do, they let me go my own way and see what's best for myself." Although he is aware that his parents' approach is very different from being merely permissive and that the freedom he is allowed puts an added strain on him, Ben accepts the challenge: "Sometimes I wish they would say, 'Do it this way' to give me an easy way out, but in the long run I know it helps me to make my own decisions."

It is not only his parents who have contributed to the development of Ben's life theme, centered on artistic talent. His grandfather, whom Ben admires greatly, served as an identity model; he displayed a great ability to enjoy himself while remaining sensitive to other people:

We were real close and it's hard to say why. He was always very calm in situations. I'd never seen him get angry. You could tell when he was mad because he would have a certain look on his face, but I've never heard him yell or scold anybody. He could work with his hands like you couldn't believe and do intricate things at the age of 75; that's something. He was very subtle about things, and I like that, not that it rubbed off on me. When certain situations come up and I'm very open about them, I look back and see that I could be subtle and it would complement the situation more, looking at him as an example.

It seems that his grandfather's subtle quality has indeed rubbed off on Ben. His ability to master experience rather than be mastered by it, and to take on increasingly more difficult challenges and find skills that "complement the situation" – all of this in the context of a unified, meaningful, and original life theme – is a feat that few adolescents are able to master. Of course Ben was fortunate to have great role models as well as supportive family and teachers.

These case studies suggest that at least some talented students enjoy working in their domain more than they enjoy almost anything else in their lives. Solving mathematical problems, singing, and designing things that look good and that work are activities that are both enjoyable in the present and can provide a core around which an entire life theme can be built. In order to provide as complete a picture as possible of how gifted teenagers feel when they are involved in the domain of their talent, we now present more detailed quantitative information based on interviews, questionnaires, and the ESM records of all respondents.

TALENT AND TIME

The simplest but in many respects perhaps the most important question to ask about the development of gifted adolescents is: How much time do teens spend involved with their talent? The answer will determine to a large extent whether future promise will be fulfilled or not. But as soon as we try to answer the question, it becomes all too clear that it is not an easy one to deal with. The main problem is determining how to quantify involvement with talent.

A gifted math student might be sitting in a math class listening to a trigonometry lecture, but her mind is on last night's TV show. Should this be counted as an instance of involvement with talent? Conversely, another student talented in science might be watching a TV program but at the same time be thinking about a biology experiment. Is he involved with talent or not? Even with the fine detail the ESM provides about what people do all day, it is sometimes difficult to decide whether a person's attention is focused on a given domain.

If we look just at what students said their main activity was at the time of the ESM signal, we conclude that the talented teens in this group spent approximately 13% of their waking hours in activities directly related to their talent. This translates into about 13 hours per week. There are noteworthy differences by domain: Students gifted in music and athletics spent almost twice as much time involved in their talent as students gifted in visual arts spent involved in art; math and science students spent intermediate amounts of time involved in their domains (ANOVA $F = 3.47$, $p < .009$).

Most of the time when involved in their talent (63% of the over 1,000 responses), students were on school premises – in class or in labs, in music rooms, and on athletic fields. They were at home 27% of the time, and the remaining 10% they were in a public place, a car, or a friend's house. Clearly the school is still the main context for the development of talent, followed at a good distance by the home – at least in these early years of adolescence.

Whenever the teenagers were involved in a talent-related activity, their thoughts also tended to be focused on it. But there were exceptions: For instance, for about 7% of the time spent working in the talent domain, students in our study were primarily thinking about such extrinsic aspects of their involvement as exams, grades, and performance. For another 7% of the time their thoughts were focused on the people involved – parents, siblings, teachers, peers – rather than on the domain itself. An additional 6% of the time was spent thinking primarily about themselves: about how they looked, how they felt, and so on. Thus we can say that for at least one fifth of the time talented teens were working in their talent area, various distractions detracted from their thorough concentration. On the other hand, we might consider it a source of satisfaction that roughly 10% of these students' waking lives was dedicated to the pursuit of a demanding discipline.

It is very important to know how much time students actually spend working to develop their gifts, but it is equally important to know how this investment of time is experienced. How motivated are these teens when they work? Are their feelings positive? Do they include those episodes of flow that provide the intrinsic rewards so important for the continued pursuit of a demanding career? Insights into these questions form the balance of this chapter.

WHY DO GIFTED STUDENTS PURSUE THEIR TALENT?

The battery of tests completed at the beginning of our study contained a short questionnaire that asked students to rate, on a scale from 1 to 6, the importance of 12 reasons for taking classes or training in the area of talent. The items included 3 clearly intrinsic reasons (e.g., "I enjoy it"), 3 strongly extrinsic reasons (e.g., "It's something that will be useful for earning a living"), and 6 reasons that were less easily classified and could be either extrinsic or intrinsic, depending on the context of the respondent's attitudes (e.g., "I'm good at it").

For purposes of the present analysis, the responses of all 223 students who completed this questionnaire were included. Each student's answers were counted only once in the group that represents the talent of her or his choice. For instance, Sheila's answers were included in the music group because, although she had been nominated as talented in science, math, and music, she herself chose music as her favorite domain.

In-Soo Choe, a student in our department, analyzed the group's responses.[4] He identified three main factors. The first included the intrinsic reasons; the second, the extrinsic rewards of a material sort (e.g., getting a better living); and the third, extrinsic rewards of a social kind (e.g., impressing people). He also found that the importance of intrinsic rewards was negatively related to the importance of the first kind of material rewards but positively related to the social sources of external rewards. The two kinds of extrinsic rewards were not related to each other.

Table 7.1 reports the ranking of the items in the three factors by talent groups and by the entire sample. The first impression from the results is that the students gifted in the five domains gave quite similar reasons for becoming involved in their respective fields. In almost all cases, the 3 intrinsic items were ranked the most important, and the 4th, which was worded negatively, was ranked among the lowest.

Looking at the last column first to determine which reasons the entire sample saw as the most important for becoming involved with the domain, we notice that the 3 items ranked highest are enjoyment, satisfaction from learning, and interest. It seems that intrinsic rewards are what keep this group of teens involved in their talent. Extrinsic social reasons are ranked lowest overall, especially the gender-stereotype item, competition, and peer pressure.

Before making too much of this interpretation, we should consider an alternative explanation for the strong showing of intrinsic reasons. Perhaps the most cogent qualification to the pattern of findings is that at this time in our culture there is a strong bias in favor of expressing preference for personally meaningful, intrinsic motives as causes for action, rather than for conformity or for the more material incentives. If this qualification is true, the findings in Table 7.1 do not mean that talented teenagers are necessarily motivated more by enjoyment than by considerations of

Table 7.1. *Ranking of reasons for engagement in various areas of talent*

Reason	Art (27)	Athletics (64)	Math (38)	Music (67)	Science (27)	Total (223)
Intrinsic						
1. I enjoy it	1	1	3	1	2	1
2. I get satisfaction from getting better or from learning	3	2	1	3	3	2
3. It's interesting to me	2	4	4	2	1	3
4. It is required (negative)	9	10	5	9	4	9
Extrinsic I (Material)						
1. It's something that will be useful for earning a living	6	8	2	8	5	6
2. It's something I get good grades in	4	7	6	5	6	4
Extrinsic II (Social)						
1. It's competitive and I like to compete	7	3	8	6	7	7
2. It's something that impresses other people	5	5	7	4	8	5
3. My friends like it, and I like their company	8	6	9	7	9	8
4. It's something that girls (or boys) are supposed to be good at	10	9	10	10	10	10

future utility, but only that they have learned to justify their actions in terms of the peculiar rhetoric of our culture. In other words, the table does not necessarily reflect experience as much as language and values.

We suspect that indeed the students' responses are – inevitably – colored by the value expectations of their time. Talented Japanese students would perhaps give greater emphasis to duty and pride than their

U.S. counterparts did. A few generations ago, during the Great Depression, U.S. adolescents might have expressed a stronger motivation to learn in order to earn a better standard of living.

Yet it would be wrong to discount the importance of intrinsic reasons as a motivation to remain engaged in a domain of talent. Certainly this motivation is not peculiar to our time and place; it has been mentioned in exalted terms in many different historical periods and cultures. The ancient Greek philosophers expressed profound delight in reflection and disputation for its own sake; the Hindu sages and the Chinese Taoist philosophers have prescribed involvement in life for its own sake as the height of wisdom; Vasari described the artists of the Italian Renaissance as so lost in their art that they failed to notice their health or physical surroundings; the Indian genius Ramanujan worked out mathematical problems on his deathbed, oblivious to his pain.[5]

The Nobel prizewinning astrophysicist Chandrasekhar, who grew up immersed in Indian culture, gives this lyrical description of the awesome feelings involved in the practice of science:

The pursuit of science has often been compared to the scaling of mountains, high and not so high. But who amongst us can hope, even in imagination, to scale the Everest and reach its summit when the sky is blue and the air is still, and in the stillness of the air survey the entire Himalayan range in the dazzling white of the snow stretching to infinity? None of us can hope for a comparable vision of nature and of the universe around us. But there is nothing mean or lowly in standing in the valley below and awaiting the sun to rise over Kinchinjunga.[6]

The strong endorsment of intrinsic rewards on the part of the teenagers in our study is not likely to be just a rhetorical device. The enjoyment they describe is consistent with the kind of experience that persons involved with the arts and the sciences everywhere and at all times bear witness to. The accounts that students like Josh, Sheila, and Ben give of how they feel when they are immersed in math, singing, and drawing have the ring of veridical reports.

Being intrinsically motivated in a domain is its own reward; yet paradoxically it brings other kinds of rewards with it. For instance, ranking instrinsic items high correlates positively with the affect students reported when involved in their talent areas ($r = .22$, $p < .01$). It also correlates positively with teachers' ratings of the students' achievement ($r = .24$, $p < .001$), and, for math and science students, with grade point average in science-related areas ($r = .49$, $p < .001$). In all of these comparisons, either kind of extrinsic motivation showed negative or nonsignificant correlations.[7]

Time devoted to talent, however, was significantly related to all three kinds of motivation. Students who had strong intrinsic motivation *or* strong material or social motivation spent significantly more time devoted to their talent domain than students whose motivational patterns were more diffuse. Thus it seems that whereas all students tend to endorse intrinsic rewards as the main reason for being engaged in their talent, those who do so more strongly benefit from it both in the short run (their affect is more positive) and in the long run (they are rated higher by teachers and get better grades).

Differences among domains

Whereas the sample as a whole strongly endorsed intrinsic reasons for being involved in talent, some interesting differences among the students involved in the various domains emerged. For example, the ranking of the items "I enjoy it" and "It's something that will be useful for earning a living" was reversed between the math students and the other four groups. For the math students, enjoyment was reason number 3 and future usefulness was number 2; for everyone else, the rankings were reversed. Obviously students gifted in math feel that having a rare and socially prized talent is reason enough for using it. This is true to a certain extent regardless of how they feel about doing mathematics per se.

Analyzing the data summarized in Table 7.1 by a one-way analysis of variance[8] showed that whereas all groups rated intrinsic reasons equally high, students gifted in art, athletics, and music rated the item "I enjoy it" significantly higher than math students, and higher, although not significantly so, than science students. But the strongest differences among the groups emerged in endorsing extrinsic reasons. Students talented in science and math placed significantly stronger emphasis on items like "It's required," "It's useful," and "I get good grades in it." On the other hand, the reverse pattern held for the two items "It impresses other people" and "It's a way to get away from my problems" (not included in the table because it did not correlate with the items in the other 3 factors). These two reasons were endorsed significantly more strongly by students in art, athletics, and music than by students in math and science. In addition, the athletes also rated the items "It's competitive" and "My friends like it" significantly higher than any of the other groups.

Thus the assumption that a dichotomy exists between the hard sciences and the arts (including athletics) in terms of the rewards they provide seems to be partially justified. As far as extrinsic rewards are concerned, the former are more utilitarian, whereas the latter provide more public recognition and a sense of escape from the troubles of everyday life. In terms of intrinsic rewards, although these were extremely important for all groups, the arts seemed to be more able to provide them than science, and especially than mathematics. The consequences of these variations for the development of talent will be reviewed later in this volume. At this point we shall turn to the question of exactly how performance in talent areas is experienced, drawing on the several thousand responses that the talented students gave to the ESM.

THE QUALITY OF EXPERIENCE WHILE WORKING IN THE DOMAIN

The power of the data collected through the ESM is that it does not represent a single global response or test score but is the result of the addition of many responses given at unexpected moments during the activities of everyday life. Thus analysis of the ESM reports can add important insights to the results obtained from questionnaires and interviews concerning how it feels to be involved in one's domain of talent.

Feelings of positive affect and potency

To ensure that students will be motivated to develop their talent, the quality of experience while working in the domain should be positive. This, however, is unfortunately not always the case. As we look through Figures 7.1–4, which report z scores while involved in talent (i.e., standardized scores expressed as deviation from each person's average score over the week), it becomes obvious that there are some important differences by domain. Figure 7.1 shows that art students were very happy and cheerful when they were doing art and that music students were quite

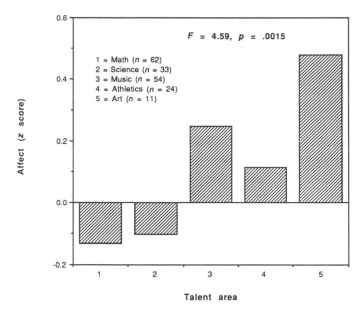

Figure 7.1. Affect across talent areas.

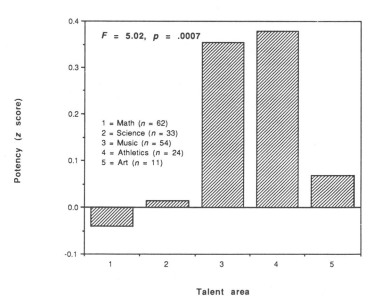

Figure 7.2. Potency across talent areas.

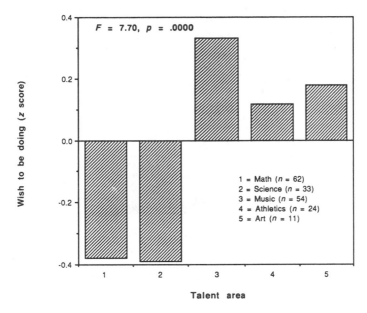

Figure 7.3. Intrinsic motivation across talent areas.

happy when they were doing music but that math and science students were less happy doing math or science than they usually were during the week. Figure 7.2 indicates that music students and athletes felt very strong and active when involved in music and sports, whereas students in the other domains felt average in terms of potency when involved in their domains. In Figure 7.3 we see that music provided the strongest intrinsic motivation and that math and science provided the least. Finally, Figure 7.4 indicates that concentration tended to be significantly higher than average in every talent area except athletics – but this is probably because much of athletics consists in waiting around for a turn in a meet, and at those moments concentration is not necessarily high.

In general, affect, potency, intrinsic motivation, and self-esteem were higher in the arts than in the sciences. On the other hand, there tended to be fewer differences in cognitive efficiency among the domains. When working on their talent, students reported high concentration, ease of concentration, clarity, and lack of self-consciousness in every domain.

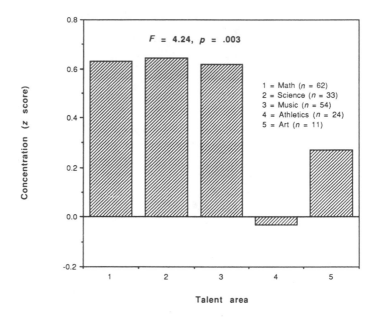

Figure 7.4. Concentration across talent areas.

Another perspective on the experience of talent is provided by Figure 7.5. This figure shows that when artists and athletes were involved in their domain they felt that they "wanted to do" it; whereas science and math students much more frequently said that they "had to do it." Students in music were evenly divided between perceiving their domain as voluntary and as obligatory.

How important is the domain?

Although math and science students did not seem to derive many intrinsic rewards from working in their domain, they knew that what they do is important, especially to others (Table 7.2). In fact, if we take the "importance to others" rating as an indication of the extrinsic rewards attached to a domain, we see a reversal of the former pattern: Students gifted in art and athletics felt that when they were involved in their area of talent, what they did was not important to others, whereas students gifted in science

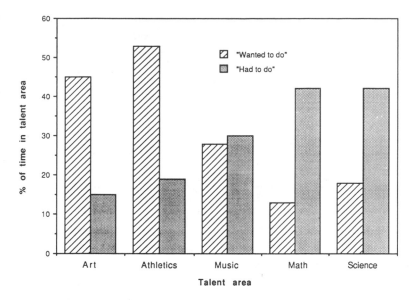

Figure 7.5. Percentage of time students felt they "wanted to do" and "had to do" what they were doing in talent area.

and math believed that their activity in the domain was important to others. Music students, as usual, were in the middle. Athletes stood out from the rest because when involved in athletics they did not feel that what they were doing was important to them.

But all groups agreed that working in the area of talent was important to their overall goals. Thus students on the whole felt that their talent was important to them, but only math, science, and music students felt that others also found their involvement with talent to be important.

TALENT AS FLOW

Another way of ascertaining the quality of experience while involved in talent is to find out whether activity in the domain produces flow. As one way to measure this, we used the questionnaire distributed in junior year, 2 or 3 years after the initial interview. The questionnaire included four

Table 7.2. *ESM rating of the importance of the talent activity as compared with the weekly average baseline*

| | Was the activity | | |
Domains	Important to you?	Important to others?	Important to your overall goals?
Art	Yes ($p < .001$)	No	Yes ($p < .01$)
Athletics	No	No	Yes ($p < .05$)
Mathematics	Yes ($p < .05$)	Yes ($p < .001$)	Yes ($p < .001$)
Music	Yes ($p < .001$)	Yes ($p < .001$)	Yes ($p < .001$)
Science	Yes ($p < .05$)	Yes ($p < .001$)	Yes ($p < .001$)

descriptions of flow (e.g., "Do you ever do something [an activity] where your concentration is so intense, your attention so undivided and wrapped up in what you are doing, that you sometimes become unaware of things you normally notice?"). If the student answered yes to any of the four questions, he or she was then asked to name the activity that produced such a feeling and to describe its frequency and context. Later the activities mentioned as producing flow were rated by the respondents on 5-point frequency scales representing 11 dimensions of flow (e.g., "I get involved" and "I clearly know what I'm supposed to do" rated from *almost never* to *almost always*). At the same time, the respondents also rated on the same scales (a) the school activity they worked hardest on, (b) their favorite activity, (c) being with the family, (d) watching TV, and (e) doing homework.[9]

Of the 165 students who filled out the questionnaire, 104 spontaneously listed one or more talent areas as the activity that most typically produced flow experiences. There were, as usual, strong differences among the domains: Artists, athletes, and musicians identified their talent with flow at more than double the rate of the talented in science and math. Clearly these students had a much easier time enjoying the arts than the sciences.

Whenever the talent area was seen as flowlike, it was rated along the flow scales as indistinguishable from the favorite activity, whereas the school activity they worked hardest on, family, TV, and homework were rated as matching the conditions of flow much less closely. For instance, both talent and favorite activity were rated as not boring, not distracting, not anxiety producing, and as clear, involving, and "I would do it even if I didn't have to" (intrinsic motivation). The reverse was true of homework, television viewing, and, to a lesser extent, family activities. Perhaps the most important finding is that students who identified their talent with flow also rated the school subject they worked hardest on – whatever that happened to be – as indistinguishable from either flow or favorite activity. The same was not true for students who did not identify their talent domain with flow. The second group rated their most demanding school activity as less involving ($p < .006$), as providing less clarity ($p < .01$), as being less intrinsically motivating ($p < .02$), and as being more boring ($p < .05$), more distracting ($p < .01$), and more anxiety producing ($p < .02$). Evidently if the talent provides the intrinsic rewards of flow, this is generalized to other school subjects as well.

CONCLUSION

In summarizing the findings of this chapter, we shall focus on what is common across domains and persons rather than on what is distinctive. Some of the conclusions we have reached will seem obvious, but it is useful to state them, because in practice people often fail to reckon with their consequences.

1. The first generalization is: *No teenager can develop talent without both immediate and long-term extrinsic rewards.* It is naive to believe that good teaching alone, good textbooks, and excellent instructional facilities will lead to the development of talent. Unless students are motivated to learn, even the best learning environment is useless, and to motivate people to learn it is necessary to provide a combination of extrinsic and intrinsic rewards. From childhood on, the immediate external rewards should include recognition, praise, and support from significant others: parents, teachers, and peers. By adolescence an individual becomes aware that a lifetime commitment to one's chosen talent area is probably necessary. The innocent idealism of childhood is replaced by the sobering consideration that it is not enough to be good at math or music in some abstract sense, but that one will also have to find a way to make a living in the real world.

2. The second point is: *No teenager will develop talent unless he or she enjoys working in the talent area.* Threats and blandishments may move an adolescent to study math or practice the piano up to a point. He or she may even become proficient and become a respectable professional. But to reach exceptional levels of performance requires a single-minded dedication that will not occur unless one enjoys what one is doing. All the talented students in our study perceived intrinsic rewards to be more important than extrinsic ones in keeping them involved in their domains. In addition, those who spontaneously mentioned their talent area as being similar to a flow experience not only enjoyed working on it more but also enjoyed the rest of their academic challenges more.

This is one set of findings that educational theory and practice still have to assimilate. Textbooks and lessons that try to introduce students to a domain are often very well planned in terms of logic and reason, but just as often they do not account for the emotional impression the information will make on the pupil. Puzzlement, frustration, and anxiety, rather than the exhilarating flow experience, are the typical reactions of students being introduced to a domain of knowledge, especially the "hard" do-mains of science and mathematics. Many gifted young persons give up at the very start of their careers because of this; many more drop out later because they have never had the chance to enjoy using their talent. And when textbooks or teachers do try to appeal to the students' interests, they often appeal to their most simplistic and superficial ones. Teachers often use texts and lessons that in trying to compete with television commercials only induce ridicule and boredom. We educators still have much to learn about how to make learning intrinsically rewarding.

3. Third, *no teenager can avoid the conflicts inherent in the development of talent.* As shown in chapter 6, talented teens tend to report generally less positive emotional states overall in comparison with average peers. The vignettes of Josh, Sheila, and Ben pointed out the nature of the most common conflicts: the tension between differentiation from and integra-tion with the family, the tension between immediate enjoyment and long-term career goals, the tension between personally constructed life themes and general cultural values, and the tension between parents and peers.

Being talented means, by definition, to be different. There is no way to escape the implications of this fact. Most parents hope that their gifted children will grow up without problems and with many close friends, passing smoothly through adolescence into adulthood. But this very natural expectation is not very realistic. The saying "There is no such thing as a free lunch" applies not only to economic theory but to the economy of the psyche as well. Talented young persons have to bear burdens commensurate with their gifts: They have more responsibilities than their peers, they have to make more difficult choices, and they must come to terms with the implications of their individuality. To resolve these tensions is not an easy task.

It does not mean, of course, that gifted teenagers must be neurotic nerds. As the longitudinal study of the Berkeley high-IQ children has shown, the popular notion that brainy children tend to be maladjusted is not true.[10] If the three typical case studies presented in this chapter show anything, they show that very talented children can be as exuberant, likable, and friendly – in other words, as "average" – as any teenager. Yet, this normality is harder for gifted children to achieve, because it does not come naturally. So in addition to the hard work necessary to cultivate talent, they also have to work hard at cultivating normality. Adults who deal with such persons should remember this; any help they can provide in this area will help prevent the erosion of talent.

4. The fourth point is: *The school is essential for cultivating talent, yet it places peculiar obstacles in the way of its development.* This conclusion will seem less obvious if we remember that until a few generations ago gifted artists, musicians, and even scientists did not learn to develop their skills in school. Talent was honed by working as an apprentice to a master or by individual enterprise, trial and error, and solitary study. This was true in the Middle Ages and continued to be so until quite recently. Picasso, for example, learned to paint from his father, who was a good artist himself; Edison was self-taught; and Einstein did not become famous by impressing his schoolteachers.

By and large, however, schools have now become the institutions entrusted with the mental development of children. Two thirds of talent-related activity takes place in school. This arrangement has some advantages: Standardized screening procedures make it more likely that truly gifted children will be identified, and attempts to provide uniform state-of-the-art instruction reduce the chances that outdated ideas and techniques will be transmitted. But mass education also has obvious drawbacks, especially for those who are talented. The uniformity of compulsory education interferes with the cultivation of unique skills. Gifted students in our study knew that the knowledge they needed could be acquired primarily in the high school. At the same time they generally felt ambivalent about the relatively impersonal obligatory, mechanical instruction that this bureaucratic institution provided. Those students whose parents could afford it supplemented their training with private tutors outside the school system.

It is an interesting question whether or not schools as we know them now will continue to provide the intellectual training for children of the future. Perhaps a combination of expert tutoring and individual computer-assisted study will supplant classrooms and teachers. Perhaps communities of the future will realize the importance of education and again make it a central focus of concern.

5. The fifth and final generalization to be made about the development of talent is: *No child succeeds unless he or she is strongly supported by adults,* usually parents, and usually both parents. The importance of family support was clearly brought out in the work of Benjamin Bloom, who detailed the great sacrifices in terms of time, energy, and money required to cultivate the talents of the gifted. It is not surprising that our study showed that the proportion of our parents who were divorced or separated was only half that of society at large, and that practically all the students lived in stable households consisting of two adults.[11] The burden of bringing up a gifted child is usually too heavy for just one adult to manage. Moreover, the modeling required to inspire a child to persist in developing her or his talent is presumably best performed by two complementary parents. It is therefore likely that gifted students who live in single-parent households will have unusual difficulties in developing their talents. Considering that by the turn of the century an estimated half of all U.S. households will be headed by a single parent – generally by a mother – we can only imagine the enormous waste of talent that will occur.

NOTES

1 Csikszentmihalyi & Beattie, 1979; Csikszentmihalyi & Larson, 1984.
2 McCormack, 1984.

3 For some ideas about the role of narrative as an interpretive method in the study of lives, see Cohler, 1982.

4 Choe, 1991.

5 Csikszentmihalyi, 1990a, p. 203.

6 Chandrasekhar, 1987, p. 26.

7 Choe, 1991.

8 Analysis of variance is a statistical method of comparing groups (in this case, talent areas) to ascertain whether such groups are significantly different from each other on some variable(s); in this case, on their ranking of rewards.

9 This way of measuring flow was an adaptation of the Flow Questionnaire and Flow Scales (Csikszentmihalyi, 1975) first used by Patrick Mayers in his dissertation (1978) and widely used since (see Csikszentmihalyi & Csikszentmihalyi, 1988).

10 Albert, 1990; Oden, 1968.

11 The relationship between family structure and talent development was studied in the doctoral dissertation of Patricia Lorek (1989).

8

How families influence
the development
of talent

In almost every chapter so far, we have stressed that for talented children to transform their potential into actuality, the support of the family, in both material and psychological terms, is essential. Because of the importance of the family for the development of talent, this chapter considers in detail those characteristics of families that seem the most important in this respect. First, however, it may be useful to present a brief historical perspective on the importance of the family for development in general.

THE HOME ENVIRONMENT

Understanding the positive role of the family in a child's development is becoming a central concern not only of parents but also of teachers, administrators, and politicians. Newspapers quote study after study comparing the United States unfavorably with other developed nations on such family health indicators as divorce rates, infant mortality, teenage pregnancy, and suicide.[1] Some social scientists read the evidence as meaning that the family as we know it is definitely on the decline – or that it never really existed in its ideal form. Others respond to the trends as an occasion for refocusing priorities on improving the quality of family life.

Our position in this debate is that the habits children develop in the first years of life and the outlooks they learn about life's possibilities are difficult to alter.[2] It is therefore essential that the early environment provide the stability and the stimulation for developing habits and outlooks that will make complex development in later life possible. It is perhaps not particularly important whether or not children are provided such stability and stimulation by two adults of the opposite sex married to each other. Yet the stubborn fact remains that in every culture we know, in the distant past as well as in the present, the vast majority of child-rearing responsibilities have been shouldered by "families," that is, by adults related to each other either genetically or by bonds of socially sanctioned commitment. Whenever other means for rearing children have been attempted – in the Soviet Union, in China, even in the Israeli kibbutzim – the experiment has been far from successful, and either total or partial family responsibility for the upbringing of children has been reintroduced. Thus it is likely that the currently fashionable accounts of the death of the family are highly exaggerated, or, if they are not, that they say more about the end of our culture than about the demise of the family.

For some children, time at home is a blessing. Their parents are warm and loving and help to create an environment full of challenging opportunities. For others, spending time at home is a nightmare. Just coping with problems at home often requires all the energy a child can muster and leaves little over for investing in growth-oriented activities. For example, one of the greatest drains on a child's resources is having to deal with the stresses and strains endemic in many single-parent families. Current statistics show that more children in the United States live in single-parent homes than in any other industrialized nation. Rising divorce rates, decreasing remarriage rates, and more women working outside the home while staying unmarried contribute to the prediction that 59% of children born in 1983 will live with only one parent at some time before the age of 18.[3]

There are probably many reasons why such a situation is less healthy for a child. One of the most important is less parental attention available to protect, guide, and stimulate the child. It is true that some children from single-parent homes may learn to do more for themselves and so gain valuable lessons about survival. But it is likely that their protected peers have more leisure to learn essential skills in their safe cocoon.

Few in the group of teenagers whom we studied, of course, fall into the troubled patterns described above. Their parents were reasonably affluent and well educated, and their divorce rate was below the national average. In almost every conceivable way, these teens had all the "advantages" on their side. The issue of whether a family environment wastes or focuses attentional energy is, however, just as relevant for these teenagers. In other words, it would be fairly easy to demonstrate that severe problems at home can greatly reduce a child's ability to concentrate. But if, even within the privileged environment of the group under study, different types of family organization had effects on the development of talent, then the importance of appropriate home conditions would be demonstrated with additional force.

ADOLESCENT DEPENDENCE OR INDEPENDENCE?

The question of what home conditions are optimal for adolescents is being answered somewhat differently now than it was even a decade ago. Traditional thinking about adolescents' needs for growing separation and independence from their parents[4] is giving way to the conception that teens grow more competent and self-directed through a renegotiated interdependence with parents.[5] Although the onset of puberty and attendant cognitive changes alter the tenor of parent–child relations, most of these major transitions are accomplished without excessive turmoil and separation.[6] Studies are beginning to show that disengagement from family too early leaves teenagers more susceptible to negative peer influence and may lead to lower academic achievement.[7] In general, healthy development is increasingly seen as happening in a context where both autonomy and attachment and connection with parents are highly valued.[8]

Thus it appears that optimal conditions for teenage development (and it could be argued for adult development as well) are not very different from what is necessary for nurturing infants. In other words, just as infants need continuing security and support for the emergence of exploration and independence,[9] so do all persons, no matter their age. Even iconoclastic, "free-thinking" university professors have to count on the tenure system to protect their freedom of thought.

That a sense of dependence is necessary to feel independent is not as contradictory an idea as it may seem at first glance. It calls to mind, for instance, the observations of some biologists concerning human development. It seems that because of the lengthy period of human dependence, during which parents must invest time and energy in taking care of their children (a condition called neoteny in biology), human infants gain more opportunities to play and explore their environment. This playful exploration is a viable evolutionary strategy because it facilitates behavioral flexibility and cognitive development and thus helps humans avoid the rigid patterns of instinctual behavior that characterize lower species.[10]

If we extend this reasoning to adolescent development, teens who maintain some reliance on parents can reap the benefit of extended periods of exploration. The flaw in this argument, though, may already be apparent: It assumes that the attention that is set free by allowing an individual to be dependent is invested in a way that encourages further growth and development. Obviously a safe and secure teenager who is allowed to play video games all day long will not develop satisfactorily, nor will the one who takes advantage of the situation by spending less and less time at home and more time with peers experimenting with drugs. On the other hand, the young person who can rely on parents for moral, emotional, and physical support when they are needed is probably better prepared to spend time perfecting the backstroke, practicing the viola, or developing meaningful friendships.

A reverse danger from the abuse of free attention is that of becoming overdependent. As teenagers grow up, some dependence must be relinquished. Otherwise the adolescent's narcissism may increase from excessive care and attention, while the parents may be overindulging their sense of being needed and in control. Consider, for instance, a devoted father who lives for his son's Friday night basketball game because his own prestige is enhanced, or the equally devoted son who struggles to play ball in college even though he thinks it's a waste of time, just because his father used to encourage him.

AN EXPLORATORY MODEL: COMPLEX FAMILIES AND TALENT DEVELOPMENT

The dynamics described above can be represented more formally in the theoretical model of complexity already introduced.[11] The bonds of connection between family members are an instance of *integration,* or the stable condition whereby the individuals feel a sense of support and consistency. *Differentiation* refers to the fact that members are encouraged to develop their individuality by seeking out new challenges and opportunities. Families that are both integrated and differentiated can be thought of as *complex*. If these two forces in the family – one pulling together for stability and one pushing away toward growth and change – are not adjusted over time to maintain complexity, the debilitating possibilities of overintegration and overdifferentiation could prevent healthy development. Finally, a further possibility, also undesirable, is the lack of both dimensions in a family. Such an organization can be thought of as *simple*, because family members' energy produces neither increasing order nor variety in relationships. Although all these family types can produce children who will develop talents, outside help – or luck – is more likely to be needed if the family lacks complexity.

Complex families are expected to be the best stimulus to teens' talent development. Bloom's interviews with 120 individuals at the top of their respective professions in athletics, art, music, math, and science suggest that high levels of both support and challenge have a positive effect across all talent areas. The parents of the accomplished individuals were child centered; they devoted great amounts of time and energy to meeting the needs of their special children and often made them the center of their attention. On the other hand, the parents served as models for and expected a strong work ethic and drive toward disciplined independence. They encouraged the productive use of time, the setting of high standards, and dedication to doing one's best. They provided challenging opportunities by making sure lessons and materials were available in abundance. They set aside areas of the home where the child could work privately without interruption, and they excused the child from household chores and work outside the home in order to conserve time and energy.

The advantages of this type of family environment are being described with increasing frequency in other family studies, but understanding why such a pattern works well has not been achieved. Our perspective based on this study is that family complexity enhances children's investment of attentional energy in growth-producing activities and so facilitates the quality of their subjective experience both at home and in school. What is special to the present approach is thus its emphasis on the importance of attention and the quality of experience for understanding what makes a family context effective. In adopting such a perspective, we have placed a greater significance on the numerous experiential episodes that build toward positive long-term outcomes. Few family studies have investigated how children actually feel at home, despite the fact that extensive research into optimal experiences, such as interest, flow, intrinsic motivation, and peak experiences, suggests that how children feel is among the most important influences on whether they will fully utilize their potential.[12]

When people are interested or are in flow, they use attention in two seemingly opposing ways at the same time: They are more receptive, spontaneous, and open to the immediate environment, yet more active, goal-directed, selective, and controlling.[13] In everyday life these qualities are usually divided: We are often passive and pleasantly at ease (but unfocused), as when watching television; or we are alert and concentrated (but not too happy), as when having to read a textbook. Conditions in an integrated and differentiated family create a context for optimal experience by facilitating both of these states of attention.[14] For instance, in an integrated family there would be stability and trust. This would reduce the need for defensiveness and conflict, thus making it easier for children to feel at ease and become absorbed in whatever they are doing. On the other hand, a differentiated family would promote independence, provide challenges, and discourage the wasting of energy through idleness and thus promote attentional involvement in activities that require self-discipline. The combination of dimensions provides the best conditions for optimal experience.

Patterns of perception and experience assimilated at home are likely to be carried over to new contexts, such as school. In other words, teenagers socialized in supportive families that encourage the pursuit of difficult challenges are likely to become persons who are able to enjoy whatever they are doing and who choose to undertake activities that require effort and promote future growth. Complex family environments breed complex, autotelic personalities – in other words, individuals who habitually react to a boring situation by seeking stimulation and challenge and to an anxiety-provoking one by increasing skills.[15]

This is not to say that a typical ideal family is a necessity for the development of talent. There are many examples of successful creative individuals who grew up in single-parent homes, who were orphaned early, or whose parents provided a tense and conflictive environment. But we suggest that in all of these exceptions some other influence in the individual's milieu is likely to have provided the support and stimulation that allowed for the development of talent. Thus family complexity is really a shorthand expression for the complexity of the interpersonal network that surrounds a child in her or his early years.

Is there a connection between how complex the family is and how well an adolescent is able to experience interest or flow at home and in school? And if so, does such positive experience enhance her or his talent development? Though much has been written separately about the benefits of optimal experiential states and the benefits of integrated and differentiated families, to our knowledge there have been no studies that have investigated the family's impact on such experiences, as well as their role in successful talent development, until ours.

Measuring the complexity of families

To determine which families were complex and which were not, the Complex Family Questionnaire (CFQ) was designed to measure family integration and differentiation. All the adolescents in our study filled it out (see Appendix 8.1). Family integration was composed of two subfactors, *support* (e.g., the teen is sometimes the center of attention, others modify plans on her behalf, others had empathy for his failures) and *harmony* (e.g., the household is organized efficiently, there are clear home rules, the behavior of family members is consistent). Differentiation was also composed of two subfactors, *involvement* (e.g., the family encourages individual intensity, tolerates competitiveness, has pride) and *freedom* (e.g., the teen's interests are not always interrupted by family chores and obligations, he can find quiet at home to think, she has privacy to escape to her "own world").

Adolescents who had high integration scores (i.e., were above the median values for support and harmony) and high differentiation scores (i.e., above the median for involvement and freedom) were classified as having complex families. Those who ranked high in just the integration dimension are referred to as integrated; those who ranked high in just the differentiation dimension are called differentiated. Finally, those low in both dimensions were classified as having a simple family organization. The last classification is not used in the derogatory sense of simple-minded; it attempts rather to describe a type of family that lacks both the stability and the push for growth present in complex families.

This way of organizing the data yielded four groups of teens who differed in their perceptions of the family but who were remarkably similar in other important respects (see Appendixes 8.2 and 8.3). For instance, there were no significant differences between groups in terms of parents' reported income or level of education. A chi square analysis of family size, sibling position, and marital status showed that the proportions of small and large families, first-born and later-born children, and married and divorced parents were similar across all four family types. Mean scores indicated that 38% of the teenagers were first-born or only children, 74% of them had at most only one other brother or sister, and 88% of their parents were married. Ethnic and religious backgrounds were also similarly dispersed across groups, as were differences in talent area and sex. Finally, adolescent levels of intelligence, based on the standardized PSAT test (Math score and Verbal score), were not significantly different. In fact, the scores were very similar, with teens in the integrated family group having slightly higher scores.

These preliminary analyses showed that the family typology used in our study is not an artifact of middle-class values and is not simply a correlate of education or intelligence. Demographic factors do not seem to determine it; almost anyone apparently has a chance of creating a complex family.

Parental perceptions of the family

Because the CFQ relied upon teens' reports, the problem of response bias was addressed with parental questionnaires. In other words, if the adolescents had been accurate reporters about their home context, the parents in the various family groups should differ in ways that correspond to their children's perceptions of differing support, harmony, involvement, and freedom at home. Although based on past research a high level of agreement between parents' and adolescents' perceptions cannot be expected,[16] some correspondence between parents' and children's reports would provide an important check of validity.

Four parental measures were used to compare adolescents' perceptions of their families with parents' responses (information from both parents was available for only about 100 of the 165 adolescents who filled out the CFQ). The Rewards in Interaction measure was a nine-item questionnaire ($\alpha = .83$) that asked parents to rate how rewarding it was to interact with their child (e.g., enjoying doing things with her/him, getting pleasure from her/his accomplishments, helping her/him develop). A Parental Disagreement measure was an eight-item scale ($\alpha = .85$) that asked parents to assess "the extent of agreement or disagreement between you and your mate on the following items": finances, recreation, affection, friends, sex, morality, philosophy of life, and in-laws. Parental Life Satisfaction was a one-item measure on a 7-point scale (*completely dissatisfied/unhappy* to *completely satisfied/happy*) used to assess parents' personal life satisfaction. Finally, Parental Intrinsic Career Expectations was a five-item scale ($\alpha = .78$) designed to assess parental expectations about the intrinsic rewards for their children (e.g., "In terms of your child's future job or career, how much would you prefer that each of the following qualities characterize her/his job: job fitting interests/skills, challenging or stimulating work, enjoyment, opportunity for learning, sense of accomplishment?").

Table 8.1 summarizes the results of the comparisons. Parents from families in which children reported varying levels of integration and differentiation also reported different interaction rewards ($p < .05$), disagreement ($p < .10$), life happiness ($p < .05$), and intrinsic expectations ($p < .05$). Parents in complex and in integrated families reported the highest rewards from interacting with their child, the most agreement with their spouse, and the highest expectations for their child to find intrinsic rewards in a future career. The parents in the complex and the differentiated families – those where we might expect a greater measure of personal freedom and independence – reported the highest personal life satisfaction. Finally, all the comparisons between the complex and simple groups were significant: Parents from families that teens described as more complex reported more rewards in interaction, less conflict, more personal happiness, and greater intrinsic expectations. Thus the children and their parents did in fact agree about the quality of their family lives.

QUALITY OF HOME EXPERIENCE

Teenagers from complex homes were expected to report more positive experience and flow while at home. Perhaps, however, those who said

Table 8.1. *Parents' descriptions of family interactions, experiences, and expectations: Comparison of mean scale scores across complex family types*

	Complex (n = 27)[a]	Integrated (n = 21)	Differentiated (n = 15)	Simple (n = 30)	F	t[b]
Rewards from interacting with child	61.9	61.7	57.9	58.1	2.97**	2.31**
Disagreement with spouse	36.0	34.5	37.3	40.1	2.27*	-1.97**
Personal life happiness	10.8	10.1	10.9	9.3	3.15**	2.70***
Expectations for intrinsic motivation in child's career	46.0	46.7	44.4	44.4	2.89**	1.93**

[a] In each group *n* represents the number of couples: mothers' score + fathers' score divided by 2.
[b] Complex vs. simple, one-tailed *t*-tests.
*$p < .10$. **$p < .05$. ***$p < .01$.

positive things about their families on the CFQ when asked about their experience at home are already biased to respond that they are more happy, concentrated, and so on. In other words, if it is the case that some adolescents are more inclined to rate their families and their experiences more positively (because they want to "look good" to outside researchers and readers), then their reports of more optimal experience would not be the result of favorable home conditions, as is suggested here, but simply the result of a response bias.

The parents' responses reported earlier make such a bias explanation less likely (i.e., one would have to argue that parents shared in their children's distortions), but to further avoid the possibility of bias, an additional criterion was proposed: If more than response bias is involved, teenagers' reports of optimal experience should be sensitive to different contexts of activity. In other words, whereas we would expect most contexts of adolescents' lives to be improved by the quality of their family life, passive leisure activities, such as watching TV, that do not require a concentrated investment of attention to yield enjoyment[17] should be experienced about the same by all teens. Thus, the analyses presented next contrast passive leisure activities, including TV watching, with other activities presumably more important for talent development, such as homework.

The first measure of quality of home experience was based upon the Flow Scales first used by Mayers[18] and was used to assess the intensity of teens' flow experiences when with their families and while watching TV. This questionnaire, which was introduced in the previous chapter, consists of 11 questions that focus on the characteristics of flow (e.g., "I get involved," "I clearly know what I am supposed to do," "I would do it even if I didn't have to," "I do not get distracted"). The results showed that family complexity was significantly related to the amount of flow reported in family interaction ($p < .001$). Those who perceived their families as complex reported the most optimal experience; the differentiated and simple groups reported the least. Being with the family provided more optimal experience than watching TV ($p < .001$), and there was a significant interaction between family type and type of activity ($p < .001$). That is, teens in all four groups reported similar subjective rewards from watching TV but varied widely in their responses concerning the quality of experience with their families.

ESM analysis of experience at home

The measure of flow above provides a retrospective look, from the teenagers' point of view, at their quality of experience at home. We learn from it how students remember feeling when they think back on times they spent with their families, but we learn nothing about their reactions of the moment to events at home. Also, because the retrospective data were collected at the same point in time as reports concerning family integration and differentiation, we cannot be sure to what extent optimal experience was part of their time at home in previous years. These questions are addressed next, using the Experience Sampling Method (ESM) reports, which were collected 2 and 3 years before the CFQ was filled out.

Observing adolescents at home is especially difficult because teens, it could be argued, are more aware than small children of the disturbance caused by the presence of strangers in the home. However, the ESM lets us see the students at home in their natural context, without the intrusion of strangers. Furthermore, these random snapshots allow unique opportunities for assessing family experiences that are not readily observable with any other method. For instance, the pager caught Jerry, an art student who perceives his family as both integrated and differentiated, helping his dad one Saturday afternoon shovel dirt in the backyard. His subjective mood was positive: He wanted to help his dad, and he felt in control, good about himself, alert, happy, and involved. Nevertheless the shoveling was giving Jerry a sore back, and the challenges he perceived in the activity were low in comparison with his skills. A couple of days later he was with his parents talking over a problem encountered at school. Again Jerry wanted to do what he was doing, but his overall mood was less positive (only "some" alertness, happiness, and control). It seems that discussing the particular problem (with a geometry teacher) had dampened Jerry's mood. However, he described his conversation with his parents as very "involved" and "open."

Such experiences are typical of the kind the pager sampled. Teens reported their subjective states in numerous activities, and eight ESM variables were chosen to represent the major dimensions of subjective experience that we were interested in: Affect (happy/cheerful), Activation (alert/excited), Expectations (living up to own/others' expectations), and Goals (activity is important to self/important to overall goals). Consistent with our theory, teenagers' momentary moods and energy levels (i.e., affect and activation) were expected to be more strongly associated with family integration. Simply stated, families that were warm, consistent, and supportive would have children who felt better at home. On the other hand, we expected the orientation toward personal intensity, involvement, and self-control in differentiated families to be more strongly associated with teenagers' positive evaluations of future expectations and goals.

Table 8.2 reports the four significant differences ($p < .0001$) between the subjective experiences of the groups for times when teens were at home. Those from complex families reported the highest affect and activation, and most often indicated that they were living up to their expectations and that they were pursuing important goals. All of the comparisons with teens from simple families were significant ($p < .001$). Follow-up analyses confirmed our expectation that the first two results were due to family integration and the latter two to family differentiation. In other words, whereas family complexity was uniformly the optimal context for experience, both integration and differentiation made unique contributions: The former accounted more for teenagers' buoyant moods and energy and the latter for positive evaluations of future expectations and goals.[19] Complex families thus appear to encourage optimal experiences that combine spontaneity with goal directedness and enjoyment with seriousness.

Focusing attention on productive activities at home

Beyond providing an improved quality of experience, a complex family should also encourage involvement in productive activities. Teenagers given a measure of freedom tend to develop initiative if they come from a warm and harmonious environment; such a setting is thought to create ideal conditions for focusing their attention on productive activities. Such conditions, however, should not affect the way they experience TV watching, which does not require much effort.

To measure the quantity as well as the subjective quality of teens' investment of attention in productive activities, we used the ESM in the following analyses to estimate the percentage of time students spent doing productive work. To do this, we extrapolated from the percentage of ESM signals that randomly caught them doing such work. For example, if a

Table 8.2. *Adolescent quality of experience at home (mean z scores)*

ESM variables	Complex	Integrated	Differentiated	Simple	ANOVA F	t
No. of ESM signals	689	559	392	765		
Affect & activation						
Happy/cheerful	0.28	0.10	−0.30	−0.08	10.2****	3.9***
Alert/excited	0.37	−0.03	−0.44	−0.05	20.1****	4.7***
Expectations & goals						
Living up to own/others' expectations	0.56	−0.18	−0.02	−0.10	21.2****	6.7***
Importance to self and overall goals	0.33	−0.32	−0.14	−0.04	15.0****	4.0***

Note: All results are also significant ($p < .05$) when aggregating first by individual student and then comparing family means. Follow-up ANOVAs (high/low integration by high/low differentiation) on affect and activation showed main effects for family integration (not differentiation), and further analyses of expectations and goals showed main effects for differentiation (not integration).

***$p < .001.$ ****$p < .0001.$

student responded 20 times to the pager at home and 5 times he or she was doing homework, we estimated that 25% of that student's time was invested in doing homework.

Based on the approximately 2,400 ESM responses that occurred at home, we investigated time use in four major activities: home routines (eating, dressing, picking things up, chores at home, and so on), leisure (TV, listening to music, reading, hobbies, playing games), productive (98% homework and study; 2% job-related work), and interaction (general talk, socializing, telephoning, and so on). Percentage scores indicate the ratio of the total number of ESM signals per family group in a particular activity to the total number of signals responded to at home (e.g., if 200 of 600 signals for the integrated groups occurred in leisure activities, the percentage of leisure for the group would equal 33).

Results showed that the four groups had differing time budgets ($\chi^2 = 20.6$, $p < .01$, $df = 9$, one-tailed). Complex families showed the most "efficient" pattern of time use: average amounts in leisure and interaction, the least in home routines (35%), and the most in homework (20%). Conversely, teens who reported low family integration and low differentiation (a simple family organization) showed the least efficient pattern: 42% of the random ESM signals caught them in routine activities (the highest of the groups) and only 14% doing homework (the lowest). They also interacted at home the least: 10%. The integrated family group, who like the complex families spent relatively little time in home routines (36%), invested the most time in leisure (36%). They were the only group in which home routines did not take up the highest percentage of ESM signals. Differentiated families had the highest mean (14%) in interaction.

One explanation for these results is that the greater cooperation in complex families has made everyday routines more automatic and hence more efficient. Presumably teens from simple families found it difficult to coordinate plans with other family members in order to take care of daily necessities, a fact that may have contributed to their lower time investment in homework. Teens from integrated families, like those from complex ones, spent relatively little time in home routines. In turn, they invested this saved attention in leisure. Leisure activities accounted for 43% of the time that adolescents in integrated families spent with their parents, a full 8% (or about 8 hours each week) difference from the next closest family type. Thus, though they were conserving attentional resources in the smooth functioning of the family, they seemed to lack challenging opportunities to invest that attention.

The next analyses addressed the question whether teens from complex homes, in addition to spending more time doing productive activities, were also more energetic and goal directed while doing them, and whether they experienced passive leisure in a way similar to their peers. The variables "alertness" and "importance to overall goals" were contrasted across the groups for times when teenagers were (without parents present) engaging in productive or leisure activities.

Figures 8.1 and 8.2 show that family type did affect teens' alertness ($p < .01$) and their goal directedness ($p < .05$), with teens from complex families reporting the highest levels in productive activities – most of which consisted of doing homework. All teenagers were slightly more alert while doing homework than in leisure ($p < .10$), and they perceived homework to be of much greater importance to their overall goals ($p < .001$). Both alertness and goal-directed levels also depended upon the interaction between family type and activity type ($p < .05$). These joint effects are illustrated by the figures and also by the comparisons of the complex and simple groups: (a) the combination of family complexity and productive work produced a greater increase in alertness for teens from complex families ($p < .01$), but family had no effect on alertness in passive leisure activities; and (b) homework was seen as more important to goals in complex families ($p < .01$), but the opposite was the case in regard to passive leisure; that is, teens from simple families perceived it as of somewhat greater importance to their goals ($p = .07$, two-tailed). Finally, once again follow-up analyses of productive work (not summarized in the figures) showed that differences in teens' alertness were associated with their perceptions of family integration (but not differentiation) and that goal directedness was related to differentiation (but not to integration).

In sum, teens from complex families reported more positive home experiences. They reported more flow experience with their families. They also reported higher happiness and cheerfulness and greater alertness and excitement (results presumably due to family integration), and they were more often living up to their own and others' expectations and doing things more important to themselves and their goals (results related

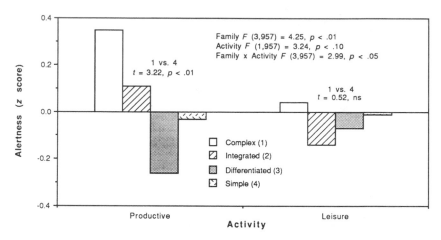

Figure 8.1. Alertness while engaging in productive and leisure activities at home.

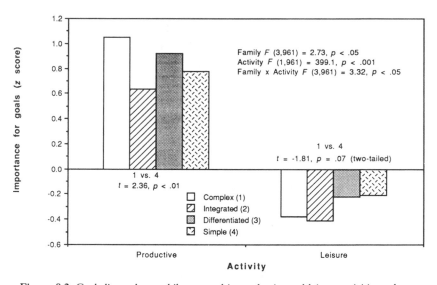

Figure 8.2. Goal-directedness while engaged in productive and leisure activities at home.

to family differentiation) in response to the pager signals. In addition, teens from complex families showed more efficient attentional investment in productive activities in terms of both quantity and quality: They put more time into study and homework (an estimate based on their ESM reports would suggest 2–3 hours more per week), and they were more alert and goal directed while doing it. Yet teens from all four family types – complex, integrated, differentiated, and simple – appeared quite alike in terms of watching TV, listening to music, playing games, and pursuing hobbies at home. They spent similar amounts of time in these pursuits and reported similar amounts of alertness and goal directedness.

QUALITY OF EXPERIENCE IN PRODUCTIVE ACTIVITIES

The next analyses compared the same family groups in regard to students' overall productive activity, most of which occurred in school. This group of ESM signals was the most comprehensive representation of students' productive work; it included times when students were either working in their talent area or on other schoolwork, regardless of place or social context. In other words, it included all homework, study, and class times as well as any signals during talent-related work. The variables compared were the same ones used for experience at home, and hypotheses predicted the same associations between family integration and teens' affect and activation, and between differentiation in the family and longer-term expectations and goals.

Results (see Table 8.3) showed that when teenagers were productively engaged, family context was related to teens' affect, activation, expectations, and goals ($p < .0001$). Those from complex families reported the highest means for each variable, and their reports were significantly higher than those from simple families ($p < .001$). Follow-up analyses again showed that affect and activation were more strongly related to family integration, and reports of living up to expectations and pursuing important goals were more related to the dimension of differentiation, regardless of whether we looked at general or talent-related schoolwork.[20]

Using the same group of productive signals, the next analyses explored the amount of time teens in each family group spent in the flow quadrant. The percentage of time in flow was derived from an individual's ratio of

Table 8.3. *Adolescent quality of experience in overall productive work (mean z scores)*

ESM variables	Complex	Integrated	Differentiated	Simple	ANOVA F	t
No. of ESM signals	767	520	403	745		
Affect & activation						
Happy/cheerful	0.40	0.11	−0.23	−0.15	16.0****	5.9***
Alert/excited	0.36	−0.10	−0.39	−0.09	19.2****	5.1***
Expectations & goals						
Living up to own/others' expectations	0.46	−0.09	0.16	−0.31	23.4****	8.1***
Importance to self and overall goals	0.38	−0.42	0.09	−0.09	21.7****	5.1***

Note: All results are also significant ($p < .05$) when aggregating first by individual student and then comparing family means. Follow-up ANOVAs (high/low integration by high/low differentiation) on affect and activation showed main effects for family integration (not differentiation), and further analyses of expectations and goals showed main effects for differentiation (not integration).

***$p < .001$. ****$p < .0001$.

skills and challenges in the following way: If the student responded to the pager 20 times in productive work, and 10 responses reported the perception of above-average skills and challenges, the corresponding percentage in flow would be 50.

Family context, according to the results, did have an effect on the percentage of flow quadrant responses ($F = 3.57, p < .05$). Teens from complex families reported the most flow (approximately 45% of their signals revealed above-average challenge and skills), and those from integrated families the least (approximately 25%). The comparison of percentage of flow between the complex and simple family groups was also significant ($t = 2.13, p < .05$). To contrast productive activities with passive leisure, as was done above in the home context, the overall productive category was contrasted with times when teens were watching television. As expected, however, no differences emerged among the four groups ($F = 0.63$, NS). On the average, TV viewing fell within the flow quadrant less than 10% of the time; teens felt either bored (skilled but unchallenged) or apathetic (unskilled and unchallenged) over 90% of the time they were watching television.

In sum, using a great variety of different methods of measurement, family complexity appears to be associated with teens' positive subjective experience in productive work. Teens from complex families reported more happiness and cheerfulness and more alertness and excitement. They also indicated more often that they were living up to their own and others' expectations and were doing something that had personal and long-term importance. In addition, more of their ESM reports in productive work were in the "balanced" category of high challenge and high skill (a good indication that they were experiencing more flow). Using the same measuring instrument, however, we found that these differences disappeared in passive activities, such as watching television, and that teens' profiles look surprisingly similar in these activities, regardless of family type. Presumably these activities require a minimal attentional investment that all teenagers can muster.

ADOLESCENT PERFORMANCE AT SCHOOL

Is family complexity associated with superior school performance? Students' ESM reports indicated the connection between complexity at home and increased amounts of attention invested in productive work, greater energy and goal directedness, and improved quality of experience (i.e., more flow and so on). However, the subjective ratings of the teenagers may not accurately reflect objective events – in this case, academic performance. It could be argued that more positive subjective ratings are in themselves an important indicator of student performance, but corroborations from independent sources would enhance the meaning and validity of the findings reported thus far. Therefore two performance measures were utilized: (a) percentile class rank, based on multiple teacher grades, and (b) teachers' ratings, given only by teachers in the talent area. The former provided a measure of students' general school performance; the latter, an indication of students' talent area performance.

Figure 8.3 reports class ranks for the four groups across their first 3 years of high school. Teens from complex families, despite the fact that their PSAT scores for intellectual ability were slightly lower than for both the integrated and simple family groups, achieved significantly better (i.e., lower) rankings, indicating superior performance in the general high school curriculum in each of the three years. Also better was their performance in their particular areas of talent, as indicated by their teachers' ratings. Family context had a significant effect on talent performance, and teachers reported that teens from complex families, in comparison with those from simple families, concentrated better, were more often performing to potential, enjoyed and preferred difficult challenges, and were more independent, original, and involved. Teens from differentiated families received the second highest teacher ratings, and those from simple families, who had the highest class rankings, also received the lowest teacher ratings.

To determine whether the superior talent performance of teens from complex families represented a general trend across all five talent areas or was confined to just one or two of them (i.e., perhaps family complexity is only associated with superior performance in math and science), teacher scores were reanalyzed crossing family type and talent area. Results showed the alternative explanation above to be implausible: No interaction between family type and talent area was observed. Teens from complex families received higher ratings in four out of the five talent areas; the exception was athletics, where they scored below the differentiated group.

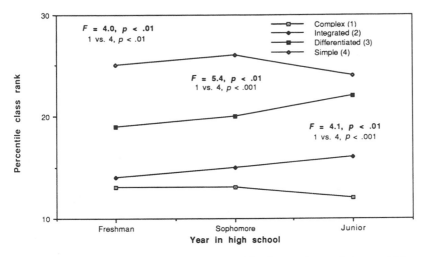

Figure 8.3. Average class rank by family context. *Note:* Lower class rank denotes higher academic standing.

FAMILY COMPLEXITY AND TALENT
DEVELOPMENT: CONCLUSIONS

All of the various measures suggest that teens from complex families experience and perform productive work with more enjoyable intensity. The data also converge in suggesting that teens who perceive their families as being neither responsive to them nor demanding much from them (i.e., a simple organization) have a lower quality of experience and performance in productive work. Contrasts between these two types of family contexts were significant across the majority of measures, *except* at times when teens were involved in such passive leisure activities as watching television. Presumably, passive activities requiring little selective effort are experienced in a similar way by all teenagers, regardless of the attentional habits they have developed.

The importance of a complex family is thus not a matter of helping a child enjoy watching television or playing a game. Children will probably enjoy these activities regardless of family support or stimulation. Rather, a complex family context will help young persons enjoy serious activities, such as studying, that normally are avoided whenever possible because they require too much mental effort. To enjoy a highly challenging activity requires a correspondingly high amount of psychic energy if the difficulties are to be mastered. A family that provides a teenager with a sense of support and consistency, and encourages her or his intensity and self-direction, enhances attentional capacities for finding challenges and for mastering them. Thus complex families create autotelic contexts that improve the quality of experience for their members.

The focus in this chapter is on young people who have superior talents, but the implications of the findings need not be confined to talented adolescents. The findings should apply to all teenagers (and presumably to younger children as well). In fact, complex families might have a stronger effect on the lives of teenagers in an average population, where the range of parenting is wider than in the present sample of generally "good" parents.

Do these observations mesh with what is known about the backgrounds of individuals who are actually at the top of their fields? Do eminent persons come from similar families? The answers to these questions are mixed: The observations of Bloom, for instance, are very consistent with those reported here; others, less so.[21]

Many studies of exceptionally talented and creative individuals point out the frequent turmoil found in their family backgrounds. For instance, Goertzel and Goertzel comment, "In the homes which cradle eminence, creativity and contentment are not congenial."[22] Only 58 of the 400 famous men and women whose biographies they studied had homes they classified as comfortable, content, warm, and untroubled. They argue that such homes tend to produce well-adjusted, competent, and stable personalities but not necessarily creative ones. When extremely talented individuals come from such harmonious homes, they are more likely to be scientists, physicians, and statesmen than great artists or musicians. On the other hand, the Goertzels claim that almost all of the homes of the 400 individuals they studied could be characterized as having a strong drive toward intellectual or creative achievement. At least one parent promoted the attributes and qualities of individual differentiation: curiosity, risk and experimentation, physical vigor, dedication to principle, and love of learning with personal involvement.

The seeming primacy of family differentiation in the development of eminent talent is in one respect supported by the results of the present study. Family differentiation had a stronger impact on the teacher ratings of talent development and on the students' ratings of flow experience in talent-related work, whereas family integration was a better predictor of general school performance.[23] This profile seems to corroborate the Goertzels' point. Integration promotes the socialization of well-adjusted and competent individuals, not necessarily talented or creative ones. However, previous studies that lacked a conceptual classification for families with a balanced tension of support and stress were forced to classify families in an either–or fashion: as (something like) integrated or (something like) differentiated. This black-and-white approach, as shown by the present study, may miss entirely the possibility that a family that is both integrated and differentiated is the most effective in developing talents.

No one claims that a complex family context is *the* necessary ingredient for the achievement of eminence. Such a thesis could easily be disproven. The claim is rather the more obvious one that potential eminence in any field is the result of an individual's sustained attention to productive tasks relevant to that field. A complex family context, through its everyday influences and its cumulative socializing effects over time, is thought only to improve the likelihood that children will grow into young adults capable of such ongoing involvement.

Ultimately it is the organization of psychic energy, not the family, that underlies talent development. The importance of the family is in helping to shape that organization. There are many eminent individuals who do not come from supportive and stimulating families; their development may be more readily accounted for by inborn talent, sociocultural conditions, or perhaps the overcoming of some personal tragedy or disability. In such cases, complex attentional habits are shaped by other factors. The results reported here, however, suggest that a home environment in which one is secure enough to feel cheerful and energetic, and challenged enough to become more goal directed, increases teenagers' chances of progressively refining their talents.

NOTES

1 According to the American Humane Association (1989), reports of child abuse and neglect in the United States escalated 300% in the 10 years prior to 1986,

from under 700,000 to over 2,100,000. For the 600% increase in births to unwed mothers in the last 40 years (they now total 25% of all live births), see Harris, 1990. For a review of the condition of families and children around the world, see the UNICEF report *The State of the World's Children* (1990).

2 A good review of what children need in order to develop to a healthy adulthood, and especially of what parents can do to facilitate their development, is in the recent volume by M. Konner (1991).

3 Hodgkinson, 1985.

4 Blos, 1979.

5 Baumrind, 1987; Cooper, Grotevant, & Condon, 1983; Damon, 1983; Hauser et al., 1984; Hill, 1987; Maccoby & Martin, 1983.

6 Offer, 1969.

7 Dornbusch et al., 1985; Steinberg & Silverberg, 1986.

8 Irwin, 1987.

9 Ainsworth, Bell, & Stayton, 1971; Matas, Arend, & Stroufe, 1978.

10 Fagen, 1981.

11 See also Rathunde, 1989a,b, 1991a; Rathunde & Csikszentmihalyi, 1991a.

12 Amabile, 1983; Csikszentmihalyi, 1975; Csikszentmihalyi & Csikszentmihalyi, 1988; deCharms, 1976; Deci & Ryan, 1985; Dewey, 1913; Groos, 1898; Harter, 1978; Maslow, 1968; White, 1959.

13 Rathunde, 1991a.

14 Rathunde, 1989a,b, 1991b; Rathunde & Csikszentmihalyi, 1991a,b.

15 Rathunde, 1989a,b.

16 Maccoby & Martin, 1983.

17 See Kubey & Csikszentmihalyi, 1990.

18 Mayers, 1978.

19 Rathunde, 1991b.

20 Ibid.

21 Bloom, 1985.

22 Goertzel & Goertzel, 1962, p. 130.

23 See also Rathunde, 1989a, 1991b.

9
Schools, teachers, and talent development

Natural ability is a great advantage in learning to enjoy a field of talent. It is the key that unlocks the potential for flow in activities that others experience as difficult, tedious, or boring. But neither great ability nor the support of a complex family guarantees the realization of talent. Unless a young person has access to a well-ordered domain and to a responsive and accessible field, potentials will probably never reach full flower. Even in the case of prodigies, as Feldman notes,[1] a time comes when the exercise of pure ability must give way to the guidance of adults "greatly gifted in the ability to catalyze potential into durable achievement." This chapter considers the influence of the adults who most often introduce young people to particular fields of performance: their teachers and coaches. The major question the chapter considers is whether the relationships among flow, complexity, and talent development imply new directions for teaching the talented.

CLASSROOM LIFE AND EVERYDAY ALIENATION

An unfortunate by-product of the standardized curricula of most modern schools is the depreciation of the role of teacher to that of information technician. Although teachers may be industrious and even inventive purveyors of knowledge across diverse domains, they are rarely practicing mathematicians, scientists, or musicians – that is, individuals who enjoy working in the domain.

This rift between practice and formal instruction is a relatively recent development in educational institutions. For centuries the dominant model of talent development centered on the establishment of reciprocal relations between the practitioner master and the apprentice pupil. This approach was not without its flaws. Students were often forced to adopt the ideas and techniques of the master, and the ultimate success of a relationship depended on the fit between two unique and often incompatible individuals.

Nonetheless, when it worked well the apprentice system provided, at the least, two important benefits. It identified early those unsuited to the demands of the discipline, and it granted able pupils an extended period in which to emulate a master committed to a craft. Such masters were capable of profoundly influencing the emerging selves of their pupils, in many cases helping them to reshape their lives to deal with the problems posed by the received tradition. For example, Donatello, the greatest sculptor of the early Renaissance, had for an apprentice the goldsmith, painter, and sculptor Andrea del Verrocchio, whose apprentices included Leonardo da Vinci and Perugino, the latter in turn becoming the teacher of Raphael. Each generation of students learned much from its master but was well prepared to innovate as well. Beyond the mere demonstration of competence, the committed teacher served as a daily model of the deeply interested life, a life of full participation in the world of challenges afforded by the domain.

But because the role of the teacher has largely evolved from a practitioner in a domain into that of a transmitter of information, the ethos of modern schooling discourages the development of just such extended and transforming relationships. Instead, modern curricula even in the arts tend to depersonalize even the transmission of information. In the name of diversity and efficiency, relations between teachers and students are kept highly specialized, programmatic, and brief. The rapid transfer of facts to masses of learners is stressed, not the slow cultivation of a unique individual's diverse gifts. The roles and goals available to teachers within these standardized curricula are in turn impersonal. They emphasize external mass performance standards, the delivery of uniform services, and the insulation of the curriculum from the interests of the particular person conveying it. Some depersonalization is inevitable under such conditions, for teachers and students alike.

But is this sort of experience also true for talented adolescents? After all, shouldn't they enjoy school more and be more motivated, given the

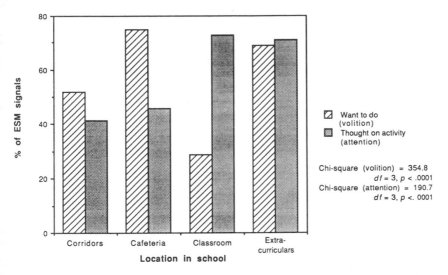

Figure 9.1. Volition and attention across four everyday high school locations.

extra attention and resources they receive? Unfortunately, the Experience Sampling Method (ESM) suggests otherwise. Figure 9.1 compares four common high school settings – lockers and corridors, the cafeteria, classes, and extracurricular settings – along two ESM measures of daily experience: how often students want to be doing what they are doing (volition) and how often they are thinking about what they are doing (attention). The resulting combinations underscore three important points about the talented adolescent's typical school day.

First – and here the experience of talented adolescents appears very similar to that of other teens in large high schools – both volition and the level of attention varied greatly across school locations. In fact, the differences across locations for both measures, and especially for volition, reach high levels of statistical significance (volition $\chi^2 = 354.8$, $p < .0001$; attention $\chi^2 = 190.7$, $p < .0001$). Second, the degree of linkage between volition and attentional focus is also highly variable across the school day. Locker areas, corridors, and the cafeteria clearly are places where students can relax and engage in activities that do not require much thought. In these settings concentration is typically below average, easy to maintain, and accompanied by feelings of happiness and self-esteem. In the classroom, by contrast, attention is quite focused – an outcome that distinguishes talented from average adolescents.[2] Yet motivation is quite low. Three fourths of the time when the talented teens reported from the classroom they did not want to do what they were doing. When they did want to do what they were doing, they tended to be doing and thinking about something other than academic work. The pager found them talking with classmates, falling asleep, daydreaming, or planning the next free period.

A third feature of Figure 9.1 is also important. The strength of both volition and attention in extracurricular settings indicates that there is nothing in structured school activity per se that necessarily sets volition and focused attention at odds. In fact, extracurricular activities evoke levels of concentration that rival the intensity of classroom examinations. Yet they do so in a way that sustains voluntary involvement.

Figure 9.2 in fact suggests that the one fourth of the time when classes produce a sense of wanting to be there, they look much more like extracurricular activities than like the majority of classes. Here we selected only those ESM signals in which students said that schoolwork was the primary focus of their attention in class. The one fourth of the time when classes were experienced as voluntary, students did not have such strong feelings of potency, skill, and involvement as they did when involved in extracurriculars, but they reported equally strong feelings of success, satisfaction, and meeting one's expectations (self-esteem). Moreover, the level of challenge was typically higher than in extracurricular activities. When classwork was experienced as obligatory, on the other hand, students reported feeling worse at a statistically significant level than how they felt when involved in either voluntary classwork or extracurricular activity, on all measures of experience except challenge. Obligatory classes appear to pose challenges that outstrip and depress a student's sense of skill and most other indicators of psychological well-being. Faced with such experiences, it is no mystery that teenagers typically do not want to be in class, even teenagers whose academic success might lead us to expect otherwise.

But if wanting to focus on hard work in the classroom can be so rewarding and energizing in its own right, why then do students experience these rewards so rarely? Why were teens so seldom in a focused and

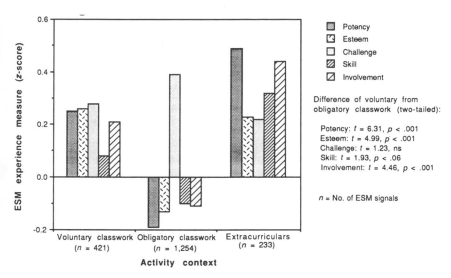

Figure 9.2. Quality of experience of voluntary and obligatory classwork and of extracurriculars.

positive frame of mind when in class? Many factors contribute, most of them beyond the control of individual teachers. However, what appears to set some teachers apart as motivators — and makes them memorable to their students — is their ability to transcend institutional roles in favor of a more personal approach to teaching.[3] Such memorable teachers are relatively few when we consider how many teachers a student encounters in the first 12 years of schooling. Yet their success at supporting, challenging, and empowering students can have a decisive impact. These themes were repeated again and again as the talented teens in our study talked about their best and worst experiences with teachers.

MEMORABLE LEARNING EXPERIENCES

Two examples from our study will perhaps give an idea of the kinds of expectations and responses that talented students singled out to illustrate their experience in school.

Judy

Judy had reached high school clearly aware of her natural singing ability, a talent firmly grounded in both hard work and her family's long history of musical giftedness. Yet as a freshman in such a large and seemingly impersonal high school, Judy found herself struggling for self-confidence and assurance. The tension between self-confidence and self-doubt sparked a crisis during her first high school audition. As her turn to audition approached, the jitters took hold. She began to worry about what "they" were looking for and how "they" would judge her. But luckily some friends intervened and all but carried her up to the stage, music in hand. To her surprise, the sound of the piano seemed to sweep her fears away. She regained control of her feelings and vocal cords and went on to win a coveted place in the chorus. "I was good enough that they didn't have to call me back. . . . That gave me a lot of confidence."

Like most students, Judy responds best to supportive teachers, those who "don't give up on me when I give up on myself" and who encourage her to "keep on trying." Yet Judy expects more than a nice manner and a positive attitude. She expects passion when it comes to music, in contrast to the boredom and anxiety of most classes. School, she says, "just doesn't have the thrill" of singing. In fact, school is "not really work, to me it's not really work." In her vocabulary "work" has a positive connotation; it is something serious, something worth doing. Real work is getting a passage just right while achieving the total concentration that only singing has for her. Judy doesn't mind vocal exercises as long as they take her back to that level of intensity.

At the same time, Judy's thirst for musical focus makes her on occasion temperamental. She particularly dislikes interruptions. "I hate it when they have to ruin the whole challenge for me by stopping me, saying, 'Stop,' trying to show me something." For Judy, that's just rude behavior – it is, as she says, the musical equivalent of "Shut up!" Such acute sensitivity to the quality of her experience while singing makes her very critical of teachers' critiques. Like many of her peers committed to a talent, Judy is often impatient as she seeks to attain perfection. The teachers who are most helpful in this quest seem to be those who can constantly stimulate their students to take on the next challenge while tolerating the students' shortness of temper, which almost inevitably follows when the search for perfection is frustrated.

Gwen

As early as the first grade, Gwen can remember enjoying math. She especially liked the clear feedback and sense of achievement that daily progress in math could provide. "The only thing I remember is one day being out in the playground, and I was finishing up my math workbook. At the end of all the workbooks there were coins, and then you can make change. I was punching out all of my coins." Perhaps in part because her mother is interested in math and encourages her to stick with it, Gwen continues to find math interesting. But most math teachers, in her words, "haven't been that great."

Gwen especially enjoys the fascination of seeing the world and its possibilities more clearly through the lens that math provides. "I like math as you can use it during the rest of your life. Not just what you should do to finish a problem. That's boring. But when you can use it to figure things out, then it's helpful and not just a job that you have to do." She particularly enjoys word problems because they require unique and unconventional solutions. "I like math because you can figure out your own way to do a problem. It's not like just studying a certain way to do a problem. . . . And if your background is good enough, it'll work, and then you can try it another way, and it'll work."

As Gwen sees it, though, most teachers do not share her interest in the concrete everyday applications of mathematics. "They'll give you the material, but they can't help you with why or when you use it. That takes a lot away from it." Other teachers do little more than "sit at the overhead [projector] and write theorems." Most teachers deflect her questions about applications with responses like "Well, don't worry about that right now." But this leaves Gwen unsatisfied. "Once you have the theorem down, it would help to know how you could use it, instead of just strictly what it is. I think it makes it more interesting, and easier to learn."

Judy and Gwen are unusually articulate about their needs, and they are probably among the more serious (and demanding) students whom we followed. But their responses illustrate a powerful theme that insistently reasserted itself throughout the interviews: Talented teens are unusually sensitive to the quality of teaching in their talent areas. They can give very specific details about the styles of teaching in their fields that motivate them, annoy them, and turn them off, and they become especially animated when relating memories of their most and least favored teachers.

This sensitivity, of course, does not necessarily make model students of them. Serious students like Judy and Gwen would try the patience of any teacher from time to time, with their insatiable curiosity and singleness of purpose that may seem occasionally selfish or arrogant. Less disciplined but equally talented students are, of course, even more frustrating, for their attention readily drifts at the first sign of a teacher's uncertainty or inflexibility. But even among those least engaged with a talent, the memory of times when an influential teacher ignited their desire to realize a potential fully remains strong and enduring. There are many ways to characterize what has made these teachers and their classes so memorable, but three dimensions of such memorable teaching seemed to surface with particular regularity.

INFLUENTIAL TEACHERS ARE
INTERESTING PEOPLE

Previous research suggests that teenagers are singularly uninspired by the lives of most adults they know.[4] Often their parents and teachers are not interested in their jobs; they spend long hours in drudgery for the sake of earning a living, and wait for their weekend free time, which in its turn is filled by activities that are passive, uninteresting, and fleeting. The majority of teens worry about this situation, at least from time to time, and wonder how they can avoid a similar fate. But many lack the skills and focused motivation to prevent daily life from slipping into similar patterns.

Little wonder, then, that teenagers – talented and average – are captivated by examples of adults, such as star athletes and entertainers, who enjoy what they do and achieve fame and riches in the process. More surprising is the ability of some exceptional teachers to find a permanent place in their students' memories.[5] What most intrigues students about these teachers is their enthusiasm for subjects that seemed boring and purposeless in other teachers' classes. Memorable teachers challenge students to expect more than just recognition or a paycheck from the work they choose. Why is Mr. Phillips so fired up about differential equations? How could Ms. Petrelli get so excited about the Crusades? Sometimes it is an encounter with just such a teacher that inspires students to reconsider the intrinsic rewards of exploring a domain of knowledge.

Talented teens experience apathetic or lackluster instruction with an especially acute sense of disappointment. More than most teens, they reach high school already interested in a particular domain and its subjective rewards. This awareness makes them, like Gwen, intolerant of teachers who go through the motions.

On a more positive note, they remember best those teachers who model interest in teaching and a professional life. It was the "really genuine" commitment of a high school science teacher, for example, that spurred one student to focus on environmental issues. "We talked about all the environmental problems and he made me see how important they are. He told us a lot of interesting facts and it got me interested in his concerns." Students almost invariably dislike the lecture mode, but one talented artist enthusiastically recalled a teacher whose lectures embodied his commitment to art. "A lot of other teachers say the same things over and over. This was the first teacher who really knew a lot about art and was really interested in it and knew all aspects of it." An admiring music student with professional aspirations saw his current clarinet instructor as "a lot more professional" than his prior teachers. "She's set a good example, and makes me want to practice more. . . . [I]t's kind of stupid, but I imagine I'm a professional too."

PACING THE MATCH BETWEEN CHALLENGES AND SKILLS

Teachers who enjoy their subject have a distinct advantage in being able to focus the attention of their students.[6] But only those teachers who translate their own interest into flow conditions for students will succeed in catalyzing talent development. Memorable teachers might be thought of as alchemists of consciousness whose art lies chiefly in transmuting abstract symbol systems into problems that matter to students. These are problems that pique curiosity and mobilize the skills of receptive learners. Such optimal conditions afford the close, well-paced match between task complexities and individual skills that is the hallmark of the flow experience.

Figure 9.3 illustrates just how critical the relationship between immediate challenge and perceived skill can be to the quality of classroom experience. Here again we selected only those moments in the classroom when the pager found students engaged in academic work. The ratings of challenge and skill were divided at the mean and crossed so as to yield four challenge–skill combinations, or quadrants, for academic classwork. Only when challenges and skills were felt to be high and working in tandem did all the varied components of well-being – cognitive, emotional, and motivational – come together for the students. Concentration was far above its normal classroom level, and self-esteem, potency, and involvement also reached their highest levels.

Other combinations of challenge and skill exacted varying psychic costs. Skill without challenge protected esteem and permitted relaxation, but only at the cost of low involvement and a dispersion of concentrated attention. Challenge without skill constrained attention effectively but took an evident toll on students' sense of self-worth. The worst profile of experiences, however, came when both challenge and a sense of exercising skill were absent. Here all four measures of experience fell significantly below average classroom levels and were most inferior to the measures of high challenge/high skill activities. This situation, which accounted for almost a third (29%) of all classroom activities, consisted mostly of reading, watching films, and listening to lectures.

Whereas active classroom pursuits like problem solving and exams were more likely to induce higher levels of challenges and skills ($\chi^2 = 45.6$, $p < .001$, $df = 3$), so-called passive activities remained well represented in all four challenge–skill combinations. In fact, evidence of what students were doing under various conditions of challenge and skill indicates that a variety of approaches to teaching may optimize classroom experience. Methods that emphasize greater activity can only improve the prospects for talent development. But what matters even more is the vision behind the method, especially because the method affects a student's sense of active immersion in the learning process.

Of course, although teenagers may prefer some challenge over monotony in the classroom, it is possible that they would still rather coast than seriously test their limits. Adults, after all, commonly fault adolescents for what they perceive as laziness, lack of discipline, and a counterproductive defiance of authority. But what came through clearly in our study was an

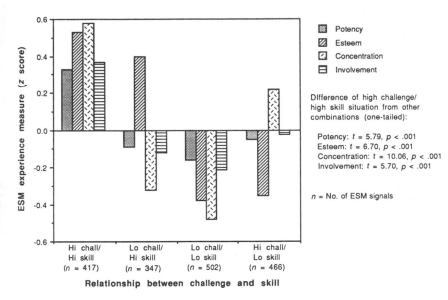

Figure 9.3. How the balance between challenge and skill alters the experience of classwork.

avid willingness to accept challenges and overcome obstacles when the problems were interesting and the necessary skills were within the individual's reach. Becoming engaged in such challenges yielded useful feedback about ability, and permitted deep and sustained immersion in activities that began to become rewarding in their own right. Asked when he most enjoyed drawing, one student responded, "When I know I've tried really hard and it's gone the way I wanted it to. It may start out bad, but if you keep at it then it just gets better, maybe better than what you thought it would be." A math student mentioned similar rewards. "I like math most when there is a hard problem and I can figure it out. When it's really hard at first and then I look at it and see the light – that's when I like it." Comparing academics with volleyball, one talented athlete remarked, "Both are difficult, but volleyball is more fun; it's not easier, but I get more satisfaction. I have the capability. The point is to use it."

In turn, students appreciated teaching that focused on all the conditions that promote a close fit between challenges and skills. What particularly distinguished such teaching was a sense of timing and pace, an understanding of when to intervene and when to hold back, of how to turn mistakes into information that can lead to improvement. One student captured this knack of pace in trying to describe the good math teacher. "I see a good teacher as one who lets you try and figure things out. She tells you what homework you have and it's not graded or anything and they try and let you figure it out. If you don't they explain it and then they give you another problem just like it to see if you can figure that – it's like trial and error." Addressing the same question, another math student added, "They explain math well, and they help you out with it." An art student related appreciatively the impact of one teacher on her progress as an artist in similar terms. "She wouldn't settle for anything less than the best. I thought I did something pretty good last semester. But she made me do it over a few times until she knew that it was the best that I could do. I didn't feel good about it at the time, but I do now."

Perhaps only talented students appreciate being challenged to their limits. But other evidence suggests that in fact everyone tends to describe the most enjoyable experiences in her or his life as having tension between opportunities for action and capacity to act.[7] A person does not get really involved in a tennis game unless skills are stretched. A book that makes no demands on the imagination is likely to be boring. Thus what talented students want from their teachers is likely to be a more urgent and clearly stated version of what every student would wish to experience in school.

ABIDING CONCERN

Often the demands of life become overwhelming, and anxiety may take over the gifted student's mind. At such times the skillful intervention of a concerned teacher can be crucial. Thus a third characteristic that distinguishes memorable teachers is their unusual ability to perceive the emerging needs of often insecure young people. Favorite childhood teachers were especially remembered for their reassuring kindness and genuine desire to be helpful. Citing his elementary teachers as "really supportive," one science student continued, "They influenced you to do better in school because you got the feeling that more people wanted you to do well. That helped you learn faster." Another student told of a sixth-grade teacher who was almost continually available for support and encouragement during her parents' divorce. A third student remembered an experimental school where "the teachers were all helpful and guided you. They helped you with your skills but basically they let you develop your own style about everything. They didn't push their own way on you."

These same teacher qualities remained important when students began to confront the new social and intellectual challenges of high school. Many complained about the distance between students and teachers. "They don't have much time to spend with you, even though I see so many teachers every day. They seem to be looking for the perfect student." But others expressed gratitude to individual teachers who had set aside time to counsel them through personal problems or discuss special concerns.

In the particular context of talent development, students remembered most vividly instances when teachers had boosted their confidence by taking them and their abilities seriously. An excited music student remembered a recent conversation with his professional teacher. "He told me that if I wanted to I could be making easily 150 grand per year. . . . He said that since I'm so tall and my arms are so long I'm great on the viola, and if I wanted to I could turn professional at 17." A math student remembered a teacher who "recommended I take more computer stuff, and told me I was real good in architecture. So I took that." In many cases, students credited teachers with recognizing in them potentials that they themselves had not suspected were there.

Sometimes a teacher's skillful and thoughtful attention to a student's interests even precipitates what Walters and Gardner call a "crystallizing experience."[8] One art student recalled how an English teacher had challenged her to expand her current interests. "When I had to do a report last year in English class, I wanted to do something on David Bowie. But my English teacher wouldn't let me. She said that I was a creative person who was ahead of her time, and that I would like reading about Coco Chanel. Then she gave me the book and I enjoyed it. She just knew, it was weird. I liked that more than I would have liked David Bowie. After that I became a lot more interested in clothes – fashion design never really hit me until then."

FLOW IN TEACHING AND TALENT
DEVELOPMENT

Transforming outcomes like the one just described may be uncommon in everyday teaching. But they demonstrate what can happen when teachers go beyond the scripted curriculum and actively attend to talented teenagers as emerging persons. The intuition that prompts a teacher to recommend Coco Chanel is almost certainly not a random occurrence, a shot in the dark. It is the culmination of an extended period of attention by the teacher to the trajectory of that student's developing interests. Further, it expresses the teacher's excitement about the implications of the subject matter for this student's personal development and quality of experience. In turn, the teacher's excitement convinces the student to trust the teacher's judgment and accept a new challenge, even if it does not coincide with her interests at the time.

But how do teachers learn to anticipate the steps that will challenge students to test their abilities? How do they establish the trust necessary to persuade them that those challenges are really opportunities for discovery? We are still far away from constructing an exact science of influential pedagogy, even though it has been known for a long time what kind of teaching does not work. As Alfred North Whitehead wrote, "Lack of attention to the rhythm and character of mental growth is a main source of wooden futility in education."[9]

The three dimensions that became evident in our interviews do suggest a number of ingredients that teachers can add to classroom life in order to encourage the development of talent. In particular, the evidence suggests that learning flourishes in environments and relationships that take the cultivation of passionate interest as a primary educational goal. We refer to such environments as autotelic, or self-rewarding contexts – more simply, flow classes – because they consistently foster the enjoyable experience of flow in learning. Much like the complex families discussed in the previous chapter, flow classes create and sustain a shared arena of interest among often disparate individual interests. Like successful families, they bring into dynamic tension the complementary tendencies toward differentiation and integration, pooling individual energies in cooperative efforts that enhance the skills and experience of all.

Flow classes are even more remarkable than successful families when we consider the odds against their occurrence. They not only lack the biological ties and societal norms that help to bind family members into a unit but have the added disadvantage of having to gain the interest of adolescents in settings that, as we saw earlier, mandate attendance and thus alienate attention. Such conditions mean that it is the teacher who must supply most of the initial energy required to create a social entity out of a psychologically wary and reluctant group of teenagers. What sets flow teachers apart are the distinctive ways in which they allocate their attention to create safe havens for flow in learning. These distinctive concerns of the autotelic teacher do not provide a blueprint for the flow class, but they do suggest some promising steps for promoting optimal experience in the classroom.

First, flow teachers never stop nurturing their own interest or take their skills at conveying that interest to others for granted. Whether as volunteer conservationists, musicians, or local artists, the teachers in our study were often involved in activities related to their domain outside of class time, as a matter of choice. Moreover, they seemed determined to help students experience the same rewards that they found in the continuing exploration of their domain. This suggests that the professional development of those who would foster talent among young people should entail more than the acquisition of techniques for classroom management and information transfer. From the start and throughout the teaching career, professional development should incorporate time for the nurture of those interests that attract teachers to their specialty in the first place. It is by keeping their own interests alive and by challenging their own abilities that teachers most often inspire the young to express their unique talents. The same strategy, we might add, is the best buffer against the everyday pressures and frustrations that so frequently exhaust even the most efficient classroom managers.

A second distinguishing focus of flow teaching is attention to those conditions that enhance the experience of intrinsic rewards. Specifically, flow teachers minimize the insidious impact of extrinsic pressures like competition, grades, needless rules, and bureaucratic procedures. Instead, they do all they can to center students' attention on the challenges and inherent satisfactions of learning something new. In doing so, flow teachers have for years put into practice what educational researchers have only begun to appreciate – the crucial difference between feedback focused on controlling the skilled performer and feedback focused on informing skill development.

Controlling feedback is outcome-oriented and – at best – experience-neutral. It seeks to constrict behavior by forging rigid links between a limited set of desirable responses and a scarce supply of external rewards. What these rewards are – and modern education has been endlessly inventive in their manufacture, from gold stars to hall passes to college scholarships – is less important than their eventual impact on motivation. For they divert attention away from the activity at hand and toward the new game of winning prizes, avoiding punishments, and ingratiating oneself with those who mete them out. In the process, students cease to cultivate sources of self-reward that yield only undivided concentration and sustained immersion in a challenging task.

Informational feedback, on the other hand, is focused on the ongoing activity. It thrives on trial and error, gamely but unobtrusively assisting the student to search out that next adjustment – that needed bit of knowledge essential to achieving a further step in competence. Its temporal frame is the present; its response, timely and ongoing; and its experiential focus, autotelic. That is, it is responsive to signs of the flow that emerges when a close fit between task demands and developing skills is realized.

This does not mean that teaching in an informational mode must be indulgent, fuzzy, or noncompetitive. Indeed, it is often the toughest teachers who are most respected, precisely because the feedback they provide is clear, relevant, and impervious to external considerations. It does mean, though, that the required standards are within the reach of effort and will allow learners progressively greater control over the trajectory of their own development. Flow teachers often expect much of their pupils, but they translate these expectations into modes of practice that model critical reflection, chronicle personal accomplishment, and authorize mistakes as clues to further improvement.

A third distinguishing focus of flow teaching is closely allied to the second. It involves reading the shifting needs of learners. The experience of flow involves a confluence of factors – feelings of choice, clarity, a lack of self-consciousness, and a merger between action and awareness. These in turn correspond to a synthesis of conditions in the learning environment that must be kept in balanced tension if flow is to continue.

Yet as complexity increases, it becomes difficult for the learner to coordinate the set of conditions necessary to achieve this confluence. Flow at advanced levels of mastery demands of the teacher or coach a flexible, dynamic attentional style. This style entails close attention to the complex interaction between the learner and her or his activity, and a willingness to move between moments of intervention and withdrawal and of critique and encouragement as the learner strives to match skills to challenges.

In chapter 8 we specified four characteristics of the parent–child relationship that enhance the child's ability to enjoy intrinsic rewards. These four dimensions – support, harmony, involvement, and freedom – are equally relevant to the sort of fluid attentional focus that teachers must maintain in pacing talent development. In attending to freedom, flow teachers create opportunities for students to tailor learning situations to their own interests and styles of learning. This includes chances to select materials and themes of study, and also the freedom, wherever possible, to control the pace of the process. Perhaps because schooling has traditionally militated against individual expression, a measure of choice is arguably the ingredient most crucial to the realization of intrinsic rewards in the classroom.

But though freedom is critical to student motivation, it cannot ensure in itself the long-term cultivation of talent. There are times when teachers must draw on their experience to help students conserve and channel their limited attentional resources. In challenging students to become involved, flow teachers act to match their students to increasingly complex activities that keep pace with their interests and extend the reach of their current skills. To optimize those challenges, teachers must ensure that the goals of each student's activity remain in harmony with other demands on her or his energies, and that their performance expectations for the student are explicit and realistic. By centering student attention, flow teachers minimize external distractions and provide feedback to performance that is timely, unambiguous, and effective in precipitating the concrete here-and-now consciousness of flow. Finally, the support that flow teachers give students recognizes them as more than mere learners. They see their students as complex human beings and give attention to the emotional as well as cognitive and motivational needs of the person as he or she grapples with failure and uncertainty. Without the mutual trust that grows from such efforts, teens remain wary of the threats to self-esteem that the acceptance of new challenges inevitably entails.

FLOW TEACHING IN DIFFERENT DOMAINS

Does what it takes to enhance the intrinsic rewards of learning differ for teachers across the five talent areas? A detailed examination of this question is not possible – our study focused on students and not teachers – but some interesting differences are worth noting. Math and science students in our study complained most often of the standardization and rigidity of the curriculum and of their teachers' reluctance to deviate from highly structured programs. Whereas challenges were high and goals relatively clear, in these areas opportunities for choice remained minimal, especially with regard to the pace of instruction. These conditions were very evident in the daily ESM reports of experience in math and science classrooms. These classes typically commanded unusually high levels of concentration, but they also produced unusually high levels of tension and confusion and caused a dramatic drop in self-esteem. Students in the sciences felt best about teachers who knew their subject well, were clear in their presentation, and provided helpful feedback on frequent practice exercises well in advance of formal exams.

Talented art and music students, on the other hand, reported much more favorable and enjoyable daily classroom experiences. Classes in the arts were far more likely to provide a sense of control and of skill than were science classes. Arts classes clearly engaged students much more frequently in activities that they genuinely wanted to do. When arts students were critical, they tended to fault their teachers for failing to challenge them sufficiently. They were particularly enthusiastic about teachers who helped identify their strengths and structured a demanding program that led to the synthesis of a distinctive personal style. Student athletes had the least to say about their instructors. It may be that sports provide such a ready structure for enjoyment that the contributions of coaches fade into the background. But it may also be that coaches tend more often to instruct players as members of a team than as individual athletes, and that those most in need of assistance are of least value to the team effort.

Those coaches who did stand out were appreciated for their sensitivity to the needs of teens in crisis moments and their emphasis on the participatory rewards of enjoyable competition.

TEACHING AND ENJOYMENT: CONCLUSION

Far more striking than the differences were the similarities in style and sensibility that united the young people's perception of influential teachers across the talent areas. By attending to their own interests and intelligently nurturing students, these teachers realized some of the strengths of the master–apprentice model mentioned at the beginning of this chapter. It should be stated that whereas talented teens did require competence in their instructors, they did not demand omnipotence or the possession of star quality. What teens noticed instead were signs of an adult who had learned to enjoy the expression of talent as one vital ingredient in a meaningful, compelling way of life, one that was worth sharing with others. This should be good news for teachers, especially those who work with teens whose talents are sometimes daunting even by adult standards. But the traits that make teachers influential with talented students are the same that would make a teacher influential with any student. Teachers who encourage integration by providing support and harmony and who stimulate differentiation by making involvement and freedom possible will be successful with the autistic as well as the prodigiously gifted.

The problem with our technologically inspired views of education is that we have come to expect learning to be a function of the rationality of the information provided. In other words, we assume that if the material is well organized and logically presented, students will learn it. Nothing is farther from the fact. Students will learn only if they are motivated. The motivation could be extrinsic – the desire to get a well-paying job after graduation – but learning essential to a person's self must be intrinsically rewarding. Unless a person enjoys the pursuit of knowledge, learning will remain a tool to be set aside as soon as it is no longer needed. Therefore we cannot expect our children to become truly educated until we ensure that teachers know not only how to provide information but also how to spark the joy of learning.

NOTES

1 Feldman, 1986.
2 Csikszentmihalyi & Larson, 1984. In a typical history classroom where the teacher was lecturing about Genghis Khan's invasion of China and conquest of Beijing in 1215, only 2 out of 27 students were thinking about China when they were signaled. One of the 2 was remembering the meal he had when he last ate out with his family at a Chinese restaurant, and the other was wondering why Chinese men wore their hair in a ponytail. None mentioned Genghis Khan or Beijing or 1215.
3 Csikszentmihalyi & McCormack, 1986; Mayers, 1978.
4 Csikszentmihalyi & Larson, 1984; Youniss & Smollar, 1985.
5 Csikszentmihalyi & McCormack, 1986.
6 Plihal, 1982.
7 One of the most widely mentioned dimensions of the flow experience is the balance between challenges and skills (Csikszentmihalyi, 1985, 1990a). This is true whether the respondent is a man or a woman, young or old, rich or poor, American or Asian. This balance is important regardless of the nature of the activity; e.g., it is as true of competitive sports as of meditation, where the challenge consists in direct control over consciousness itself.
8 Walters & Gardner, 1986.
9 Whitehead, 1929, pp. 29ff.

PART III

The cultivation of talent

10

Commitment to talent and its correlates

In the preceding chapters we described how talented teenagers differ from their less exceptional peers, how talent is experienced and expressed in adolescence, and how families and teachers can nurture the difficult development of superior abilities. The implications of what we learned are not limited to talented teenagers; they suggest what needs to be done to develop any skill, whether athletic or mental, possessed by any student, whether exceptional or otherwise. What we can see clearly in the case of talented students applies to the growth and maturation of every adolescent.

At this point we are ready to turn to a new question and a new set of issues: Which students will continue to develop their talents through high school, and which ones will lose interest along the way? For the really important question about talent is not so much who has it and how much, but rather what one does with it. Among knowledgeable people the remark is often heard that talent is cheap, meaning that being potentially able is not enough. For potential talent to be useful, it must be translated into actual accomplishment.

OBSTACLES TO TALENT DEVELOPMENT

When this study was begun, we expected that a sizable proportion of the gifted teens nominated by teachers at age 13 would no longer look as promising at 17. In the 4 years of high school many things can happen to derail the development of talent: Parents may lose their jobs or divorce and no longer be able to provide the emotional or material support

199

needed for cultivating their adolescent's gift; the teenager may lose interest, develop different interests, and become alienated from teachers or from peers. In fact, the possibilities for disengagement in those 4 years are almost endless.

Of course just because an adolescent who is talented in science decides by the time he or she is a junior to go into journalism or business does not necessarily mean a regrettable waste of potential talent. Such a student may turn out to contribute to society much more than if he or she had stayed in science. For example, when Winston Churchill became a roving reporter as a young man, it might have seemed that he was squandering his gifts; in his case, it was not until he was approaching middle age that his awesome talents began to find expression. In fact, it is not at all unusual to find, especially among creative individuals, that their youth involved several false starts and sudden changes in direction.

Yet for the majority of people who contribute to a given field, a line of continuous development is more typically the case. The reasons for this are fairly obvious. A person with a musical talent cannot afford the luxury of dropping out from practice for any length of time without becoming rusty. To remain competitive, a gifted young scientist or mathematician must go through a fairly rigid curriculum and keep up with advances in the field. It is rather rare for a young artist to switch to science in midstream successfully or vice versa. Hence it makes sense to assume that talented students who have disengaged themselves from their area of talent during high school have in fact lost a rare opportunity. They may be happier doing this than if they remained in their domain, they may later switch to something much more important and useful, and they may have been absolutely right in disengaging – nevertheless the fact remains that from the viewpoint of the present, the neglect of their gifts is not to be taken lightly. To the extent that exceptional skills are by definition few and far between, it is a great loss for humanity as a whole, and for the particular society concerned, when even one of these skills remains undeveloped. It is for this reason that the chapters that follow are so essential to the theme of this volume. In many ways they deal with the most crucial issue: How can we facilitate the commitment to talent through high school and thus avoid disengagement? Even though we focus on talented students, the answers have repercussions far beyond the narrow circle of the exceptional. Whatever we discovered in our study about preventing disengagement from talent can make it easier to help the development of every kind of human potential, no matter how small.

MEASURING COMMITMENT TO TALENT

How can we tell if an adolescent is committed to developing her or his talent or is becoming disengaged from it? Extreme cases are easy to distinguish. For instance, a student who is taking all the most difficult courses in the talent area, who intends to pursue a talent-related major in college and to make a career of it, and who is seen by teachers to be living up to early promise can safely be called committed. On the other hand, a student who has stopped taking advanced courses, who has lost interest in the domain and is not planning to continue it in college, and who is judged to be an underachiever by teachers is a clear case of disengagement. Such a student may accomplish many great things but is unlikely to develop this particular talent to its fullest.

But such extremes are relatively rare. Many students cannot be so clearly labeled as either committed or disengaged. Some show middling levels of commitment on all dimensions of engagement; others seem highly committed in terms of one dimension – say, teachers' opinions – but seem disengaged in other dimensions, perhaps in terms of future plans. There is no generally accepted single scale for measuring whether a young person is committed to developing a talent; we had to develop our own measures for purposes of this study. The sections that follow describe four ways in which commitment to talent can be measured. Then we go on to see to what extent the various indicators collected in our study can predict which students will stay committed to their talents through high school and which will not.

Teachers' Ratings

The easiest – but not necessarily the best – way to measure whether a student continues to cultivate her or his talent is to ask teachers. After all, they are the experts in the field who know the student's performance best. Twice during our study teachers who taught our students in their talent area were asked to rate them on 10 dimensions of performance. The first teachers' ratings were collected at the end of the first year of the study and the second at the end of the third year, as students finished either Grade 11 or 12. The commitment measure based on teachers' ratings is the sum of 7 items of the second teacher ratings. These items include realization of potential, quality of attention, enjoyment of challenge, degree of involvement with work in talent area, originality, ability to do independent work, and preference for working on difficult tasks. Teachers were asked to give their responses on a 7-point scale ranging from *not at all* to *very much*. The 7 items are highly correlated with one another; all of them have high loadings on the same factor in the factor analysis performed on the responses.[1]

Subjective Commitment

Although the teachers' ratings gave a good indication of progress as seen by experts, they did not reflect how committed the students themselves felt. To get at this aspect, each respondent was interviewed either at the end of the third year or at the beginning of the fourth year of the study. Of the many questions asked in the interview, the ones relevant to the issue of commitment were: (*a*) "How often do you do things related to [talent area] right now?" (Students were asked to select one of the following: "every day," "once or twice every week," "a couple of times every week," "more than once a month," "less than once a month," or "never.") (*b*) "How would you compare your interest in [talent area] now to 2 [or 3] years ago?" (Students selected one of the following options: "become more interested," "interest remains unchanged," or "become less interested." (*c*) "How would you compare your skills in [talent area] now to 2 [or 3] years ago?" (One of the following choices might be picked: "improved," "the same," or "less skilled.") (*d*) "How would you compare the challenge of [talent area] now to 2 [or 3] years ago?" (Students were asked to choose among the following: "more challenging," "the same," or "less challenging.") (*e*) "Do you think that you will continue with [talent area] as an interest in college?" (The options were "yes," "maybe," and "no.") (*f*) "Do you think that you will continue with [talent area] as a major in college?" (Again, students were asked to select one of these responses: "yes," "maybe," and "no.")

Responses to each individual question were coded so that a high score reflects a high level of subjective commitment. The score of the first question has a range of 0 to 6. All other questions have scores that range from 0 to 3. Scores for each question were then added for each person to provide a Subjective Commitment score with a range of 0 to 21.

Highest Talent Level

An easy and compelling measure of commitment is how far a student chooses to go in taking courses in the talent domain. For instance, a student could graduate from these particular high schools with only 2 semesters of math. Some students, however, took at least one math course each semester and rapidly exhausted the extensive offerings of the math department. Such eagerness to absorb information in the field is a good prima facie indication of how committed a student is.

We set up the Highest Talent Level measure separately for each subject matter, with the help of the relevant high school faculty. Most courses, especially in math, science, and music, are hierarchically arranged; a student may not take a higher-level course before passing a lower-level prerequisite. With the help of the teachers in the subject area, we assigned a level of difficulty to each course, ranging from 1 (lowest) to 6 or 8 (highest, depending on subject matter). A student who had an 8 on this variable was assumed to be more committed than a student who had a lower score.

Composite Engagement Score

In an attempt to get a single measure of engagement, Teachers' Ratings and Subjective Commitment were added to yield a composite score. It should be noted that none of the four indicators we just described included such "hard" measures of academic success as grades. We did not feel that grades were directly relevant to the issue of whether a student was committed or not. A person could get low grades for a variety of reasons, including less native ability, competing claims on attention, personal problems, and so on yet be very committed and doing the very best he or she could in the given circumstances. Conversely a student could get a high grade point average (GPA) by taking only easy courses. Our attempt was to measure commitment, not success. Nevertheless we collected exhaustive data on academic achievement as well, including GPA, GPA in talent courses, grade in highest talent course, and so on. Whenever appropriate we shall also report results concerning such indicators.

Correlation among the measures of commitment

As was to be expected, the various measures of commitment did not perfectly agree with one another. In fact, although the correlation among them was statistically very significant, the lack of overlap remained quite substantial (see Table 10.1). Only about 19% of the variance was held in common between Teachers' Ratings and Subjective Commitment,[2] suggesting that quite often students whom the teachers thought highly of already felt disengaged from their talent and vice versa. The Composite Engagement score overlapped about 71% with each of its two subscales, and so it seems a reasonable measure of both.

The Highest Talent Level measure was strongly correlated to the three other indicators, but again the overlap was not very high: 8% with Teachers' Ratings, 25% with Subjective Commitment, and 19% with Combined Engagement. Thus, how far a student chooses to go in high school, though having a strong face validity as a measure of how engaged with talent the student is, does not necessarily reflect the other ways in which commitment could be measured.

When this matrix of correlations was repeated separately for each of the five talent areas, the same pattern of correlations and the same relative strength of relationships were obtained. For example, the correlation coefficient between Teachers' Ratings and Subjective Commitment was .31 ($p < .05$) for students with talent in math, .46 ($p < .01$) in science, .59 ($p < .01$) in music, .48 ($p < .01$) in athletics, and .43 ($p < .05$) in art. In other words, regardless of the student's talent, when the relevant teachers rated that student as living up to potential, then that student was significantly more likely to say that he or she was still interested and involved – even though the overlap between the two measures ranged from a mere 9% in math to 35% in music.

What does this mean? Clearly the various measures agree in describing

Table 10.1. *Correlation among the measures of commitment*

	TR	SC	CE	HTL
Teachers' Ratings (TR)	1.0	.44**	.85**	.28**
Subjective Commitment (SC)		1.0	.84**	.50**
Composite Engagement (CE)			1.0	.44**
Highest Talent Level (HTL)				1.0

Note: The statistics are based on a sample size of 160, because several students lacked one or the other measure of commitment.

**$p < .01$, one-tailed.

an underlying process. But it is equally clear that this process is not unitary, is not all of a piece. A student who is taking all the possible math courses in high school is not necessarily determined to major in math in college. The students who are most convinced personally that they will become musicians may or may not be the ones that teachers rate as living up to their potential. Commitment – or its opposite, disengagement from talent – is not an all-or-nothing process. There is a great deal of tentativeness and much trial and error as a young person chooses a future that fits and makes sense to the self. A young man of 17 may seem to his teachers to be a promising scientist, but deep down he may be having doubts about dedicating his life to science. A young woman of 17 may seem frivolous to her teachers, but in her heart of hearts she is developing a firm resolve to become a concert pianist. Which of these four indicators is a surer sign of things to come? Only time will tell. Eventually the various lines of commitment are bound to converge even further, until after some more years it will be clear to all that yes, this young man is no longer a scientist, but a successful businessman; and that yes, this young lady has indeed turned into a fine concert pianist.

Were any of the signs of commitment related to what we knew about the students beforehand? For instance, are students from more advantaged families more likely to persevere? To what extent does the quality of experience while studying predict future involvement in the area of talent? Are youngsters from autotelic families more committed? Do endurance and achievement orientation help? How important are academic abilities as measured by the Preliminary Scholastic Aptitude Test (PSAT) in predicting further development of talent? The remainder of this chapter will attempt to answer these questions, beginning with an examination of the link between socioeconomic status (SES) and commitment to talent.

SOCIOECONOMIC BACKGROUND AND DEVELOPMENT OF TALENT

Early in chapter 4 we remarked that the families of talented youngsters provided several advantages: They were better off financially and were also better off in parental education and occupational status. These results were not surprising, but they suggest the uncomfortable possibility that the development of talent itself might not be anything more mysterious than the success of white-collar children over their blue-collar peers. Therefore it becomes very important to check whether SES does or does not make an important contribution to the various measures of disengagement. None of the family SES variables show even a glimmer of a significant relation to any of the four measures of commitment (see Appendix 10.1). The correlation coefficients between SES variables and commitment measures range from .1 to −.1; all are insignificant. Thus, although an affluent, well-educated family was more likely to have a talented adolescent, material support from the family did not seem to help the child further in the development of talent. The lack of relationship we found is in part due to the restricted range of SES in the sample. Only about 20% of the families could be characterized as low SES; four out of five students came from middle- to upper-middle-class families. Obviously if more young persons from the underclass, which was almost completely unrepresented in this group, had been included, the correlation is likely to have been positive, because relatively more extremely disadvantaged children would have given up on their talent. However, children from such families did not make the cut in the first place.

Thus it appears that parental income and education do not contribute further to the development of talent in high school after the initial advantages they give children in the early years.

No differences between sexes

Another demographic variable that does not seem to make a difference as far as commitment to talent is concerned is sex. Male and female students were equally likely to continue in or to become disengaged from the domain of their talent by the end of high school. Moreover, sex did not interact with any of the relationships we shall be reviewing in the remainder of this chapter. This variable has therefore been dropped from the analyses that follow. Results for males and females are added together, and the discussion from now on will be unisex unless otherwise indicated.

PERSONALITY, ACADEMIC ABILITY, AND COMMITMENT

Two variables that differentiate talented students from average peers are certain personality and cognitive characteristics (see chapter 4). In particular, talented students are distinguished by a strong need for achievement, by endurance, and by high aptitude for academic performance as indexed by PSAT scores. These traits should also help the further development of talent. As Table 10.2 suggests, however, the results are mixed.

High achievement motivation and strong endurance contribute to the more personal measures of engagement – to the subjective sense of being committed – and they also predict positively how far students will go in taking courses in the domain. On the other hand, neither Teachers' Ratings nor grades in talent courses (not reported in Table 10.2) are related to this aspect of personality.

More surprising is the lack of significant correlation between academic ability as measured by the PSAT and any of the indexes of commitment. This lack of correlation, however, could have been because of the different role academic ability may play in the two main types of talent: the scientific and the artistic. The correlations were therefore repeated separately by talent area.

When the relationship of PSAT scores to talent development is investigated separately for the five talent areas, a complex but basically sensible pattern appears. These are its main features: (a) In the domains

Table 10.2 *Correlation between personality plus cognitive variables and commitment to talent*

	Teachers' Ratings	Subjective Commitment	Composite Engagement	Highest Talent Level
Work orientation (achievement + endurance) (*n* = 140/177)[a]	.12	.38**	.32**	.22**
PSAT 2 (verbal + math) (*n* = 167/203)[a]	.06	.04	.06	.08

[a]Numbers vary because not every student completed every test.

**p < .01.

of art and athletics, PSAT scores show no significant relation to any of the measures of commitment; (*b*) in the domain of music, PSAT scores correlate only with Teachers' Ratings (*r* = .25, *p* < .05); (*c*) in the domain of science, PSAT scores correlate with Teachers' Ratings (*r* = .40, *p* < .01) and with grades in the talent area (*r* = .46, *p* < .01); and (*d*) in the domain of mathematics, PSAT scores correlate only with the Highest Talent Level course a student took (*r* = .44, *p* < .01). This pattern suggests that academic ability helps the development of talent mainly in the sciences, but even there it seems to have little to do with subjective feelings of commitment, and mainly seems to influence teachers' opinions and grades.

THE QUALITY OF EXPERIENCE AND COMMITMENT TO TALENT

The obvious advantages that should help students develop their talent – material support from the family, the relevant personality traits, and superior academic potential – do not seem to make much difference. Let us, then, turn to the more subtle influences that might be involved. These have to do with the quality of experience that students have while involved with work in their domain of talent.

One of the central expectations of this study, based on the flow theory, was that if a teenager talented in math enjoyed the experience of doing math, he or she was more likely to continue doing it through high school and to become a mathematician. The same reasoning would hold, of course, for teens talented in other areas. In order to test this hypothesis, the Experience Sampling Method (ESM) self-reports collected in 1985 were correlated with the commitment measures collected in 1988.

There are many reasons why this test should not work. In the first place, the week during which the ESM was collected may not have been truly representative of a student's feelings toward her or his talent. Some students happened to be paged only once or twice during the week as they were involved in their area of talent – would this be enough on which to base a prediction? Even if the ESM did provide a valid assessment of how students felt about their talent, would this feeling say anything about commitment 3 or 4 years later?

Despite all these good reasons why we should not have found any significant relationship between moods while doing talent-related work at age 13 and commitment to talent at age 17, we did in fact find several relationships. The first criterion of commitment, Teachers' Ratings, is the one least related to how students felt when engaged with their talent 3 and 4 years earlier. Only three variables were significantly related to Teachers' Ratings: Students who felt more open and unself-conscious and who felt they were living up to the expectations of others tended to be rated as more committed by teachers.

In contrast, two other outcomes, Subjective Commitment and Highest Talent Level, were predicted by seven experiential variables each. Those who felt cheerful, strong, excited, open, and successful while engaged with their talent were more likely to want to continue, and they actually did take more advanced courses in their talent area.

The rows of Table 10.3 reveal that some experiential variables show a stronger relationship with commitment measures than others. "Open" seems to have a more positive relationship with all commitment measures: Students who reported being more "open" than "closed" were more committed by the end of high school. Other strong variables are "cheer-

Table 10.3. *Statistically significant correlations between quality of experience while working in talent area, as measured by the ESM, and commitment to talent measured 3 years later*

Experience	Commitment			
	Teachers' Ratings	Subjective Commitment	Combined Engagement	Highest Talent Level
Affect				
Happy	—	—	—	—
Cheerful	—	.17*	.19*	.20*
Sociable	—	—	—	—
Potency				
Strong	—	.15*	—	.20*
Active	—	—	—	—
Alert	—	—	—	—
Excited	—	.17*	—	.16*
Cognitive efficiency				
Concentration	—	—	—	—
Open	.18*	.19*	.21**	.19*
Clear	—	—	—	—
Unself-conscious	.22**	—	—	.25**
Motivation				
Wish to be doing	—	.17*	—	.26**
Involved	—	—	—	—
In control	—	—	—	—
Self-esteem				
Feeling good	—	—	—	—
Successful	—	.17*	.17*	.18*
Living up to own expectations	—	—	—	—
Living up to others' expectations	.17*	—	—	—
Other				
Skillful	—	.24**	.20**	—

Note: Dashes indicate statistically nonsignificant correlations.

*p < .05. **p < .01.

ful," "strong," "excited," unself-consciousness, intrinsic motivation ("wish to be doing"), "successful," and "skillful." Each of these experiential variables was significantly correlated with at least two commitment outcomes.

The pattern that emerges from the table confirms both the earlier findings about the personality of talented young persons and the flow theory of intrinsic motivation. The importance of openness as a cognitive style was mentioned in chapter 4. Lack of self-consciousness while immersed in talent-related activities, intrinsic motivation, and feelings of skill and success are dimensions of experience predicted by the flow theory. Finally, positive affect and potency also add to the kind of experience that makes it more likely that students will want to continue developing their talent.

Relationship between experience and commitment after other variables have been controlled for

It would be possible to argue that the relationships shown in Table 10.3 might be contaminated by other variables not included in the table. For instance, conceivably students whose personality traits include a strong work orientation enjoy working on talent more, so that the correlation between enjoyment and commitment is a spurious result of the underlying and stronger correlation between work orientation and commitment.

To test for this possible alternative, the correlations reported in Table 10.3 were repeated, this time using statistical controls to eliminate the effects of three other potentially confounding variables. These were (a) the student's PSAT scores (combined Verbal and Mathematical), which measure academic aptitude; (b) the autotelic family score, which indicates the effect of parental influence; and (c) work orientation, or the Jackson Personality Test factor that is most strongly correlated with academic achievement.

Controlling for these variables, the same correlations that were significant in Table 10.3 remained significant. Some, such as motivation and the student's perception of her or his success and skill, became statistically more significant after the contributions of the controls were removed. In addition, some new experiential variables showed a strong relationship with commitment. For example, how important students thought working in their talent area was to their overall goals correlated both with Subjective Commitment ($p < .05$) and with Highest Talent Level ($p < .001$) when PSAT, family type, and work orientation were held constant. Thus believing that one's talent will be important to one's future appears to be a significant ingredient in continuing involvement, apparently even compensating for relatively lower abilities and for the lack of other facilitating conditions.

Motivation and commitment

Besides using the "wish to be doing" item to measure motivation, we assessed the level of motivation by examining whether students perceived their work in the talent area to be voluntary. Each time students responded to the pager they had to indicate the reason they were doing what they were doing. The options were "because I wanted to," "because I had to," "because there was nothing else to do," or a combination thereof. In the present analysis we assumed that whenever a student marked the option "because I wanted to" while working in the talent area, that student was endogenously motivated.[3] In other words, the student saw the choice of working in the talent area to be a personal and voluntary choice.

Table 10.4 reports the relative contributions of academic ability (combined PSAT scores), autotelic family context, personality (the combined factors of achievement and endurance), and the ESM measure of intrinsic motivation to the three measures of engagement with talent used earlier, plus a fourth one: the grades that students received in the highest level course they took in their talent area.

Teachers' Ratings are best predicted by students' academic ability and by their family context. Neither personality nor motivation affects Teachers' Ratings. Academic ability is the sole predictor of the grades that students received in their most difficult talent course. In contrast, Subjective Commitment is strongly influenced by students' needs for achievement and endurance, marginally by their motivation, and not at all by ability or family context. How far students will go in taking courses in their talent area is best predicted by their motivation, then by personality, and worst by their ability.

Again the data suggest that the various outcome measures respond to different student characteristics: Teachers' Ratings and grades are more

Table 10.4. *ANOVA testing the relative contributions of academic ability, family context, personality, and endogenous motivation while working in talent area to commitment to talent measured 3 years later*

	Measure of commitment (F)			
	Teachers' ratings ($n = 142$)	Grade in highest course ($n = 152$)	Subjective commitment ($n = 170$)	Highest talent level ($n = 152$)
Academic ability (PSAT combined)	4.3*	8.7**	0.2	5.4*
Autotelic family context	4.0	2.1	0.1	0.4
Personality (achievement + endurance)	0	0	10.4**	8.6**
Motivation (ESM "wanting to do" talent)	2.6	0	3.1*	11.6***

*$p < .05$. **$p < .01$. ***$p < .001$, two-tailed.

dependent on ability, whereas the distance that students will go in their talent area and their personal feeling of involvement are more dependent on motivation and personality. In other words, knowing students' motivation and personality will not help us predict grades or teachers' opinions of students; on the other hand, knowing how good students are academically and how well supported they are by their families will not help predict how far they will go and how personally committed they will be. The patterns for all of the five talent areas are almost identical.

FLOW AND COMMITMENT TO TALENT

Another of the main expectations of this study was that students who in their early exposure to a talent area were able to experience flow would be more likely to persevere. This hypothesis follows from the more general proposition according to which any activity that is enjoyable will be repeated.[4]

A simple way to measure whether a student did or did not experience flow in the talent area was to use one of the sections of the Flow Questionnaire students filled out in their third year of high school. This section included four brief vignettes describing the flow experience (e.g., "Do you ever do something where your concentration is so intense, your attention so undivided and wrapped up in what you are doing, that you sometimes become unaware of things you normally notice?"), and each description was followed by the questions "Have you ever felt this way?" and "And if yes, what were you doing?" Students who responded by listing their talent area after any of the three questions were assumed to have experienced flow while involved in their talent.

About half the sample listed their talent area as an example of flow experience, but there were large differences among domains. Only 9% of the talented young scientists and 17% of the mathematicians did so. On the other hand, 62% of the talented artists, 68% of the musicians, and 74% of the athletes gave examples of flow from their respective talent areas. These results, while unsettling, are not unexpected. The real question is: Does it make a difference whether a student has flow while engaged in her or his talent? The answer is given in Table 10.5, where an analysis of variance contrasts the relative contributions of flow, academic ability, autotelic context, and personality to the various measures of commitment. The results show that whether or not a student claims to experience flow while involved in talent is vastly more predictive of commitment than is academic ability, family support, or personality. The only outcome for which flow is not the best predictor is grade in highest level talent course. However, it is the only variable that predicts significantly all four outcome variables.

Table 10.5 vividly demonstrates that the four predictors are differently related to the four outcomes. Academic ability and autotelic family context have the strongest relationship to Teachers' Ratings but are not related to Subjective Commitment or to Highest Talent Level. Personality and flow both predict Subjective Commitment best, but personality is unrelated to either Teachers' Ratings or to grade in highest level talent course.

Figure 10.1 illustrates the fact that the difference in commitment between students who do and do not mention their talent as a flow experience is uniformly significant across all five talent areas. Here only the

Table 10.5. *ANOVA testing the relative contributions of academic ability, family context, personality, and flow in talent area to commitment to talent*

	Measure of commitment (F)			
	Teachers' Ratings ($n = 185$)	Grade in highest course ($n = 183$)	Subjective Commitment ($n = 210$)	Highest Talent Level ($n = 183$)
Academic ability (PSAT combined)	10.2**	5.0*	0.2	1.6
Autotelic family context	7.6*	6.7**	0.1	0.2
Personality (achievement + endurance)	0.3	0.3	34.4***	5.3*
Flow (mentioned talent as flow experience)	21.4***	5.7*	65.3***	22.7***

*$p < .05$. **$p < .01$. ***$p < .001$, two tailed.

Combined Engagement outcome is used, comprising the sum of Teachers' Ratings plus Subjective Commitment. The 9 math students who mentioned doing math as a flow experience had an average Combined Engagement score 1.5 standard deviations above that of the 39 math students who did not mention math as flow ($F = 11.1, p < .01$). The same difference in engagement separates the 4 science students for whom science produced flow from the 35 for whom science was not associated with flow experiences. The largest difference was for students talented in music: Here the 41 students who associated music with flow had an average engagement score 0.5 standard deviations above the mean, whereas the 14 who did not had an average score 1.3 below ($F = 21.1$, $p < .001$).

The figure can also be interpreted another way. It suggests that talented artists and athletes are unlikely to stay committed unless they enjoy what they are doing. On the other hand, talented science and math students are likely to stay at least moderately committed even in the absence of intrinsic rewards – presumably because extrinsic rewards in these fields are enough to ensure some involvement. In math and science, however, the

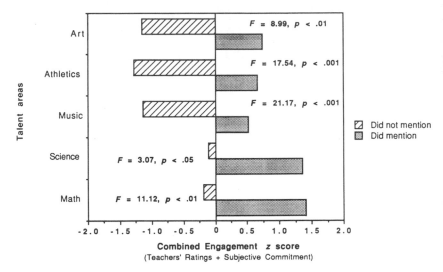

Figure 10.1. Average Combined Engagement scores for students who did and did not mention talent area as flow experience.

relatively few who do experience flow are likely to be supercommitted to their talent area or areas.

SUMMARY AND CONCLUSIONS

It is not easy to determine how commitment to talent should be measured. It could be defined as the impression one makes on teachers, the difficulty of the courses one takes, or the resolve to continue cultivating one's talent in the future. Each of these ways of measuring commitment overlaps significantly with the others but by no means completely. It would seem to follow from this lack of convergence that it is impossible to predict the characteristics that will lead to future commitment. Yet there is one exception to this bleak conclusion: If a teenager experiences talent as enjoyable, chances are that he or she will continue, no matter which measure of commitment is employed. But before reviewing the relationship of flow to continued involvement with talent, it will be useful to summarize briefly what predicts each of the various outcome measures.

Teachers' Ratings.   Whether teachers think a student is living up to expectations in her or his talent area is related to whether the student thinks of talent as a flow experience, to his or her academic ability, and to a supportive family context. In addition, teachers give higher ratings to students who feel open, feel unself-conscious, and feel that they are living up to other people's expectations while involved in their talent. Equally important to understanding the relationship between Teachers' Ratings and commitment is to know which variables are unrelated to Teachers' Ratings. Whether a student is happy, strong, self-confident, or motivated when doing talent is irrelevant to Teachers' Ratings, and so are the two crucial personality dimensions of achievement and endurance.

Grade in Highest Talent Level.   How well students do in the highest level course in their talent area shows the same pattern of relationships as Teachers' Ratings. In other words, flow is a good predictor,[5] but in this case academic ability and family context are even better.

Subjective Commitment.   A student's feeling of continued involvement and expectation of continuing in the area of talent are also most powerfully related to experiencing flow in the talent area. But in this case personality also plays a role: Those who have higher needs for achievement and endurance are more likely to be personally committed. Students who feel cheerful, strong, excited, open, successful, skillful, and motivated while actually working in the talent area are more committed years later. However, academic ability and family context, which are strong predictors of Teachers' Ratings, do not seem to play any role in Subjective Commitment.

Highest Talent Level.   Perhaps the ambition of a student to continue developing talent is best revealed by the difficulty of the courses taken in high school. The tendency to take the most challenging courses is again related most strongly to whether talent provides flow or not, and somewhat less to personality. Family context and academic ability do not seem to be involved; the relationship to PSAT scores is significant only in the domain of mathematics, and it drops below significance when flow is taken into account. The ESM variables that correlate with Highest Talent Level achieved are: cheerful, strong, excited, open, unself-conscious, successful, and intrinsically motivated.

This pattern suggests that there are two basic forms of commitment: one that manifests itself in terms of external success (e.g., Teachers' Ratings and grades in highest level talent class) and one that reflects an inner drive (e.g., Subjective Commitment and Highest Talent Level). The first of these depends to a large extent on a student's ability and on the support he or she receives from a complex, autotelic family that encourages both differentiation and integration. The second form of commitment is more a function of such personality traits as achievement and endurance, and it is helped by the positive feelings a student experiences when involved with the talent area.

Educational implications

Perhaps the most important finding is that when students experience flow while working on their talent, the likelihood that they will keep on developing their gift increases significantly, no matter which measure of commitment is being used. It would be hard to underestimate the significance of this finding. It suggests that teachers can achieve their educational objectives best by focusing their efforts on making learning enjoyable. Every time a student tastes the exhilaration of creating a difficult mathematical proof or designing a novel chemical experiment, the motivation to continue exploring the domain becomes stronger. The importance of turning learning into a flow experience appears to be especially urgent in math and the sciences. As we have seen, students talented in music, art, and athletics have no trouble enjoying their talent; for them the obstacles are external, rather than internal – finding a viable career so they can continue doing what they love to do. But for students talented in the "hard" domains, the problem is lack of intrinsic motivation. For too many of them, math and science remain arid subjects, useful in the long run but not enjoyable in the present.

Part of the blame for this state of affairs must rest squarely on the shoulders of educators. Teachers and parents have traditionally assumed that serious learning cannot be enjoyable. "No pain, no gain," a motto used by certain athletic coaches, seems to underlie much of our educational philosophy. Yet when scientists or mathematicians describe their work, the importance of enjoyment is so obvious as to be overwhelming. Their lyrical accounts of how it feels to discover a new solution are no less ecstatic than the accounts of artists and composers talking about their works.[6] If practicing scientists and mathematicians know how important enjoyment is to their work and how satisfying it can be, why can't we communicate that understanding to beginners?

Contemporary educational practices appear to suffer from an acute case of split personality as far as the transmission of learning is concerned. On the one hand, we are obsessed with the goal of breaking down knowledge into its logical components and of presenting information in the most rational form possible. From the "new math" to all the various curricula inspired by computer programs, the preoccupation of the educator is to follow a particular theoretical outline, regardless of how it will be experienced by the learner. On the other hand, most textbooks and many teachers have succumbed to the reverse tendency. Inspired by pop graphics and telemontage techniques, textbooks try to present information in the most garishly attention-grabbing ways, hoping that colorful sidebars, changes in typography, and vivid pictures will get students to absorb some of the content. Similarly many desperate teachers resort to various forms of showmanship in order to attract the attention of students. These tactics can work in the short run, but unless they are promptly followed by more challenging methods, the attention of students will soon wander again.

Education today lacks a sound understanding of the intrinsic motivation that keeps students wanting to learn and to take on increasingly demanding intellectual challenges. This motivation has very little to do with the mindless relaxation induced by television programs or other forms of entertainment that are currently used as models for making learning more palatable. It has much more to do with the active enjoyment of learning to ride a bike or to swim or to solve a difficult puzzle or to build a table. In other words, intrinsically rewarding learning produces an experience of growth and of mastery, a feeling that the person has succeeded in expanding her or his skills.

The flow model helps to explain how such an experience could be induced. As we saw in the preceding chapter, it is essential for a teacher to present clear and feasible goals to students, goals that initially relate to the students' present aspirations. The intellectual challenges perceived by the student should match as closely as possible the student's capacities, being neither too difficult nor too easy, so that the likelihood of success is about fifty–fifty. For students to remain involved, it is important that their performance be monitored so that immediate and constant feedback is available. This feedback should be informational rather than controlling; in other words, the less students' egos are threatened, the more unselfconsciously they can become immersed in their work.[7] Outside interruptions should be minimized. As long as students look at a domain of knowledge as a subset of their everyday reality, the domain will seem pale and unimportant. But once they see math or music as separate realities with their own peculiar goals, rules, and rewards, they can free themselves from the preoccupations of everyday life and lose themselves in exploring and discovering these endlessly fascinating domains.

Of course it is not easy to implement such a time-consuming educational strategy. But considering how much money and effort are spent trying to transmit knowledge in ways that are boring and painful, to change priorities may not involve a great additional burden. If we refocused on learning to emphasize challenge and enjoyment, at least we would look at education with greater hope than many of us do now. We would know that we are not only building solid foundations for the future but enriching the lives of our young people in the present as well.

This chapter has shown how important it is for students to enjoy their talent if they are to develop and stay with it through adolescence. In the chapter that follows we shall show how the theoretical model of complex growth helps to interpret the differences between students who are committed and those who are not, thereby providing a more coherent picture of what is involved in the development of talent.

NOTES

1 A factor analysis is a statistical method of finding out whether responses to different items on a test or questionnaire form different clusters. In this case, the seven items "load" on a single cluster, suggesting that Teachers' Ratings, although purportedly measuring such different dimensions as "realization of potential" or "enjoyment of challenge" may in fact be taken as measuring a single dimension of engagement.

2 The variance in common between two variables is equal to the square of their correlation coefficient. The correlation between Teachers' Ratings and Subjective Commitment reported in Table 10.1 has a coefficient of $r = .44$; hence the

common variance is $.44 \times .44 = .19$. If two variables were exactly the same, the common variance would be 100%; if they were completely unrelated, it would be zero. A shared variance of 19% means that the two variables are significantly related even though four fifths of their variances do not overlap.

3 Csikszentmihalyi, 1982.

4 Csikszentmihalyi, 1975, 1988b; Csikszentmihalyi & Csikszentmihalyi, 1988.

5 The verb "predicts" is used here interchangeably with the passive form "is correlated with" to designate a variable correlated with an outcome, when that variable has been measured earlier than the outcome. For instance, academic ability and family context were measured 2 or 3 years before the outcome variable "grade in highest talent course" measuring commitment. Hence we are inferring that academic ability etc. predict commitment even though, strictly speaking, correlation does not imply causation.

6 Griessman, 1987; Schlick, 1934.

7 Amabile, 1983; Deci & Ryan, 1985; Nicholls, 1990.

Cultivating talent
throughout life

John Dewey, writing earlier in this century, understood clearly the connection between enjoyment and learning. In his book *Experience and Education* he wrote:

Everything depends upon the *quality* of experience which is had. The quality of any experience has two aspects. There is an immediate aspect of agreeableness or disagreeableness, and there is its influence upon later experiences. . . . Hence the central problem of an education based upon experience is to select the kind of present experiences that live fruitfully and creatively in subsequent experiences.[1]

Thus Dewey based his educational philosophy upon a connection between momentary and future concerns. True education, according to Dewey, was a spiral and dialectical process. The task of the teacher consisted in stimulating enjoyable experiences in students in a learning context, so that they would want to repeat such experiences on their own:

It is part of the educator's responsibility to see equally two things: First, that the problem grows out of the conditions of the experience being had in the present, and that it is within the capacity of students; and, secondly, that it is such that it arouses in the learner an active quest for information and for production of new ideas. The new facts and new ideas thus obtained become the ground for further experiences in which new problems are presented. The process is a continual spiral.[2]

Yet Dewey's philosophy, although universally acclaimed for its insights, has provoked much controversy, most notably between those who endorse progressive views of education and those who endorse the traditional. Proponents of each ideological stance often misunderstand the flexibility needed for authentic education. Traditionalists want more classroom discipline and the teaching of basic skills, and progressives argue for freedom and sensitivity. One administrator who works at an elementary school in the Chicago area described the problem this way: "When you mention Dewey, most teachers think of putting kids in a large room with lots of toys, and letting them do whatever they want." Although Dewey saw this misguided debate brewing, his efforts were unable to prevent it.

A lack of appropriate methods for measuring the quality of experience is certainly one reason why these misunderstandings persist. The point that needs to be proven is that short-term enjoyment and long-term involvement are intimately related in the process of education and therefore in the development of a talent. The Experience Sampling Method (ESM) is a method that can be used to begin to test that assumption. This chapter explores these two dimensions from the perspective of teens working in their talent areas.

The contrast between short-term and long-term involvement is another manifestation of the dialectics of integration and differentiation. At this level of analysis, short-term, spontaneous, or momentary involvement corresponds to integration in consciousness. That is, students do not feel overwhelmed or alienated by the talent-related work at hand but rather experience themselves and their actions as a seamless whole; they are "into" whatever they are doing. Long-term, goal-directed involvement, on the other hand, indicates differentiation in consciousness. That is, students are aware that what they are doing at the moment is something new and challenging that has ramifications for their growth and for their futures. A state of consciousness that has both these dimensions would be complex; that is, students would feel that their talent activity – in addition to being a means for growth and change – is also an enjoyable end in itself. In our study we expected that the students who were the most committed to developing their talents would show such a complex state of consciousness more often.

EXPERIENCE AND TALENT DEVELOPMENT

As in previous discussions of personality and family context (e.g., chapters 6 and 8), the notion of complexity will be used here to represent the simultaneous presence of integrating and differentiating forces. A complex personality and a complex family context have been described as optimal for growth because they are multidimensional, that is, oriented toward both stability and growth. In the present chapter this general dialectic will be applied to the quality of experience. A complex experience is one that is enjoyable yet related to future concerns and growth. In this sense a complex experience is one in which intrinsic and extrinsic motivation are fused and the immediate rewards of an activity are related to expectations of future rewards. To the extent that students' mode of engaging their talents is characterized by this dialectical tension, it is likely that their talents will grow.

As discussed in chapter 10, our study has partially confirmed these observations. For the sample as a whole, the ESM data predicted engagement with talent 2 years later. Students who had reported being open and excited when working on their talent were more likely to persevere, as were those who perceived what they were doing as being important to their overall goals. In other words, momentary interest and involvement and long-term goals were both linearly related to various dimensions of engagement. Apparently neither of these qualities can be ignored when we talk about talent development.

On the other hand, the results reported in chapter 10 tell us little about the synergistic relation between these variables. Is involvement enough to predict talent development? Or is awareness of the long-term importance of what one is doing enough to carry one successfully through the high school curriculum? It may be the case that those students who are most engaged will be simultaneously enjoying the present moment and also aware of the connection between their present activity and future goals.

The relationship of flow experience to talent development described in the preceding chapter suggests the same dynamic considerations. High skills can provide a platform for enjoyable and effortless involvement with new information, but if there is no perception of a challenge for growth it is unlikely that flow will occur. Thus another issue discussed in the present chapter is whether the most committed students demonstrate a synergistic relation between skills and challenges.

In line with Dewey's insight, talent development is conceived in this study as a dialectical or spiral process marked by a certain mode of engaging experience. The metaphor is *a path with a heart*,[3] or the feeling of approaching a destination while enjoying the journey as an end in itself. To measure momentary involvement, the combined ESM scores of the variables "involved," "open," and "excited" were used; long-term goals were measured with the single item "How important is this activity in relation to your overall goals?" An experience was classified as complex when a student responding to a particular pager signal indicated both high involvement and high importance to future goals (i.e., *above average* on each variable). In addition, three other modes were distinguished: high involvement and low importance, high goal importance and low involvement, and low involvement and low importance (see also chapters 6 and 8). Committed students were expected to indicate the simultaneous presence of involvement and importance more often than the uncommitted.

The flow model[4] provided a second way to explore a complex experiential mode. Again four types of experience were considered: high skills and challenges (the best condition for flow experiences), high skills and low challenges (potential boredom), high challenges and low skills (potential anxiety), and low skills and challenges (apathy). We expected that high talent engagement would be characterized by the "productive tension" of high skills and challenges.

Undivided attention: The experiential mode of committed students

Immersion in the task at hand is not all a teacher asks for when requesting students' undivided attention. If it were, the point of the lesson might not go beyond the classroom door, being forgotten as soon as the bell rings and the students leave. What the teacher truly desires is that students' attention not be divided between wanting to learn just enough material to get decent grades and at the same time using every bit of attention left over to fantasize about the next date or the next game.

To explore the questions of how short-term enjoyment and involvement in long-term goals interacted with talent commitment, we first selected a committed group of students in each talent area, students who by the end of high school exemplified ongoing engagement with talent. The criteria were simple and straightforward. Using two questions from the Subjective Engagement scale (see chapters 2 and 10), we classified students as committed if they (*a*) were doing talent-related activities every day and (*b*) planned to major in their talent area in college. In other words, committed students were defined as those who at the end of high school were still investing much energy in their talent and were planning to invest much energy in the future. Together these two components seemed to provide a good measure of commitment even if they did not indicate level of achievement (i.e., grades, ratings, and so on). Based on this method of selection, we classified as committed 31 students who also had sufficient pager responses in their talent area. Of these, 5 were committed in more than one domain of talent. This resulted in 12 students committed to math, 6 to science, 11 to music, 2 to athletics, and 5 to art. Because of the small sample in athletics, we excluded it from some of the analyses across talent areas.

Students in the committed group had impressive profiles of talent involvement. Kyra, who "always had a dream of going to Juilliard," typifies the kind of student selected. Her week – both at home and at school – was structured around devotion to music. Unabashedly she said, "I have to give up everything else just so I can make it my life." She performed with the high school orchestra and was accepted in two others outside school. She traveled to downtown Chicago for private music lessons, spent a good deal of her time practicing, and at the time of her interview was preparing an audition tape for a prestigious summer program of studies. She said she put so much energy into music because "I can hear myself getting better and better. . . . I've come this far, I can't stop. I don't want to, but [even if I did] I just can't."

Despite overwhelming levels of dedication, however, the students in this group did not differ from the uncommitted students in important ways. Their family incomes were about equal, their mothers and fathers had attained comparable levels of education, and their scholastic aptitude (as measured by the Preliminary Scholastic Aptitude Test) was not significantly different (committed group = 101.08; uncommitted = 98.50). Neither were the two groups of students different in terms of the prestige of their fathers' occupation, their position in the order of siblings (i.e., first or only child vs. not), the size of their family (one or two vs. two or more), the marital status of their parents (married or divorced), or their sex.

Quality of experience and commitment to talent

Before proceeding to the main question of whether or not such committed students were characterized 2 years earlier by a more complex experiential mode, we first compared the committed and uncommitted students on the ESM measures of quality of experience in their talent areas. These comparisons confirmed the relationship between positive experience and talent development suggested in the preceding chapter, and showed that when the most committed students are compared with the rest, these relationships become even stronger. For instance, significant differences ($p < .05$, one-tailed) were observed for the following variables: happy, cheerful, strong, active, sociable, proud, involved, excited, open, skilled, succeeding, wish to be doing, important to overall goals, and unself-conscious. Figures 11.1–3 represent these trends, using the composite ESM variables Affect and Potency and the motivational variable "wish to be doing." The figures also compare students across talent areas.

Committed students in math, science, music, and art were feeling more positive affect, greater potency, and stronger intrinsic motivation while they were engaged in their talents. These figures also show consistency across talent areas. This means that there is no interaction between quality of experience, commitment, and type of talent. Thus the positive correlations reported in the last chapter cannot be explained as an artifact of talent area. It was not, for example, that music or art students were primarily responsible for the positive relationship between engagement and quality of experience; the same pattern held also for students in science and mathematics. Even though music and art students tended to report higher levels of affect, potency, and intrinsic motivation overall while working in their talent areas, committed math and science students were comparable to students in the other domains.

Complex experience and talent development

Exciting moments unrelated to plans of action and purposeful but unpleasant moments represent two failed sides of a vital link in education. Thus we might expect that students who are committed to the development of their talents would less often experience these two modes. Instead, committed students should report a more complex experiential mode, that is, one characterized by both short- and long-term interest, one playful and serious at the same time.[5] Dewey certainly used the concept of interest in this way, carefully avoiding the association of interest with purely momentary excitement and stimulation. And current research on the concept of interest and its importance to educational

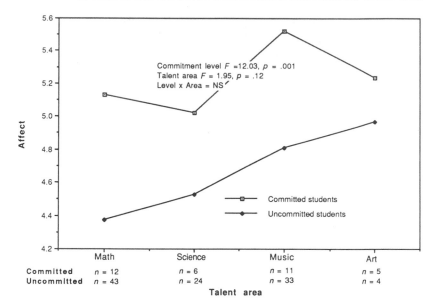

Figure 11.1. Affect of committed and uncommitted students while engaging in talent-related activities.

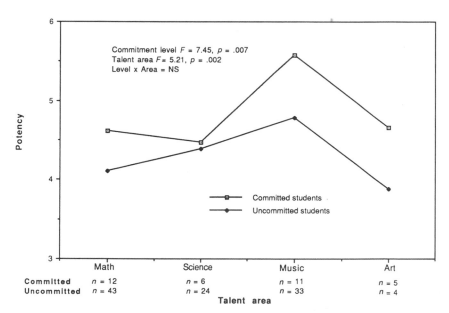

Figure 11.2. Potency of committed and uncommitted students while engaging in talent-related activities.

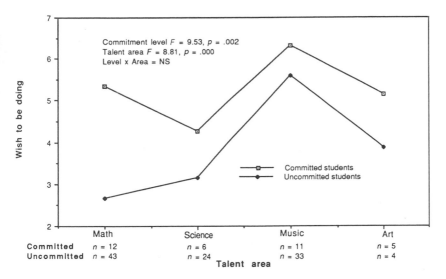

Figure 11.3. Motivation of committed and uncommitted students while engaging in talent-related activities.

theory[6] emphasizes both positive emotional involvement and intrinsic motivation as well as the cognitive importance given to future goals.

As mentioned above, momentary involvement was measured by adding the ESM items "open," "involved," and "excited." The relationship between experience and long-term goals was measured by the single ESM item "How important is this activity to your overall goals?" On the basis of median splits on the distributions of these two variables, we classified all of the talent-related pager signals into one of four quadrants: high momentary involvement/high importance to goals, high involvement/low importance, low involvement/high importance, and low involvement/low importance. Then each student's ESM signal responses were aggregated, yielding a percentage score for each of the four quadrants. In other words, if a particular music student responded to four talent-related signals while in music class, and one fell in each quadrant, then the corresponding percentage in each would equal 25.

Figure 11.4 presents the comparison of committed and uncommitted students, using the method just described. As expected, committed students reported being significantly more often in situations characterized

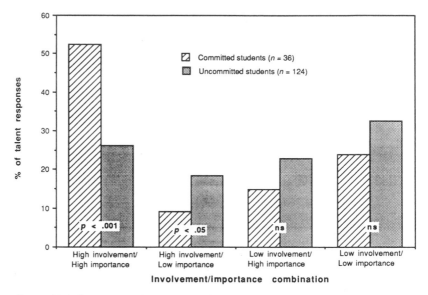

Figure 11.4. Comparison of committed and uncommitted students on levels of momentary involvement and importance to goals.

by momentary enjoyment plus importance given to long-term goals. This manner of dealing with their talents characterized their experience over 50% of the time (twice as much as the uncommitted students), and it was by far their predominant mode of operation. In contrast, the primary mode of talent engagement for the uncommitted students was low involvement/low importance of goals, which characterized their talent engagement over 30% of the time. These relationships held across each talent area; that is, committed math, science, music, and art students all had higher percentages in the high/high mode.

The other significant difference between the two groups was that the uncommitted students tended to be more often in situations where they were momentarily interested in their talents but did not feel them to be relevant to their long-term goals. It may be that some of the uncommitted students still enjoyed talent-related tasks – perhaps because they were good at them – but they had stopped thinking of them as offering important opportunities for the future.

Whereas the coincidence of short- and long-term interest is important for commitment in each domain of talent, as discussed in chapter 6, we expected that committed and uncommitted students might have different profiles in the high involvement/low importance mode and in the low involvement/high importance mode, depending upon whether or not they were involved with the arts (i.e., music, athletics, or art) or the sciences (i.e., math or science). We found in our study that in general students working in the sciences more often perceived the importance to their long-term goals of what they were doing while feeling low momentary interest; in contrast, those in the arts were more often feeling involved at the moment while not seeing the future importance of their talent-related tasks.[7]

Students who became committed to their domain of talent were able to compensate for the temporary lack of relevance or enjoyment. Table 11.1 shows how students who became committed to the sciences were more able to enjoy themselves at the moment, whereas those in the arts learned more often to relate what they were doing at the moment to their long-term goals. Thus those in each committed group were distinguished from their uncommitted peers significantly by their greater percentages in the high/high mode, and this mode characterized their talent activities most often. It is, however, important to keep in mind the variability between the committed young scientists and artists: In the former group, only 46% reported high involvement and high importance to goals, compared with 59% for the latter group. Thus even among committed students, math and science compared unfavorably with music, athletics, and art in terms of the opportunities each provided for optimal experience (see chapter 6 for an extended discussion).

We expected that those students whose interest remained divided, who weren't able to add the dimension that was lacking in their domain, would be less likely to develop their talents. In other words, science students who couldn't enjoy the day-to-day work and students in the arts who couldn't see in their work any future were the ones most likely to remain uncommitted. Table 11.1 confirms these expectations. Uncommitted science students were three times more likely to see the importance of what they were doing than to enjoy it. Uncommitted students in music, athletics, and art were more than three times as likely to be enjoying what they were doing in school than to be able to relate it to their future goals. Clearly the major obstacle to the development of talent in the sciences is

Table 11.1. *Comparison of students talented in arts and sciences on levels of momentary involvement and importance to future goals (percentage of time working in talent area)*

| | Math and science students | | | |
	High involvement/ high importance	High involvement/ low importance	Low involvement/ high importance	Low involvement/ low importance
Committed (*n* = 18)	45.5	11.6	11.6	31.3
Uncommitted (*n* = 67)	20.2	14.7	32.4	32.7
	$p < .01$	NS	$p < .05$	NS
	Music, athletics, and art students			
Committed (*n* = 18)	59.3	6.5	18.1	16.2
Uncommitted (*n* = 57)	33.4	22.6	11.4	32.6
	$p < .01$	$p < .05$	NS	NS

lack of enjoyment, whereas the major obstacle in the arts is lack of viable future prospects. This finding underscores the need for teachers and parents to help students correct the imbalance of conditions that inhibit full interest and involvement and hence the possibility of growth.

Flow and commitment to talent

The perception of high skills and challenges provides the psychological preconditions for flow experiences. The productive tension between high skills and high challenges is another manifestation of integrated and differentiated modes of experience. A highly skilled science student is likely to find new material understandable and stimulating. However, if the material does not, in Dewey's words, "[arouse] in the learner an active quest for information and production of new ideas" (i.e., if it does not challenge the student), the student is unlikely either to enjoy or to learn the material. Conversely, if a science student is constantly bombarded with new information yet feels alienated from the work, the connection between experience and education is subverted. The focused flow of attention is likely to occur only when the interaction of challenges and skills creates a balanced tension. This tension sets up the dialectical movement between order and change that stimulates development.

To determine when students perceived themselves to be in a high skill, high challenge state, two flow measures were computed from the ESM data. The first was based on the percentage of a student's talent-related signals for which he or she reported perceiving challenges and skills higher than his or her *own* weekly average. For example, if a student was paged four times and reported above-average challenges and skills on two of these occasions, the flow percentage would be 50. The second flow measure was similar, but it computed percentage of flow by the perception of above-average challenges and skills compared with the *group's* weekly average. In other words, a flow response according to the latter measure would indicate a student's perception of higher challenges and skills than was typically perceived by her or his classmates. By the first measure, every student was likely to have at least some flow experiences; by the second, it would be possible for one student to be always in flow (i.e., above the group's average in challenges and skills) and for another to be always in boredom or in apathy.

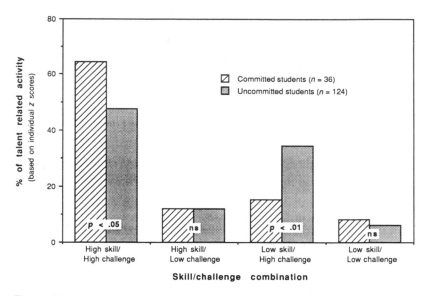

Figure 11.5. Comparison of committed and uncommitted students on levels of skills and challenges in talent work.

Figure 11.5 again suggests that optimal experience is associated with commitment to talent and that the committed students' predominant mode of engaging their talents is more complex. Collected 2 and 3 years before the commitment information, these measures reflect the students' natural way of experiencing their talents. Teens in the committed group reported high skill and challenge 65% of the time when they were doing talent-related work. This means that, compared with their average weekly perceptions of challenges and skills, working in the talent area fairly consistently generated the dynamic conditions for flow. In contrast, less than half (48%) of the uncommitted group's talent-related signals were flow responses. And these relationships held across talent areas; that is, committed students in both arts and sciences had similar proportions of flow when working in their respective talent areas.

Whereas committed students more often experienced the conditions for flow when engaged with their talents, the uncommitted were more often in the low skill, high challenge context that tends to produce anxiety. This finding replicates previous studies with different groups of talented students[8] and suggests one reason why some students disengage from their talent. The major obstacle to momentary involvement seems to be the feeling of anxiety – a fact that is important for educators to keep in mind.

When group averages were used to construct the flow quadrants, the results were virtually identical, with significant differences between the committed and uncommitted groups for the flow and anxiety quadrants. This similarity of results is important because it indicates that when students in the committed group reported relatively high challenges and skills (compared with their own average), such perceptions were also high by absolute group standards. Thus, using either method of measurement, the committed students were more likely than uncommitted students to perceive high challenges and skills while working in their talent areas.

THE LONG-TERM EFFECTS OF POSITIVE EXPERIENCE

We have argued that integration and differentiation are important components of social and personality systems. As characteristics of a person's social environment or as relatively stable personal dispositions, these qualities facilitate optimal experiences. A complex family or personality system both is stable and contains opportunities for growth. Such families and personalities are related positively to talent development.

Not all teenagers, of course, have such supportive social environments and personal habits. Can enjoyable experience in a domain of talent compensate for their absence? This is the question addressed through the case of a student whom we call Ron Schwartz. The troubling information he provided about his family and personality would have led us to believe that Ron would give up on his musical talent, but this turned out not to be the case.

The case of Ron Schwartz

Ron is a saxophonist who prefers the freedom of playing show music, blues, and jazz to the structured forms of classical music. He describes himself as serious, moody, capable of emotional extremes (which he feels is typical of artists), accepting, and friendly but also demanding. Ron more than adequately demonstrates the dedication and the accomplishments to justify his inclusion in the committed category. He devotes a tremendous amount of time to music, which he considers an "essential part of life" and the only "pure form of communication." By his own estimate, he spends over 60 hours a week involved with music, playing for the school choir, in a jazz band, and in a blues band as well as playing for several local and professional theater groups outside school. He is an instrumentalist and occasional musical director for the theater groups, where he is in charge of musicians who are sometimes twice his age. His precocity has been noted by many, including the community newspapers.

Music is, in his own words, the force that keeps him together. He does not play for money, which he says he hates from the bottom of his heart because it's a bother and "destroys all your dreams" but rather because he feels compelled to reach the goals he has set for himself. This goal-directedness not only allows him to focus attention enjoyably but also directs his attention away from a host of other problems. Here is a telling passage from his interview:

All my life I've always set goals, I mean one goal after the next after the next. . . . And I just work and work and work. I like that. It makes me feel good when I can reach goals, but now they're getting bigger and bigger. . . . My whole life is goals. I could really sit down and think about my family and get so screwed up. So I've just completely shut out my family. . . . You know, *it's shutting off all realization that my family exists.* It would be nice if they could just wait a couple of years until I'm out of high school to have their difficulties, and then I just could worry about that. But now when I have 10 million other things to worry about along with this, I have to shut out some stuff.

Music is Ron's shield, a protection from the psychic entropy that would result if he spent time worrying about his family problems, particularly the divorce that his parents are going through. "It's to the point now where I don't do anything with my family," he comments. "It would be nice to come home to people who were really happy." There is little doubt that Ron's devotion to music is in part the result of the narrowed concentration he achieves in order to avoid unhappiness. His motivation thus appears to be an unusual blend of intrinsic and extrinsic reasons: In part, it is escapism and the need to get away; in part, it is the joy of playing music. Ron is well aware of the highs that emerge from successful performances and the good feelings that come from reaching goals and doing "better and better and better." In this sense, his mode of engagement is complex: enjoying the activity as an end in itself and as a means to an end.

Ron's ESM responses also provided a dramatic example of how his deep interest in music helps him to rise above other problems. One evening during a rehearsal for a local production he answered four ESM signals over a 3-hour period. The first came at 5:15 p.m. when Ron was carrying his saxophone into a theater and getting ready to rehearse a show's music. He saw that his fellow band members (whom he was responsible for) had not yet arrived, so he decided to cram in some homework while waiting. He commented on the self-report form, "Why can't a day be 36 hours." At this time, he was feeling a bit tense, but his moods were not particularly negative.

Approximately 15 to 20 minutes later a second signal arrived, and the members of his band had still not shown up. Now he was clearly worried and reported feeling self-conscious, not in control of the situation, very irritable, ashamed, and tense. The third signal came at 7:00 p.m.; he was still alone, wandering around the theater and thinking about "why and how people can be so cruel." Apparently his friends had finally shown up for rehearsal, but he felt that they didn't care about him and he was wondering, "Am I that shitty of a person?" His mood had grown much worse: He was now having difficulty concentrating and was feeling "lonely" and "closed" in addition to the tension and sense of shame he was still feeling.

These negative feelings were partly the result of the importance Ron placed on his friends in music. He maintained close relationships with teachers, some of whom were quite a bit older, and he enjoyed the company of the members of the band. Because relations with his parents were so poor, the time he spent with these friends seemed to have added importance. Perhaps because of his insecure family situation, he was susceptible to self-doubt and depression concerning his value to others. By the time the third ESM signal came at rehearsal, he was lost in one of his moody introspections (a scenario that was repeated on other nights when he was with his friends). His mood had sunk so low that his ESM report at 7:10 represented his worst mood of the entire week.

Yet miraculously, at 8:30 he responded to the pager signal with the best mood of the week. What had made such a profound difference and turned black depression into elation? He was playing the saxophone for the show and was apparently having a flow experience. He reported perceiving high skills and high challenges (9 on each scale, the highest possible response) and was very much in control, *quite* happy, cheerful, sociable, open, relaxed, alert, clear, concentrated, intrinsically motivated, involved, and feeling that what he was doing was important to his overall goals. Once again we can see the crucial role of music for Ron. It provided him with opportunities to involve himself in something enjoyable and important to his future as well as with a way in which to avoid "falling apart" because of personal problems. As long as he could keep himself together until he could get his hands on his instrument, and if he could listen to music while showering and doing other mundane things that might allow his mind to wander, then he was happy and had a sense of satisfaction.

Ron's life illustrates the point that whereas it is *more likely* that commitment to talent will be associated with complex families and healthy personalities, a high quality of optimal experience during talent-related activities can help a young person overcome stress that might otherwise be overwhelming. The overcoming of personal troubles is a familiar story to those who study the development of creative talent. Numerous biographers and researchers have interpreted negative events as providing the initial impetus toward remarkable accomplishment. The point we wish to make here is the similarity between courses of development stimulated by negative and by positive events. In other words, what is essential to talent development – regardless of whether positive or negative factors are involved – is that relevant problems in a domain of talent are a high focus of attention over long periods of time. We have argued how the complexity of fields, domains, families, teachers, and personalities can help in focusing attention, which is necessary for talent development insofar as these factors facilitate a student's need to grow through the processes of integration and differentiation. However, as the case study just described shows, other factors can also motivate concentration.

It would be a mistake, though, to overstate the importance of negative factors, which are all too often romanticized in our culture. We tend not to believe such revered figures as T. S. Eliot, who commented near the end of his life that he had given up too much for his poetry. For every Ron who is successful in shutting off the "realization that his family exists," there are probably many others who are immobilized by their personal problems. Furthermore the foundations of a talent that rests on such "negative" motivations may be precarious.

For instance, seeds of later problems may already be planted in Ron, even though music is still masking their existence. His ESM responses show flirtation with drugs and alcohol when music is not available to provide an emotional outlet. These alternative paths of escape could someday compete with music for his attention disastrously. In addition, success in shutting out his family problems may only be temporary. Ron lives with contradictions. At one point in the interview he suggested that he wanted to make a lot of money in music so his parents could quit their jobs. By removing their everyday burdens (financial and otherwise) he hopes to make them less miserable. Thus two of his nemeses – money and family – become entwined in his fantasy to help everyone live happily ever after.

One thing is certain at this crucial point in Ron's development: He enjoys music. It provides a way for him to live enjoyably in the moment and to look to the future – to set goals and to maintain the discipline needed in order to bring these goals to fruition. As is typical of others in the committed group, Ron's experience with talent is complex and not easily classified as either hedonistic enjoyment or hard work. These gifted youngsters are open and involved with what they are doing, and they are aware that it is important to their long-term goals. They feel highly skilled and highly challenged and thus seem able to maintain the tension between the need for continuity and the need for change.

CONCLUSIONS

There are many reasons why it is important to understand better the connection between experience and education,[9] not the least of which is to resolve the ideological differences that plague many families and schools. There are often two seemingly antagonistic educational philosophies at work in modern society. One group of parents and teachers is convinced that a stronger emphasis should be placed on impulse control, discipline, and hard work; another group sees true education as hinging upon students' enjoying and being excited about learning. Thus some parents are "serious" about educational matters, and some stress playful freedom and self-initiative; some teachers strive for a reputation of enforcing strict discipline and teaching "by the book," and others see themselves as liberated, "fun," and interesting. The more conservative group is afraid that too much playful interest will undermine the work ethic, and the more liberal group is afraid that an emphasis on discipline will restrict the joy of inquiry.

The results presented in this chapter suggest that such entrenched positions are based upon an inadequate understanding of the relationship between experience and education. The profile of committed students indicates that it is erroneous to believe that serious goal-directedness cannot be united with a sense of enjoyment and excitement over the task at hand. The fact that adolescent talent development was predicted by the presence of high momentary involvement and high importance given to goals, high skills, and high challenges (as well as being associated with complex families and personalities) suggests why an either–or philosophy of education won't work. The very nature of complexity defies such reasoning, and perhaps the function of complexity in these various systems is to defy the obstacles to growth that such one-sidedness entails.

This chapter has provided empirical support for the importance of dialectical models in the study of talent development, or development in general. Despite the difficulty in measuring integration and differentiation, and despite the attraction of supporting either the side of play or that of seriousness, what is gained in terms of insight into development makes it worth the effort to keep the tension between these alternatives alive.

The committed students in our study defy easy description. They enjoyed their talent work, but they were not hedonists who avoided hardships and discipline. Indeed, they worked very hard, but they were not anxious and pressured while doing so. Although they were an elite subsample of an already elite group of young students, and although some researchers may object to trying to understand development from such a perspective, Maslow was probably correct in claiming that the study of health is at least as important as the study of pathology.[10] We can learn much about average development by examining positive extremes.

Even Ron Schwartz has much to teach us about talent development. Despite any other weaknesses he may possess, or perhaps because of them, he has found a way to let music turn disorder into order. In previous studies we borrowed the term "dissipative structures" from the field of biology to help explain how living systems are able to exploit chaos and make use of dispersing energy to create order.[11] Psychic dissipative structures are attentional habits that exploit conflicting information to create order in experience.[12] Ron seems to use involvement with music to order his life. Whether in time it will become a genuine dissipative structure and help Ron transform his problems and not just avoid them, it is too early to tell. However, his story speaks about the power of human consciousness to turn disadvantage into advantage.

If the enjoyment of complex experience is central to the work of the most engaged high school students, it is useful to ask how often it is missing from the average student's day. To help all young people fulfill their potential, it seems urgent to place a higher value on the importance of enhancing the quality of educational experience for *all* students. If parents and educators acted to implement this knowledge, much waste of gifts could be avoided.

NOTES

1 Dewey, 1938, p. 27.
2 Ibid., p. 79.
3 The phrase "a path with a heart" is adopted from Castaneda (1971); it was used by the Yaqui sorcerer Don Juan to describe a life based on personal choices.
4 Csikszentmihalyi 1975, 1990a.
5 Rathunde, 1991a, in press.
6 See Schiefele, 1991.
7 See also Rathunde, in press.
8 Nakamura, 1988.
9 Dewey, 1938.
10 Maslow, 1968.
11 Csikszentmihalyi, 1978; Prigogine, 1980.
12 Csikszentmihalyi & Larson, 1984.

12

What have we learned?

What our study disclosed matches in some respects what other researchers have also reported, or what common sense would suggest. For instance, it should come as no surprise that young persons with a strong desire to achieve do advance farther in their area of talent. Other findings, like the importance of lack of self-consciousness when involved in one's talent, could only have been revealed by an instrument able to capture fine detail, such as the Experience Sampling Method (ESM).

But to us the most important result of this study does not lie in the richness and concreteness of its details. We feel that the most remarkable conclusion we have drawn from our investigation is the unity that underlies the diversity of particular patterns of data. Stated in its simplest form, what we have come to realize is the importance of *psychological complexity* as the organizing principle for making sense out of the multitude of factors affecting the development of talent. Complexity – or the simultaneous presence of differentiating and integrating processes – distinguishes the personalities of talented teens, their families, and their approach to learning. We found the same operation of differentiation and integration underlying the later development of the talent.

Complexity is important as an organizing concept because it helps resolve some dangerous theoretical misconceptions that have bedeviled educational and personality psychology for some time. The concept of complexity helps synthesize tendencies that psychologists and educators have artificially set apart and against each other: the need to achieve versus pure curiosity; narrow concentration versus openness to novelty; extrinsic versus intrinsic motivation. These and many other opposites are reconciled in talented people and in their environment. Based on this insight, we can build a model of optimal human development – one that turns out to have been anticipated by some of the great psychologists of the past, in particular William James and John Dewey. If we achieve nothing beyond alerting parents, teachers, and our colleagues in the profession to the fact that one must take psychological complexity into account when trying to understand human behavior, we feel that the importance of this volume will be established.

But before reviewing the holistic implication of this study, it is important to summarize once more the conclusions based on the empirical results. What did the data show, and what did they suggest about enhancing the development of talent?

SUMMARY OF FACTORS ASSOCIATED WITH TALENT DEVELOPMENT

1. Although this might seem too obvious to deserve mention, children must first be recognized as talented in order to develop a talent, and therefore they *must have skills that are considered useful in their culture* – in our case spatial–mathematical, musical, athletic, or artistic gifts. But the further implications of this statement are not so obvious. For instance, there are many skills that children have that are not recognized because there are no established domains or fields to support them. Some persons will have extraordinary sensitivity to smells or to the moods of other people; others have extraordinarily developed moral sensitivities. Shouldn't these be recognized as talents?

Conversely, the statement also implies that parents, teachers, and teenagers must realize that talent alone is no guarantee of future success. Every potential talent needs to be cultivated and nurtured with great discipline for many years if it is to be applied usefully. A great musical gift at age 10 will make little difference at age 30 unless it has been turned into a usable skill.

2. Talented students *have personality traits conducive to concentration (e.g., achievement and endurance) as well as to being open to experience (e.g., awareness, or sentience, and understanding).* These four characteristics distinguish both talented males and females from average teenagers. This implies, first, that the talented are less sex stereotyped than average stu-

dents and are thus freer to explore a deeper range of human potentials. (Achievement orientations are more typical in males, and sentience is usually a female characteristic, yet in our sample males are sentient and females achievement-oriented – as well as having the characteristics typical of their own sex. Other findings also suggest a more androgynous profile; see chapter 4.) Second, and more important, talented teens have complementary qualities that in tandem are likely to produce a powerful autotelic combination. While openness to experience helps them recognize new challenges, endurance and achievement orientations are essential for sustained application of skills.

These complementary qualities are necessary also at the highest levels of talent development. The prominent German poet Hilde Domin describes her writing as consisting of two phases: deep involvement with the verbal formulation of an experience and then a stepping back, that is, finding a relatively objective perspective from which to evaluate what she has done. This idea is expressed in these lines from one of her poems:

> Man muß weggehen können
> und doch sein wie ein Baum:
> als bliebe die Wurzel im Boden,
> als zöge die Landschaft und wir ständen fest[1]

Eminent scholars often remark that successful colleagues have an ideal balance of qualities: an ability to pour themselves into their work and assimilate necessary information plus the ability to know when to shape, bring closure to, and quit a particular topic. Both points recall the profile of talented teens: achievement and endurance orientations, needed to work hard, and openness to experience, needed to find new challenges.

3. Talent development is easier for teens who *have learned habits conducive to cultivating talent.* For instance, talented students spent less time just socializing or hanging out with friends. Instead they shared more active and challenging pursuits with friends, for example, hobbies and studying. They learned to modulate attention: more concentration in school and less when socializing, doing chores, and watching TV. They also spent a greater amount of time alone, which is essential for anyone building future skills. More solitude and more productive activities probably accounted for more somber weekly moods than average teenagers. But talented teens had learned to tolerate negative moods and reported

being more happy, cheerful, active, and motivated than average teenagers when productively engaged.

Other characteristics that distinguished the talented group were more directly attributable to family context. For instance, such teens in our study did not have to invest much attention in such practical tasks as chores and jobs. This is not surprising, given their parents' education, job status, and incomes. Talented teens, compared with average teenagers, also reported that their families were more psychologically supportive, that is, cohesive and flexible. The ESM showed that they tended to spend more time with their families and had more one-to-one contact with their parents. These material and psychological supports seemed to help establish more efficient patterns of attentional use. In other words, teens who have financial worries and jobs, many chores at home, and more tension with parents are likely to waste valuable time on routine activities and on coping with problems.

There is no denying that some of these beneficial habits and characteristics are due to being born into financial security or to having "good genes," but the basic principle of making the best use of one's energy applies across the board to individuals of all social classes and ability levels. Therefore the findings suggest the importance of looking for opportunities to keep from investing energy in nonessential tasks and of diverting it to more productive uses. Are teenagers' jobs really necessary? Much research suggests that teenagers' part-time jobs contribute little to positive developmental outcomes.[2] Can family chores be taken care of more efficiently? How much time is the TV set on? Would there be less distraction if the teenager worked alone in another room? The list of questionable activities to consider can be extended indefinitely to include habits that were not discussed here. For instance, how much time is spent eating and getting dressed in the morning?

Such questions may seem tedious or insignificant, but they sometimes provide ideas for even the most productive and creative individuals. One popular story about Einstein is that he wore the same kind of clothes every day in order to cut the time needed to choose them each morning. Many teachers believe that reintroducing school uniforms would improve the attentional focus of students and eliminate the time they waste comparing themselves with others. Even a small factor like style of dress can have an impact on the way attention is used. Cultivation of other time-saving habits is more obvious. A noted research biologist used to hate two very different aspects of his job: waiting in airport terminals and writing grant proposals. One day a simple solution occurred to him: Combine the two disliked activities. Now he dictates research proposals on a tape recorder while waiting for departures or standing in line at ticket counters and customs checks, and he derives profound satisfaction from having halved his wasted time. Anyone can find ways of developing more productive habits once the goal of economizing attention is clearly established. Talented students have a head start in this regard, but every teenager is likely to benefit from better use of her or his time.

4. A fourth finding – also relevant to the economy of attention – is that talented teens *are more conservative in their sexual attitudes and aware of the conflict between productive work and peer relations.* Both talented males and females scored lower than average teenagers on the Offer Self-Image Questionnaire (OSIQ) "Sexual Attitudes" factor, which suggests that as they go through puberty, a time when emerging concerns about social and sexual competence inevitably increase the demands on psychic energy, they have adopted a relatively conservative approach to sexual issues. In addition the interviews suggested that they were highly sensitive to the conflict between investing time in friends of the opposite sex and investing it in their talent. This trend was also supported by the ESM findings just discussed, namely, that they spent less time socializing with friends in general (e.g., hanging out, going to parties) or playing sports and games, and more time studying, thinking, and doing hobbies with friends.

A recurrent issue in the Roman Catholic Church has been celibacy for priests. The idea of married priests has been rejected by the church leadership mainly on the ground that marriage would split the energy and attention that ought to be devoted to God's work; and for similar reasons, celibacy is extensively practiced by monastic orders in a great variety of Eastern religions. In a much less extreme form, the basic issue is similar for talented teenagers: The value of a conservative sexual attitude is that it allows more energy for math, science, music, athletics, and art. Teenagers can easily be swept away by the biological needs stirred up at puberty, especially when these are heightened by a constant barrage of commercially motivated exploitations of sexuality. They can lose perspective on the importance of sex in the context of a whole life. Talented adolescents, perhaps because they know they have more to lose or because they are better prepared by their families, do not let this happen. It may be that theirs is an overly careful reaction that will delay some aspects of social maturation as currently defined, but it would be a mistake to assume that the excessive concern for peers and sexuality that is characteristic of our youth culture is natural or right. There is no reason to believe that the cautious approach to sexuality shown by talented teenagers is a sign of repression, that fearsome spectre of the 20th century. We might rather say that it is the talented teens who are liberated from the need constantly to attend to the artificially fueled sexual concerns that take up their peers' energy and time.

5. A fifth conclusion is that *families providing both support and challenge enhance the development of talent.* Adolescents in the talented sample, compared with average teenagers, reported that their families were more cohesive and flexible. Those who perceived their family context as integrated and differentiated (supportive, harmonious, challenging, free) reported more flow experiences with their families and a higher quality of experience at home. Their parents also reported more rewards from family interaction, more harmony with their spouses, more personal life happiness, and greater expectations for intrinsic motivation in their offsprings' career. Teens from integrated and differentiated families spent more time doing homework and were more alert and goal-directed while doing it. These productive habits transferred to the school environment, where the same teens report being more happy and alert (a finding associated just with family integration) and more focused on important expectations and goals (associated just with differentiation). The same patterns emerged in talent-related work and in general schoolwork, and teens from complex families – according to the grades and ratings of their teachers – performed both types of work more effectively.

It is impossible to say just how parents create environments that their children come to see in such positive ways, but an example will illustrate what some families do to accomplish this goal. A colleague of ours (whom we shall refer to as Mrs. Cooper) told us the following story about her son, Andy, who is now a senior in high school and very much interested in ecology, nature, and animals. When he was in the second grade, he used to walk to school with his mother past one of their favorite sights: a statue of the Swedish scientist Linné, naturalist and inventor of the system for classifying botanical and zoological species that is still used today. One day after school Mrs. Cooper took Andy with her to her office so she could finish some work. While she was busy her son spontaneously started making charts classifying animals as "wild" and "domestic." He had several categories under each (e.g., bird, mammal, reptile, amphibian, and so on), and after completing a first draft of his charts and having his mother correct his spelling, he proceeded to make a final version, complete with pictures and definitions that he copied from the office dictionary.

When it was time to go, Andy was reluctant to quit. He suggested that they stay longer and work some more. Recognizing the opportunity to turn the project that her son enjoyed into more than just a passing interest, Mrs. Cooper suggested that he keep his charts at the office and, because they worked so well together, that he return often and complete them. She got two new folders from her office supplies and carefully put his work inside, showing that she appreciated its quality and maturity. She placed them on the bookshelf with her own folders, and they left for home. Andy was feeling extremely satisfied with the way the afternoon had progressed, and as they were walking he wanted his mother to promise that they could return two or three days a week to work together.

This story is an interesting example of how family involvement and encouragement of challenge creates a supportive context for the development of genuine interests. At the office with his mother, Andy felt comfortable and loved, the perfect safe and secure place to begin fooling around with charts of wild and domestic animals. Perhaps Andy's interest would have remained unfocused playfulness, however, if his mother had been only nurturant and not also concerned about preparing him to be more self-directed in the future. Her challenge to keep the folders at the office and return to them later showed her respect for her son's individuality and trust in his ability to work toward goals as she did. In addition to creating a context that enhanced his capacity to become involved in some activity, she created one with opportunities to expand upon an initial involvement. Such opportunities would eventually help distinguish Andy as a unique individual in the family: "This is my son Andy, he has been very much interested in ecology and animals since he was a little boy."

6. Even the best home environment may be undermined, however, by

negative learning experiences at school. A sixth finding of the study is that talented teenagers *liked teachers best who were supportive and modeled enjoyable involvement in a field.* Students said that such teachers demonstrated an abiding concern for them, could be counted on for support and stimulation, and cared about their interests. On the other hand, these teachers were themselves intense people often professionally involved in their fields outside the classroom, and they had a presence and an infectious enthusiasm that helped create an exciting environment for learning. They did not just go through the motions but wanted their students to become deeply involved in their own work. They made sure that they challenged their students in a way commensurate with their ability levels.

If a home environment fails to provide a place where the enjoyment of productive work can be learned, teachers may represent the last chance for many students to find a path with a heart. Although the connections between student and teacher are not as direct and emotionally charged as those between parent and child, teachers represent for many students the first encounter with an adult from a particular field of talent. Whether or not a teacher is sensitive and comforting and in touch with a young person's interests tells the student much about the kind of adult they may be working with somewhere down the line, and the kind of adult they might themselves become. Thus the issue of integration involves a teacher's modeling a professional identity that will be attractive to students. Opportunities for student differentiation are also essential. Students must be able to feel that they have something unique to contribute to the field and that their teachers recognize their individual skills.

When such favorable conditions are present in the classroom, it is much more likely that the pacing of challenges will match the level of skills. Teachers will know students, and vice versa; their interactions will be coordinated. Fewer mistakes will be made in giving students challenges that are too hard or too easy. Students will feel more comfortable, unself-conscious, and clear about the purpose of their activities and will be able to focus on work that is suited to their interests and abilities. Like the art of parenting, teaching requires quick reactions that seize moments that may be fateful to a student's future. Again, no one formula can suffice for guiding a teacher in this task, but these general principles are enacted in thousands of ways by successful teachers every day.

An experimental public school in Indianapolis, the Key School, which we have observed for several years, has taken several steps in this direction. Teachers work with the same students for 2 years instead of 1, and they maintain closer contact than usual with other teachers of the same grade level. All teachers must organize some of their daily lessons around schoolwide themes. Teachers must therefore be creative and work harder *as individuals*, and must *collaborate* more with their co-workers. Many successes have resulted from this approach. Students can move from geography to art to music to science and still be studying the same topic – for instance, rainforests. At three points in the school year students are allowed to choose a project of their own that is related to the schoolwide theme. Their own interests are thus given full expression (i.e., an opportunity for differentiation is supported), and they are connected like branches to the trunk of the school theme (i.e., they are integrated).

7. *Talent development is a process that requires both expressive and instrumental rewards.* Involvement with the arts (music/athletics/art) tended to evoke strong positive feelings in students, or expressive involvement; involvement with the sciences (including math), on the other hand, tended to be judged as useful to future goals, that is, offered instrumental incentives. However, talent development in either area required the synergistic combination of these rewards. In other words, successful young artists showed some of the qualities that typified young scientists, and committed young scientists felt the way artists usually feel about their work.

Several patterns in the data confirmed the widely held expressive–instrumental distinction between the arts and the sciences. Arts students more often endorsed the item "I enjoy it" in their interviews; science students more often said things like "It is useful." In chapter 6 we reported that when students in the arts were paged, they more often felt that what they were doing was involving and exciting but unimportant to their future goals. Those in the sciences reported the opposite pattern: They were thinking instrumentally, that is, that what they were doing was important but not enjoyable. In addition, those in the arts reported higher affect, potency, and intrinsic motivation while doing talent-related work and more often responded to the pager by saying they "wanted to do" it. Those in the sciences tended to concentrate more and said that they "had to do" their work. None of these findings of course would surprise many parents, teachers, or students. What was surprising – although on reflection is very reasonable – was that arts students who were not able to think ahead and science students who did not enjoy their work of the moment were less likely to become highly engaged in their talent in later years.

In chapter 11 we showed that those students who were committed to the development of their talents were the ones who 2 and 3 years earlier had achieved a synergy between momentary involvement and long-term goals, or expressive and instrumental involvement. This was true for engagement in both the arts and the sciences and for each domain: math, science, music, athletics, and art. Of course the ideal of the artist–scientist is not new. Nietzsche's "artistic Socrates," who successfully combines the Dionysian and Apollonian virtues of passion and vision, is one example among many in Western literature. However, there are very few empirical studies that add substance to these metaphors.

The findings above support the commonsense view of what goes on in schools. Teachers in the arts tend to emphasize the momentary, sensual rewards of the subject, and students from the earliest grades look forward to having "easy" music and art classes. The talented students with whom we spoke were no exception. On the other hand, students learn early that science is "serious." The typical classroom environment for these courses is more formal and directive, less mindful of students' interests, and often very dull.

Teachers certainly do not deserve all the blame for this state of affairs. The prejudices are deeply ingrained in our educational system. Educational psychologists, when they juxtapose intrinsic and extrinsic goals and motivations, add to the problem. They often look at these orientations as if they were opposites, without specifying how long-range concerns can be compatible with momentary ones. The results just reviewed about commitment in the arts and sciences illustrate the potential for confusion. An overemphasis on future goals (commonly called extrinsic motivation) is as harmful to a person's productive use of attention as an overemphasis on curiosity or playful task-related involvement (commonly called intrinsic motivation).

Much can be done to correct these imbalances by increasing opportunities to combine momentary involvement and long-term goals. The concrete and immediate impact of the arts may compel expressive involvement, and the abstract and mediate symbols of science may best fit extending vision beyond the moment. But these strengths become weaknesses when exaggerated.

To right an imbalance, the first step is always to find out what the child likes to do spontaneously and then to tease out the natural interest and curiosity with progressively difficult challenges. For instance, a child who loves cats and likes to draw them might also be curious about how fast they run, how long they live, how their bodies are similar to or different from human bodies, what part of the world they are indigenous to, why humans are attracted to them, why they appear as symbols in countless myths, or why their fur makes some people sneeze. A child could thus learn some math, biology, geography, psychology, mythology, and so on by seeing the world through love of cats. Although it is extraordinarily difficult – perhaps impossible – to help a class of 30 children learn in this way, it is in such a manner that the immediate and the mediate and the concrete and the abstract can be bridged. If a teacher (or parent) can observe what draws a child's attention and discover her or his special leverage point, exercise a bit of imagination, and do the necessary work to prepare a course of studies, the teacher (or parent) may start the child on a self-directed course of learning.

8. This brings up the final conclusion concerning the factors that facilitate talent development. Everything we have said up to now reinforces this final point: *A talent will be developed if it produces optimal experiences.* That optimal experience contributes to talent development was clearly documented by the results presented in chapters 10 and 11. For instance, whether students experienced flow in their talent area was significantly related to engagement, and it was the only predictor related to all four engagement variables: teacher's ratings, grades in talent class, subjective commitment, and highest talent level reached. Preliminary Scholastic Aptitude Test scores and complex families were the best predictors of such external standards as teachers' ratings and grades, but flow was the strongest predictor of subjective engagement and how far the student progressed in the school's curriculum in her or his talent. Furthermore the most committed students in the group (i.e., those who were working every day and planning to major in their area in college) more often perceived skills and challenges to be high and balanced when they were working in their talent area.

Other ESM variables showed that quality of experience facilitated engagement, as is suggested by flow theory. Some of the strongest experiential predictors were feeling open, cheerful, strong, excited, unself-conscious, intrinsically motivated, successful, and skillful and feeling that one was working toward long-range goals. We can say with some certainty that enjoyment of a student's talent-related work was one of the most important determinants of whether the student developed her or his talent. This was true even when taking into account other factors, such as sex, socio-economic status, and academic aptitude. Some of the other factors discussed above that were also important, such as ability, personality, productive habits, and an autotelic family and school context, reinforce this notion. In other words, all of these factors positively influence the quality of subjective experience. It is in this sense that the various findings in the study are of a piece.

Unfortunately, many adults who have not been able to pursue a vocation that they enjoy will be reluctant to accept this general conclusion. They will tend to see interest and effort, and play and work, as separate realms because that is how they normally experience them in their own lives. Yet most people remember a time, no matter how brief, when they were swept along by a sense of effortless control, clarity, and concentration on an enjoyable challenge. It may have happened on the athletic field, on a scout outing, or in a high school choir, but such moments are often enshrined in memory and turned to for inspiration in more stressful times.

Optimal experiences are important to talent development partly for this reason: Memories of peak moments motivate students to keep improving in hopes of achieving the same intensity of experience again. One of the strongest predictors of engagement – whether students reported that their talent had been the source of flow – supports this interpretation. The question related to this topic asked them to recall whether their talent had produced flow; a positive response thus indicated that they had at some point experienced an optimal moment. Emphasizing the importance of optimal experience does not mean that every talent-related moment should be intrinsically rewarding. Doing schoolwork is not the most pleasant thing even for the most committed and talented of teenagers. The connection of optimal experience to talent development should not daunt teachers who do not see rows of smiling faces in their classrooms.

It is perhaps encouraging to know that a few moments in a person's past can have such an energizing effect. A musician in an earlier study recalled his first strong flow experience: improvising before a live audience. He was 16 years old at the time, and the thought of a live performance was still intimidating. His self-consciousness was one factor that had prevented him from letting go and risking genuine improvisation. The flow experience, however, made enough of an impact that he recorded the date, time, and name of the song, along with his impressions, on a piece of paper and stuck it in the back of his guitar. Understanding the experience and how to regain it became a conscious goal, and he tried to find books that would help explain the workings of his mind. After several years he realized that such experiences often came after weeks of practicing some new skill, for example, a new scale or new fingering, and then attempting to use it while improvising. When the skill had become second nature and he risked improvising with it, he would sometimes become totally involved in an enjoyable experience. In the state of flow, he described feeling more in sync with the rhythm of the music and with his own emotions when playing something "new" with perfect execution.

In summary, talented teens had skills that were considered useful and were supported by recognized fields and domains. Second, they had personalities conducive to both hard work and openness to experience, which also made them less sex stereotyped and better prepared to sustain and expand their interests. Third, talented teenagers had cultivated efficient life habits, such as spending more time alone and with family, less time socializing, and more time in productive activities with peers, which economized their attention and diverted more of their energy into their talents. A fourth finding is related to the preceding one: Talented teens had more conservative orientations toward sex and toward opposite-sex peer relations, which helped them keep the tumultuous changes of puberty in perspective. Fifth, those talented teens who reported more integrated and differentiated home environments also reported a higher quality of experience in productive activities and performed better in school. Sixth, talented students were most influenced by teachers who created, like autotelic families, a context in which they felt supported and stimulated. Seventh, talent development was enhanced by modes of involvement that were both expressive and instrumental and both satisfying at the moment and promising of long-term rewards. Committed students in the arts and in the sciences were able to avoid the unproductive impasses that result when these two modes are seen as dichotomies. Finally, engagement with a talent was enhanced by the association of optimal experience with talent-related work.

A THEORETICAL MODEL: COMPLEXITY AND
THE DEVELOPMENT OF TALENT

The main findings summarized above reflect a diversity of factors associated with the development of talent. In this final section we shall review the implication of the study from a holistic perspective and suggest how the particular findings reflect a coherent pattern. We refer to the organizing principle that we have used to make sense out of the findings as psychological complexity, or the simultaneous presence of differentiating and integrating processes. The tensions that talented teens showed in their personalities, habits, families, and experience can, we argue, be seen as instances modeled on this general dialectical principle. Such a model does not spring full blown from this study or its data. In fact, there is precedent for it in the writings of William James and John Dewey, and their views will also be examined in order to provide a historical context for these observations.

When we look across the findings it seems that there are contradictions and incongruities, not among the findings but within them. What are we to make of a person who is oriented to hard work but who pays attention to ideas and sensations because they are interesting? who is warm and cooperative with other members of the family and yet is strongly independent? who spends more time with the family and more time alone than average teens? who likes those teachers best who demand hard work but are also fun? who acts a bit like an artist and a bit like a scientist? who enjoys the moment and yet looks ahead to the future? who feels skillful and yet feels challenged? Such a person is, like a good bottle of wine, complex and surprising, multidimensional, and likely to improve with age. At first glance it may seem that we have a group of confused individuals and a collection of perplexing results, yet we suggest that the apparent contradictions add up to a coherent pattern.

If complexity is defined as the simultaneous presence of processes that integrate and differentiate, then what our findings say is that talents are themselves a complex phenomenon and that they develop along lines of complexity, that is, through processes of integration and differentiation. A student may be always curious, but without perseverance the fruits of curiosity will be dissipated. Students who always relied on their families would not learn to stand by themselves, whereas if they rejected their families too early they might never have the strength to stand alone. Too much time alone might lead to detachment; too much time with others, to conformity. If students liked only teachers who were fun, they would become frivolous; if they liked only teachers who told them what to do, they would become compliant; and so on. If attention is so integrated that a person is never able to discover new things, then that person stops growing.

Development proceeds in a spiral process, building upon what has already been mastered as a basis for exploring the unknown and then working that into the existing pattern, thereby changing it. It is thus difficult to study talent development, or human development in general, without a flexible model that can identify patterns such as those that emerged in the present study. Some of the great psychologists and philosophers of the recent past anticipated this fact and worked toward building such a model.

James and Dewey: A context for the study of experience

Carl Jung argued that some archetypes, or patterns, recur in various cultures and times as manifestations of the collective unconscious.[3] Among these, his central interest was in dialectical patterns as represented in various trinity symbols. He pointed out the similarity, for instance, in the Egyptian, Platonic, and Christian trinities: Each developed out of unity, division, and resynthesis. It would not be difficult to list other thinkers, such as Hegel and Piaget, who worked out similar dialectical systems and had tremendous influence on modern conceptions of consciousness. The model of psychological complexity that we put forward suggests a similar movement: from integration to differentiation to (re)integration and then on again to a new cycle. Perhaps this pattern can be explained by reference to a collective archetype; it seems more likely, however, that it is better explained in terms of how attention is used in consciousness. William James and John Dewey took the latter approach and developed dialectical models based on experience.

James spoke of two "sister passions":

Our pleasure at finding that a chaos of facts is the expression of a single underlying fact is like the relief of the musician at resolving a confused mass of sound into a melodic or harmonic order. . . . The passion for parsimony, for the economy of means in thought, is the philosophic passion *par excellence*. . . . But alongside of this passion for simplification there exists a sister passion. . . . This is the passion for distinguishing; it is the impulse to be *acquainted* with the parts rather than to comprehend the whole.[4]

James disparaged neither of these passions. On the contrary, he saw them as complementary and felt that the appropriate philosophical attitude rested on a balance of these two uses of attention – hence his description of the entire man (and woman) in the fullness of living:

When weary of the concrete clash [of multiplicity] . . . he will refresh himself by a bath in the eternal springs [of unity]. . . . But he will only be a visitor . . . and when tired of the grey monotony of her problems . . . will always escape gleefully into the . . . richness of the concrete world.[5]

A dialectic is thus proposed between multiplicity and unity that is motivated by subjective states, namely, the need for "refreshment," the elimination of "monotony" and feeling "tired," and the "gleeful" escape into the "richness" of the world. Such a dialectic is never satisfied but is always propelled forward:

Hence the unsatisfactoriness of all our speculations. On the one hand, so far as they retain any multiplicity in their terms, they fail to get us out of the empirical sand-heap world; on the other, so far as they eliminate multiplicity the practical man despises their empty barrenness.[6]

James argued that systems of philosophy that either eliminated one of these needs or subordinated one to the other would never find universal acceptance: They would simply not be satisfying or interesting enough and therefore would not be *liked*.[7] He comments, "The only possible philosophy must be a compromise between an abstract monotony and a concrete heterogeneity." A balance of these two cravings allows fullness of living; it allows for satisfaction of the two human interests, the need to act *with* and the need to act *against*. The former we call an integrating process of attention, and the latter, a differentiating one.

Even a passing glance at Dewey's many writings on experience reveals a strong similarity to James. Dewey also proposed an optimal balance of contrasting qualities that he thought generated a productive *rhythm*. He juxtaposed a wide variety of terms that attempted, from various angles, to express the essence of his dialectical argument: direct–indirect, synthesis–analysis, implicit–explicit, emotion–intellect, near–remoted, sense–mind, unconscious–conscious, passive–active, concrete–abstract, identification–discrimination, apprehension–comprehension, perception–recognition, immediate–mediate, and so on. Dewey, like James, was suggesting that attention is drawn back and forth between modes of consciousness, and anything less than this – anything that subordinates or eliminates one or the other possibility – is not satisfying. In other words, the dynamic movement between them is propelled by the positive subjective reactions they engender.

In light of these comments, one can grasp Dewey's meaning in the comment "To be playful and serious at the same time . . . defines the ideal mental condition."[8] In such a mode of "serious play," both uses of attention can be exercised, and the enemies of education – fooling (playful curiosity without serious work) and drudgery (work without play) – are avoided.[9] Thus Dewey postulated that the ideal conditions for optimal interest, for example in a classroom, were ones that facilitated a student's momentary enjoyment while making her or him work toward long-term goals. When this intrinsic connection motivates attention, the ideal conditions exist for education.

These comments are sufficient to suggest a resemblance between the views of Dewey and James and the integration–differentiation model proposed in the present study. A further similarity between them is that the quality of subjective experience is emphasized and seen to depend upon the free or flexible movement of attention. Both James and Dewey placed great importance on what we refer to as optimal experiences. "For to miss the joy is to miss all," says James, quoting Robert Louis Stevenson. "In the joy of the actors lies the sense of any action. That is the explanation, that the excuse."[10] And later: "Yet in what other *kind* of value can the preciousness of any hour consist . . . if it consists not in feelings of excited significance like these?"[11] Comments Dewey about education, "Everything depends upon the *quality* of experience which is had."[12]

Given these concerns with experience, James envisioned a science of psychology at the turn of the century that was very different from contemporary cognitive psychology, of which he is often considered the father. The following clearly portray his views:

The problem [of education] is . . . how can men be trained up to their most useful [optimum] pitch of energy. . . . "energy" and "maximum" may easily suggest only *quantity* to the reader's mind, whereas . . . qualities as well as quantities have to be taken into account.[13]

Admit so much, then, and admit also that the charge of being inferior to their full self [optimum energy] is far truer of some men than of others; then the practical question ensues: to what do the better men owe their escape? and, in the fluctuations which all men feel in their own degree of energizing, to what are the improvements due, when they occur?[14]

The two questions, first, that of the possible extent of our powers; and second, that of the various avenues of approach to them, the various keys for unlocking them in diverse individuals, dominate the whole problem of individual and national education. We need a topography of the limits of human power. . . . we need also a study of the various types of human being with reference to the different ways in which their energy-reserves may be appealed to and let loose. Biographies and individual experiences of every kind may be drawn upon for evidence here.[15]

James felt that when these questions were taken as a methodological program for scientific research, "the whole of mental science and the science of conduct would find a place under them."[16] Unfortunately, James did not develop his views about a balance of multiplicity and unity and relate them systematically to "optimum energy," nor was he able to carry out a "topography of the limits of human power." Cognitive science took up James's agenda of attention; it considered seriously the importance of subjective perceptions, but emphasized only the rational forms in which psychic energy is invested.

With the face of education in the United States changing so dramatically in the last few decades and diversity becoming the norm, it might be argued that nothing very useful could be learned from studying a group of relatively well-off and talented teenagers such as the ones described in this book. However, if it is true, as James implies, that some individuals are more true to their optimum pitch of energy than the rest, and that it is an important task for psychology to discover the conditions that lead to this occurrence, then studies of talented students can fill an important role in contemporary research. If a person is curious about how the full extent of human potential can be reached, then it makes sense to study exceptionally talented individuals at their best moments (and also, but not exclusively, the most disturbed at their most pathological). To learn what psychological, social, and cultural conditions facilitate peaks is, as James has pointed out, a research agenda that has barely begun – even now.

The adolescents in our study were relatively free of the typical and obvious constraints on development. Few were ravaged by deep family conflicts or by lack of financial resources or support at home, and thus they made visible the more subtle processes that enable optimum levels of energy to be reached. If we wish for a yardstick by which to evaluate human development, and if we can no longer expect to find such standards in a priori universal principles, then studies of actual talented individuals – topographies of the heights of human power – might fill the gap.

A yardstick is needed now more than ever. All too often these days our notions as to what constitutes the best context for growth oscillate between endorsing a rigid sense of discipline and conformity on the one hand and valuing a completely unfettered personal freedom and independence on the other. It seems to be either the three R's or do your own thing. Yet those who have thought about such matters at least since Aristotle have realized that ideal growth involves a person's achieving excellence relative to her or his unique potential. Yet excellence cannot be idiosyncratic; it depends on the recognition and approbation of a community. Hence the ideal must involve a struggle to express one's individuality in ways that are meaningful to others.

As adults responsible for the growth of the next generation we should know that we are not doing our jobs unless we provide youth with opportunities to live right – that is, with chances to do their best. A just society is one in which men and women, rich and poor, the gifted and the handicapped, have an equal opportunity to use and to increase all their abilities, each according to her or his talents. We are still a long way from reaching that goal, but every step we take in that direction will make life richer and more meaningful for all.

NOTES

1 Hilde Domin, "Ich schreibe, weil ich schreibe," in *Von der Natur nicht vorgesehen: Autobiographisches* (Munich: Piper, 1974). One English translation of these lines loses their rhythm while retaining their content:

> One must know how to go away
> and yet be like a tree.
> As if the roots stayed in the earth,
> as if the landscape moved and we stood still

(Trans. Tudor Morris as "I write because I write," *Stand, 17* [n.d.], 36–39 [p. 38].

2 Greenberger & Steinberg, 1986.
3 Jung, 1958.
4 James, 1890/1950, pp. 126–27.
5 Ibid., p. 130.
6 Ibid., p. 129.
7 Ibid., pp. 128–30.
8 Dewey, 1933, p. 286.
9 Rathunde, 1991a, in press.
10 James, 1917, p. 7.
11 Ibid., p. 13.
12 Dewey, 1938, p. 27.
13 James, 1917, p. 42.
14 Ibid., p. 45.
15 Ibid., p. 57.
16 Ibid., p. 44.

Appendixes

Summary of ESM primary location codings and their frequency in final ESM sampling

Location category	No. of signals	%
In school (nontalent)		
In school (general)	120	1.5
Classroom	1,306	16.7
Halls & locker areas	269	3.4
Library	154	2.0
Cafeteria	254	3.3
Student center	126	1.6
School grounds or bus	58	0.7
Extracurricular settings	32	0.4
Other	52	0.7
In school (talent-related)		
Class: Math	395	5.1
Science	335	4.3
Music	85	1.1
Art	56	0.7
P.E.	140	1.8
Extracurricular: Music	153	2.0
Athletics	43	0.6
Art	6	0.1

Location category	No. of signals	%
In public		
Walking or biking outside	258	3.3
In automobile	177	2.3
On public transit	5	0.1
At friend's house	312	4.0
At work	137	1.8
Shop or restaurant	149	1.9
Recreational facility	38	0.5
Entertainment setting	56	0.7
Religious setting	44	0.6
At home		
At home (general)	371	4.7
Own bedroom	905	11.6
Other's bedroom	40	0.5
Kitchen	463	5.9
Dining room	176	2.3
Living room	455	5.8
Den or family room	346	4.4
Bathroom	116	1.4
Basement	105	1.3
Yard or garage	24	0.3
Uncodable	50	0.6
Total	7,811	100.0

APPENDIX 3.2

Summary of ESM primary activity codings and their frequency in final ESM sampling

Activity category	No. of signals	%[a]
Productive: Nontalent		
Classroom activities	1,745	22.3
Homework & studying	526	6.7
Preparing for exams	57	0.7

Activity category	No. of signals	%[a]
Extracurriculars	34	0.4
Job-related	102	1.3
Productive: Talent		
Homework & studying	247	3.2
Preparing for exams	33	0.4
Extracurricular: Academic	42	0.5
Music	180	2.3
Athletics	84	1.1
Art	26	0.3
Leisure		
Socializing	836	10.7
Telephoning	175	2.2
Playing (informal games etc.)	83	1.1
Watching TV	715	9.2
Attending media or events	64	0.8
Listening to music	94	1.2
Reading	234	3.0
Hobbies (nontalent)	44	0.6
Thinking & reflecting	299	3.8
Shopping	42	0.5
Personal maintenance		
Eating	374	4.8
Grooming	393	5.0
Transportation	414	5.2
Chores & errands	361	4.6
Resting or sitting	244	3.1
Miscellaneous	304	3.8
Uncodable	59	0.8
Total	7,811	100.0

[a]These frequencies do not reflect exactly the time spent in different activities, because more signals were sent when school was in session in order to get as many examples of productive activities as possible. Weighted frequencies that compensate for oversampling are reported in Table 5.1.

APPENDIX 3.3

Summary of ESM primary companionship codings and their frequency in final ESM sampling

Companion categories	No. of signals	%[a]
Family members only		
Mother alone	266	3.4
Father alone	141	1.8
Siblings alone	485	6.2
Mother & father	150	1.9
Mother & siblings	137	1.8
Father & siblings	78	1.0
Other relatives	4	0.1
Mixed family gatherings	57	0.7
School-related		
Classmates and teacher	2,255	28.9
School adult alone	44	0.6
Friends		
Friends only	1,608	20.5
Friends and family members	122	1.6
Alone		
In solitude	1,957	25.1
In public among strangers	334	4.3
Others (includes boss and co-workers)	101	1.2
Uncodable	72	0.9
Total	7,811	100.0

[a]These frequencies do not reflect exactly the time spent with different companions, because more signals were sent when school was in session in order to get as many examples of companionship in productive activities as possible. Weighted frequencies that compensate for oversampling are reported in Table 5.2.

APPENDIX 3.4

Summary of questions contained in open-ended personal interview
(Study Phase 1)

PART I: PERSONAL EXPERIENCES

1. (SELF-CONCEPT) So far we've given you a lot of forms to fill out. Now we want to give you a chance to tell us about yourself. How would you describe yourself? What do you like and dislike about yourself? What kinds of activities are important to you?

2. (PERSONAL INFLUENCES) Now I have some questions about what made you the person you are now, the influences that have shaped your personality, your experiences, and plans. I'd like you to start as far back as you can remember and tell me about influences you remember over your life until now. You can take your time in thinking about this.

3. (PRESENT GOALS AND PERSONAL CHALLENGES) In your present life, what would you say your most important goal is? What do you see as the main challenge facing you in the next few years? (*Note:* Students were probed for academic, occupational, and personal goals.)

4. (MOTIVATION FOR GOALS) Why did you come to see this as being the most important goal/challenge for your future?

PART II: TALENT DEVELOPMENT

1. (FOR MULTITALENTED STUDENTS) Which of the following subjects is the most important to you? [Interviewer lists student's talent areas.]

2. (FOR SINGLE-TALENT STUDENTS) We know that you are particularly involved with [talent area]. Is there anything else you are as interested in as you are in [talent]?

[*Note:* The remaining questions were posed with regard to the preferred or single talent area. If time remained, effort was made to pose the same questions regarding nonpreferred talents and/or new areas of personal interest.]

3. Can you tell me how long you have been interested in [talent]?

4. How did you first get interested in [talent]?

5. Did anyone encourage you in [talent]?

6. When did you first start formal training in [talent]?

7. (GOOD AND BAD TIMES) What was your training in [talent] after that? Were there any particularly good or bad times that you remember?

8. Currently, how do you feel about your interest in [talent]?
9. When do you enjoy [talent] most?
10. Do you think that you will continue with this subject through high school? If not, why not?
11. Will you major in this subject in college?
12. What role do you think this subject will play in your adult life?
13. Following is a list of reasons why some people pursue [talent area]. I'd like you to rate how important that reason is to you on a scale of one to 6 [1 = *completely irrelevant;* 6 = *very important*].
    a. My friends like it and I like their company
    b. I enjoy it.
    c. I'm good at it.
    d. It's required.
    e. It's competitive and I like to compete.
    f. It's something that will be useful for earning a living.
    g. It's something I get good grades in.
    h. It's interesting to me.
    i. It's something that impresses other people.
    j. It's something that girls/boys are supposed to be good at.
    k. I get satisfaction from getting better or learning.
    l. It's a way to get away from my problems.
    m. Other. [write-in]

APPENDIX 3.5

Questions drawn from parental questionnaire (Study Phase 1)

I. DEMOGRAPHIC INFORMATION

1. What is the last year of schooling you completed?
    SCALE: *last grammar school grade* (1) to *graduate/professional school* (4)
2. What is your total family income before taxes?
    SCALE: *under $10,000* (1) to *$200,000 or more* (8)
3. List current occupation. [*Note:* When parental report was unavailable, occupational information was drawn secondarily from student's induction questionnaire.]

II. PARENTAL LIFE SATISFACTION

1. All things considered, how satisfied are you with what you are doing for a living (. . . with being a homemaker)? Circle the number that comes closest to how satisfied or dissatisfied you feel.

    SCALE: *completely satisfied* (1) to *completely dissatisfied* (7)

III. PARENTAL DISAGREEMENT

1. State the approximate extent of agreement or disagreement between you and your mate on the following items. Circle the number under the column that best describes your relationship: handling family finances; matters of recreation; demonstrations of affection; friends; sex relations; conventionality (right/good conduct); philosophy of life; ways of dealing with in-laws.

    SCALE: *always agree* (1) to *always disagree* (6)

IV. PARENTAL INTRINSIC EXPECTATIONS

1. In terms of your child's future job or career, how much would you prefer that each of the following qualities characterize her/his job: enjoyment; job fitting interests and skills; opportunity for learning; sense of accomplishment and acceptance; challenging/stimulating work.

    SCALE: *not important* (1) to *very important* (5)

V. PARENTAL EXTRINSIC EXPECTATIONS

1. In terms of your child's future job or career, how much would you prefer that each of the following qualities characterize her/his job: good income; flexible hours; getting to make decisions; opportunity for advancement; job security; appreciation and recognition; prestige; getting out of the house.

    SCALE: *not important* (1) to *very important* (5)

VI. PARENTAL REWARDS MEASURE

1. In thinking about your child in the study, to what extent is each of the following rewarding: the pleasure you get from his/her accomplishments; helping her/him develop; the love s/he shows; feeling proud of how s/he is turning out; liking the person s/he is; enjoying doing things with her/him; being

special and irreplaceable; seeing him/her mature and change; the way s/he
gets along with siblings.

SCALE: *not at all* (1) to *extremely* (4)

VII. PARENTAL INSTRUMENTAL REWARDS

1. In thinking about your child in the study, to what extent is each of the following
   rewarding: being needed by him/her; being able to go to her/him with problems; the help s/he gives me; the meaning and purpose s/he gives me; the way
   s/he helps to change me for the better.

   SCALE: *not at all* (1) to *extremely* (4)

APPENDIX 3.6A

Mathematics mastery level codings

Level	Course or achievement
0	No participation
1	Algebra 1/2s
	Algebra 1/2A
2	A Algebra 1/2A
	Computer Programming
3	Plane Geometry 1/2
	Plane Geometry 1/2A
4	Geometry 1/2A
	Advanced Algebra 1/2
	Advanced Computer Science
5	Advanced Algebra/Trig 1/2A
	Trigonometry (238)
6	College Algebra/Trig 1/2A
	College Algebra (2462)
7	Probability & Statistics A (247)
	Analytic Geometry A (248)
	AP college Computer Science
8	AP Calculus 1/2AB
9	AP Calculus 1/2BC

APPENDIX 3.6A *(cont.)*

Level	Course or achievement
10	Advanced math 1/2A Senior mathematics award winner
11	University-level math course

APPENDIX 3.6B

Science mastery level codings

Level	Course or achievement
0	No participation
1	Biology 1/2 Biology 1/2A
2	Earth Science 1/2
3	Earth Science 1/2A Anthropology Aviation Science Environmental Science
4	Geology 1/2 Introduction to Chemistry 1/2 Physics 1/2P Astronomy
5	Physics 1/2 Chemistry 1/2
6	Chemistry 1/2A Physics 1/2A
7	Sophomore/junior departmental science awards
8	AP Biology AP Chemistry AP Physics
9	Senior departmental science awards
10	Regional/national recognition in science

Music mastery level codings

Level	Course or achievement	
	School 1	School 2
0	No participation	No participation
1	Fundamentals of Music Rock to Bach Beginner Guitar	American Music Freshman Chorus Beginner Guitar
2	Aeolian Choir Apollo Choir Concert Band Year 1 Concert Orchestra Year 1	Freshman Chorus Concert Band International Folk Guitar
3	Lyrian Choir Concert Band Years 2/4 Concert Orchestra Years 2/4 Applied Music Year 1	Sophomore Chorus Advanced Concert Band Vocal Technique Year 1
4	Treble Choir Varsity Choir Wind Ensemble Year 1 Symphonic Orchestra Year 1 Applied Music Years 2/4	Concert Choir Year 1 Symphonic Band Year 1 Symphonic Orchestra Year 1 Vocal Technique Years 2/4
5	OPRF Singers Year 1 Wind Ensemble Year 2/4 Jazz Ensemble Year 1 Symphonic Orchestra Year 2	Concert Choir Years 2/4 Symphonic Band Year 2 Symphonic Orchestra Year 2 Jazz Band Year 1
6	OPRF Singers Years 2/4 A Capella Choir Jazz Ensemble Years 2/4 Symphonic Orchestra Years 3/4	Varsity Choir Jazz Band Years 2/4 Symphonic Band Years 3/4 Symphonic Orchestra Years 3/4
7	Harmonic Theory Music Literature Years 1/2	Music Theory
8	Regional or state selection or other recognition	Same
9	All-State Vocalist or Instrumentalist Major competition finalist	Same
10	Music scholarship winner	Same

APPENDIX 3.6D

Athletics mastery level codings

Level	Description
0	No participation
1	Certificate of participation
2	Class numeral
3	Junior Varsity/Minor award certificate
4	Varsity/Major award certificate Years 1 & 2
5	Varsity/Major award certificate Years 3 & 4
6	Starting member of championship team (Varsity – conference level or higher)
7	Most Valuable Player (MVP) *Pioneer Press* Athlete of the Week *Chicago Tribune* Athlete of the Week
8	All-Area/All-Conference/All-Regional designate
9	Participates in State championship tourney on individual or small group level (4 or fewer competitors)
10	State championship finalist on small group level (4 or fewer competitors) All-State selection – second team
11	Individual state championship finalist All-State first team All-American selection

APPENDIX 3.6E

Art mastery level codings

Level	Course or achievement
0	Art for Non-Artists/No participation
1	Art Foundations Introduction to Drawing and Design Introduction to Ceramics/Jewelry Photography

APPENDIX 3.6E *(cont.)*

Level	Course or achievement
	Fashion Design and Illustration
	Architectural Drafting (Level 3)
	Introduction to Drafting
	Drafting Technology
2	Intermediate Drawing and Painting
	2-D Studio
	Commercial Design
	Intermediate Ceramics
	3-D Studio
	Advanced Photography
	Film Art
	Intermediate Jewelry
	Advanced Drafting (Level 3)
	Architectural Drafting (Level 4)
3	Advanced Drawing and Painting (Level 3)
	Advanced Commercial Design
	Advanced Ceramics
	Advanced Jewelry
	Advanced Drafting (Level 4 or 5)
	Architectural Drafting (Level 5)
4	Advanced Drawing and Painting (Level 4)
	AP Art History
5	Visual Arts Contract 3, 4
6	Visual Arts Contract 5
7	Awards or formal recognition for excellence in art competitions
8	Postsecondary art scholarship

APPENDIX 3.7

Sample teacher assessment form (Study Phase 2)

The following questions were designed to elicit the opinions of talent-area teachers about the level of development of each subject, on 7-point scales:

1. Compared to his/her potential, this student is performing
   (0 = *far below potential;* 6 = *at full potential*)

2. On the whole, this student's attention is
   (0 = *very focused;* 6 = *very scattered*)
3. Given a choice, this student prefers activities that are
   (0 = *easy to master;* 6 = *difficult to master*)
4. Does this student become deeply involved in the work at hand?
   (0 = *always;* 6 = *never*)
5. To what extent does this student's performance reflect originality or a unique personal style?
   (0 = *very little;* 6 = *very greatly*)
6. Is this student able to pursue work independent of supervision?
   (0 = *never;* 6 = *always*)
7. Does this student enjoy the challenges encountered in doing [his/her talent area]?
   (0 = *never;* 6 = *always*)
8. Compared with other students in advanced [talent] classes, this student possesses talent that is
   (0 = *below average;* 6 = *above average*)
9. Does this student possess the ability to pursue a career in [talent area]?
   (0 = *definitely no;* 6 = *definitely yes*)
10. Does this student possess the interest to seek a career in [talent area]?
   (0 = *definitely no;* 6 = *definitely yes*)

APPENDIX 3.8

Summary of questions relating to flow experience (Study Phase 2)

A. Flow Descriptions

Subjects rate each of four experiences for (*a*) if they experience it; (*b*) which activity most often provides it; (*c*) how often generally [1 = *few times a year*/7 = *few times a day*]; (*d*) how often in four specific settings (alone, with family, with friends, and with classmates).

1. Do you ever do something where your concentration is so intense, your attention so undivided and wrapped up in what you are doing that you sometimes become unaware of things you normally notice (for instance, other people talking, loud noises, the passage of time, being hungry or tired, having an appointment, having some physical discomfort)?
2. Do you ever do something where your skills have become so "second nature" that sometimes everything seems to come to you "naturally" or "effortlessly,"

and where you feel confident that you will be ready to meet any new challenges?

3. Do you ever do something where you feel that the activity is worth doing in itself? In other words, even if there were no other benefits associated with it (for instance, financial reward, improved skills, recognition from others, and so on), you would still do it?

4. Do you ever do something that has provided some unique and very memorable moments – for which you feel extremely lucky and grateful – that has changed your perspective on life (or yourself) in some way?

B. Flow Scale (Mayers, 1978)

Subjects rate the intensity of the eleven experiences below in the following activity situations: their primary flow activity; most challenging school subject; favorite activity; being with family; watching TV; doing homework.

1. I get involved
2. I clearly know what I am supposed to do
3. I feel I can handle the demands of the situation
4. I tend to get bored doing it
5. I would do it even if I didn't have to
6. I feel cheerful
7. I feel good about myself
8. I get distracted
9. I feel strong
10. It is important to me
11. It makes me feel anxious

C. Personal Interests Survey

The following questions were designed to assess each teenager's level of commitment to talent development. Each student received a questionnaire with her or his talent area(s) circled. Students assessed their talent areas by placing the number of each talent in the blank next to the appropriate response.

(1 Math   2 Science   3 Music   4 Athletics   5 Art)

1. How often do you do things related to the areas circled right now?
   _____ a. every day
   _____ b. once or twice every week
   _____ c. more than once a month

_____ d. less than once a month

_____ e. never

2. How would you compare your interest in (the areas circled) now to two years ago?

_____ a. become more interested

_____ b. interest remains unchanged

_____ c. become less interested

3. How would you compare your skills in (the areas circled) now to two years ago?

_____ a. improved

_____ b. the same

_____ c. worse

4. How would you compare the challenge of (the areas circled) now to two years ago?

_____ a. more challenging

_____ b. interest remains unchanged

_____ c. less challenging

5. Do you think that you will continue with (the areas circled) (current juniors) through high school? (current seniors) in college?

_____ a. yes

_____ b. not sure

_____ c. no

6. Do you think that you will continue with (the areas circled) as:

_____ a. an interest in college   Yes   No   Maybe

_____ b. a major in college   Yes   No   Maybe

APPENDIX 4.1A

Standardized achievement results for talented mathematics and science students

	Math (N = 40)	Science (N = 19)	Math/science (N = 28)
California Achievement			
Language	89.8	89.8	95.7
Mathematics	95.7	90.8	97.8*
PSAT Verbal	49.6	50.4	55.0*
	(90 %ile)	(90 %ile)	(95 %ile)
PSAT Mathematics	60.0	53.8	62.8**
	(90 %ile)	(88 %ile)	(92 %ile)

APPENDIX 4.1A *(cont.)*

	Math (N = 40)	Science (N = 19)	Math/science (N = 28)
SAT Verbal	558.6	578.3	618.6*
	(88 %ile)	(88 %ile)	(93 %ile)
Mathematics	655.7	613.9	691.8**
	(91 %ile)	(85 %ile)	(95 %ile)
ACT Verbal	24.4	24.6	27.2**
	(89 %ile)	(89 %ile)	(95 %ile)
Mathematics	29.1	27.6	32.70**
	(98 %ile)	(96 %ile)	(99 %ile)
Natural Science	29.5	29.9	31.6
	(99 %ile)	(99 %ile)	(99 %ile)

Note: Percentile comparisons against college-bound norms.

$*p < .05$; $**p < .01$, two-tailed significance: comparison of math/science students with single-talent students.

APPENDIX 4.1B

Academic achievement results for talented mathematics and science students during first 2 years of high school

	Math (N = 40)	Science (N = 19)	Math/science (N = 28)
Total grade point average	3.28	3.46	3.81**
Math grade point average	3.14	—	3.73***
Science grade point average	—	3.67	3.87*
Class rank percentile	85	90	96***

$*p < .05$; $**p < .01$; $***p < .001$, two-tailed significance: comparison of math/science students with single-talent students.

APPENDIX 4.1C

Athletic achievements of talented athletes and normal high school classmates by end of Grade 10

	Award level		
	Class numeral	Jr. Varsity	Varsity
Talented			
Male (N = 29)	29 (100%)	28 (97%)	5 (17%)
Female (N = 29)	29 (100%)	25 (86%)	15 (52%)
Total (N = 58)	58 (100%)	53 (91%)	20 (35%)
Normal			
Male (N = 844)	342 (41%)	281 (33%)	19 (2%)
Female (N = 867)	242 (28%)	177 (20%)	35 (4%)
Total (N = 1,711)	584 (34%)	458 (27%)	54 (3%)

Note: Percentage represents number of students who reached that level of achievement by the end of Grade 10.

APPENDIX 4.2

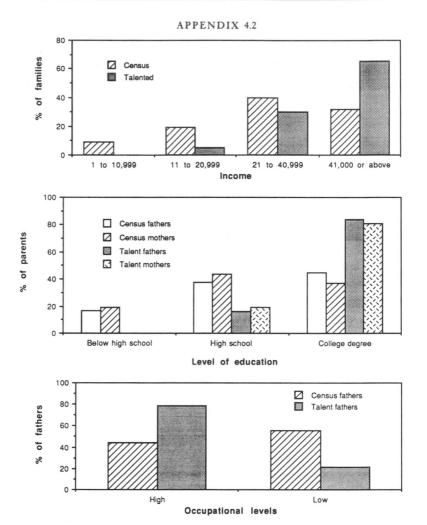

Appendix 4.2. The census figures refer to the communities in which the schools were located.

APPENDIX 8.1

Complex Family Questionnaire (CFQ) (Study Phase 2)

The following questions were rated on a 4-point scale: 1 - *definitely no; 2 = usually no; 3 = usually yes; 4 = definitely yes.*

1. Would you say there was much bickering and arguing in your family?
2. Are there objects around the house, e.g., photos, paintings, antiques, heirlooms, "prized possessions," and so on, that mean a lot (hold special memories) for family members?
3. Can family members find a quiet place at home to think?
4. Are other family members serious and intense when engaged with things that are important to them?
5. Are there clear rules that keep the house running smoothly?
6. If you are feeling depressed or are having a problem, do others notice even though you may not say anything about it?
7. Is it hard to find privacy and to escape into your "own world" at home when you need to?
8. Would you say your family is "religious" or "spiritual," even though they may not attend church regularly?
9. Do family members stay mad at one another for days?
10. Are family members critical of each other and insensitive to others' feelings?
11. When you get into something you really feel like doing, are you often interrupted by having to perform other family obligations?
12. Are members of your family indifferent to or apathetic about current world events or problems?
13. Is your home environment hectic or disorderly?
14. Does your family have traditional ways of celebrating birthdays and holidays that enhance a feeling of family togetherness and unity?
15. Do other family members modify their plans on your behalf?
16. Do you receive attention from other family members (are you sometimes the center of attention)?
17. Are members of your family consistent in their actions?
18. Is it clear to you and other family members who makes the final decisions on particular household matters, for instance, when to be home at night, if you can or cannot use the car, and so on?
19. Do you get the chance at home to listen to the music you like and watch television shows you like?
20. Is there a strong competitive spirit at home when family members play games or sports?
21. When family members do things together (for instance, go on vacations or go out to dinner), are you embarrassed or ashamed of your family?
22. Is it difficult for you to "be yourself," fool around, and have fun at home?
23. Are family members proud, do they work hard, and do they have ideals and values?
24. Are you shy or uncomfortable around your family?

APPENDIX 8.2

Family group comparison on adolescent PSAT scores and parental income and education

Variable	Complex	Integrated	Differentiated	Simple	F	p
PSAT ability score	101.7 (41)	104.3 (29)	98.5 (23)	101.8 (42)	0.40	NS
Parent education	3.4 (26)	3.1 (20)	3.5 (14)	3.3 (28)	1.30	NS
Parent income	4.8 (26)	4.5 (20)	4.6 (14)	4.4 (28)	0.32	NS

Note: The numbers in parentheses for parent education and income indicate the number of couples (mothers + fathers).

Education coding: 1 = < high school graduation, 2 = high school or some college, 3 = college degree, 4 = master's or beyond.

Income coding: 1 = < $10,999, 2 = $11–20,999, 3 = $21–40,999, 4 = $41–60,999, 5 = $61–80,999, 6 = $81–100,999, 7 = $101–200,999, 8 = $201,000 or above.

APPENDIX 8.3

Family group comparison on various confounding variables

Variable	Complex (n = 48) (%)	Integrated (n = 35) (%)	Differentiated (n = 26) (%)	Simple (n = 56) (%)	χ^2	p
Religion						
Protestant	32	31	48	33	9.98	NS
Catholic	32	34	26	46		
Jewish	4	3	4	2		
None	6	14	4	10		
Other	26	17	17	10		
Ethnic origin						
Caucasian	85	81	81	82	4.95	NS
African-American	2	6	5	2		
Hispanic	2	—	—	2		
Asian	2	3	5	8		
Other	9	9	9	6		
Talent area (preferred)						
Math	17	32	12	13	11.4	NS
Science	15	15	15	13		
Music	32	24	31	32		

APPENDIX 8.3 (cont.)

Variable	Complex (n = 48) (%)	Integrated (n = 35) (%)	Differentiated (n = 26) (%)	Simple (n = 56) (%)	χ^2	p
Athletics	23	12	31	21		
Art	9	15	8	18		
More than one	4	3	4	4		
Sex						
Male	40	43	50	46	0.91	NS
Female	60	57	50	54		
Sibling position						
First (or only)	44	32	42	34	1.73	NS
Second	56	68	58	66		
Family size						
1 or 2	77	65	81	73	2.38	NS
3 or more	23	35	19	27		
Marital status						
Married	90	94	92	80	4.80	NS
Divorced or reconstituted	10	6	8	20		

Note: Degree of freedom for ethnic origin and religion, 12; for talent area, 15; for remaining analyses, 3.

APPENDIX 10.1

Correlation between family SES variables and commitment to talent

	Teachers' Ratings	Subjective Commitment	Composite Engagement	Highest Talent Level
Father's education				
(*n* = 115)	−.01	.07	.04	.02
Mother's education				
(*n* = 151)	.04	.00	.02	−.11
Family income				
(*n* = 167)	.03	.11	.09	−.03

References

Ainsworth, M. D. S., Bell, S. M., & Stayton, D. J. (1971). Individual differences in strange-situation behavior of one-year-olds. In H. R. Schaffer (Ed.), *The origins of human social relations*. London: Academic Press.

Albert, R. S. (1990). Identity, experiences, and career choice among the exceptionally gifted and eminent. In M. A. Runco & R. S. Albert (Eds.), *Theories of creativity* (pp. 13–34). Newbury Park, CA: Sage.

Albert, R. S., & Runco, M. A. (1986). The achievement of eminence: A model of exceptionally gifted boys and their families. In R. J. Sternberg & J. E. Davidson (Eds.), *Conceptions of giftedness* (pp. 332–360). New York: Cambridge University Press.

Albert, R. S., & Runco, M. A. (1987). The possible different personality dispositions of scientists and nonscientists. In D. Jackson & J. P. Rushton (Eds.), *Scientific excellence: Origins and assessment* (pp. 67–97). Newbury Park, CA: Sage.

Aliotti, N. C. (1981). Intelligence, handedness, and cerebral hemispheric preference in gifted adolescents. *Gifted Child Quarterly, 25,* 36–41.

Amabile, T. M. (1983). *The social psychology of creativity.* New York: Springer-Verlag.

American Humane Association (1989). *Highlights of official aggregate child neglect and abuse reporting.* Denver, CO: Author.

Bamberger, J. (1982). Growing up prodigies: The midlife crisis. In D. H. Feldman (Ed.), *New directions for child development: Developmental approaches to giftedness and creativity.* San Francisco: Jossey-Bass.

Bamberger, J. (1986). Cognitive issues in the development of musically gifted children. In R. J. Sternberg & J. E. Davidson (Eds.), *Conceptions of giftedness* (pp. 388–413). New York: Cambridge University Press.

Barrileaux, L. E. (1961). High school science achievement as related to interest and IQ. *Educational and Psychological Measurement, 21,* 929–936.

Baumrind, D. (1987). A developmental perspective on adolescent risk taking behavior in contemporary America. In C. E. Irwin (Ed.), *Adolescent social behavior and health.* San Francisco: Jossey-Bass.

Beattie, O., & Csikszentmihalyi, M. (1981). On the socialization influence of books. *Child Psychology and Human Development, 11*(1), 3–18.

Beavers, W. R., & Voeller, M. N. (1983). Family models: Comparing and contrasting the Olson Circumplex model with the Beavers systems model. *Family Process, 22,* 85–96.

Benbow, C. P. (1991). Mathematically talented children: Can acceleration meet their educational needs? In N. Colangelo & G. A. Davis (Eds.), *The handbook of gifted education* (pp. 154–165). Boston: Allyn & Bacon.

Benbow, C. P., & Stanley, J. C. (1983). Sex differences in mathematical reasoning ability: More facts. *Science, 222,* 1026–1031.

Bertalanffy, L. von (1968). *General system theory: Foundations, development, applications.* New York: Braziller.

Bloom, B. S. (Ed.). (1985). *Developing talent in young people.* New York: Ballantine.

Bloom, B. S., & Sosniak, L. A. (1981). Talent development vs. schooling. *Educational Leadership, 39,* 86–94.

Blos, P. (1979). The second individuation process. In P. Blos (Ed.), *The adolescent passage: Developmental issues of adolescence.* New York: International Universities Press.

Buescher, T. M. (1987). Counseling gifted adolescents: A curriculum model for students, parents, and professionals. *Gifted Child Quarterly, 31,* 90–94.

Carney, J. (1986). *Intrinsic motivation in successful artists from early adulthood to middle age.* Unpublished doctoral dissertation, University of Chicago.

Carter, G. E. (1982). Assessing students' interests in chemistry. *British Journal of Educational Psychology, 52,* 378–380.

Carter, K. R., & Ormrod, J. E. (1982). Acquisition of formal operations by intellectually gifted children. *Gifted Child Quarterly, 26*(3), 110–115.

Castaneda, C. (1971). *A separate reality.* New York: Simon & Schuster.

Chandrasekhar, S. (1987). *Truth and beauty.* Chicago: University of Chicago Press.

Choe, I. (1991). *Types of motivation and their effects on adolescent subjective experience, time investment and achievement.* Unpublished manuscript, University of Chicago.

Cohler, B. J. (1982). Personal narrative and the life course. In P. Bates & O. G. Brim (Eds.), *Life span development and behavior* (Vol. 4). New York: Academic Press.

Colangelo, N., Assouline, S. G., & Ambroson, D. L. (Eds.). (1992). *Talent development: Proceedings from the 1991 Henry B. & Jocelyn Wallace National Research Symposium on Talent Development.* Unionville, NY: Trillium Press.

Cole, M., Gay, J., Glick, J. A., & Sharp, D. W. (1971). *The cultural context of learning and thinking*. New York: Basic.

Coleman, J. S. (1961). *The adolescent society*. New York: Free Press.

Cooke, G. J. (1980). Scientifically gifted children. *Gifted/Creative/Talented, 12*, 17–18.

Cooper, C. R., Grotevant, H. D., & Condon, S. M. (1983). Individuality and connectedness in the family as a context for adolescent identity formation and role-taking skill. In H. D. Grotevant & C. R. Cooper (Eds.), *Adolescent development in the family*. San Francisco: Jossey-Bass.

Csikszentmihalyi, M. (1975). *Beyond boredom and anxiety*. San Francisco: Jossey-Bass.

Csikszentmihalyi, M. (1978). Attention and the wholistic approach to behavior. In K. S. Pope & J. L. Singer (Eds.), *The stream of consciousness* (pp. 335–358). New York: Plenum.

Csikszentmihalyi, M. (1982). Towards a psychology of optimal experience. In L. Wheeler (Ed.), *Review of Personality and Social Psychology* (Vol. 2, pp. 13–36). Newbury Park, CA: Sage.

Csikszentmihalyi, M. (1985). Emergent motivation and the evolution of the self. In D. Kleiber & M. H. Maehr (Eds.), *Motivation in adulthood* (pp. 93–119). Greenwich, CT: JAI Press.

Csikszentmihalyi, M. (1988a). Society, culture, and person: A systems view of creativity. In R. J. Sternberg (Ed.), *The nature of creativity: Contemporary psychological perspectives* (pp. 325–339). New York: Cambridge University Press.

Csikszentmihalyi, M. (1988b). The ways of genes and memes. *Reality Club Review, 1*(1), 107–128.

Csikszentmihalyi, M. (1990a). *Flow: The psychology of optimal experience*. New York: Harper & Row.

Csikszentmihalyi, M. (1990b). The domain of creativity. In R. Albert & M. Runco (Eds.), *Theories of creativity* (pp. 190–214). Newbury Park, CA: Sage.

Csikszentmihalyi, M. (1990c). Literacy and intrinsic motivation. *Daedalus, 119*(2), 115–140. Reprinted in S. R. Graubard (Ed.), *Literacy*. New York: Hill & Wang.

Csikszentmihalyi, M., & Beattie, O. (1979). Life themes: A theoretical and empirical exploration of their origins and effects. *Journal of Humanistic Psychology, 19*, 45–63.

Csikszentmihalyi, M., & Csikszentmihalyi, I. S. (Eds.). (1988). *Optimal experience: Psychological studies of flow in consciousness*. New York: Cambridge University Press.

Csikszentmihalyi, M., & Larson, R. (1984). *Being adolescent*. New York: Basic.

Csikszentmihalyi, M., & Larson, R. (1987). Validity and reliability of the experience-sampling method. *Journal of Nervous and Mental Disease, 175*, 526–536.

Csikszentmihalyi, M., Larson, R., & Prescott, S. (1977). The ecology of adolescent activity and experience. *Journal of Youth and Adolescence, 6,* 281–294.

Csikszentmihalyi, M., & LeFevre, J. (1989). Optimal experience in work and leisure. *Journal of Personality and Social Psychology, 56*(5), 815–822.

Csikszentmihalyi, M., & McCormack, J. (1986, February). The influence of teachers. *Phi Delta Kappan,* pp. 415–419.

Csikszentmihalyi, M., & Nakamura, J. (1986, August). Optimal experience and the uses of talent. Paper presented at the 94th Annual Meeting of the American Psychological Association, Washington, DC.

Csikszentmihalyi, M., & Nakamura, J. (1989). The dynamics of intrinsic motivation. In R. Ames & C. Ames (Eds.), *Handbook of motivation theory and research* (Vol. 3, pp. 45–71). New York: Academic Press.

Csikszentmihalyi, M., & Robinson, R. (1986). Culture, time, and the development of talent. In R. J. Sternberg & J. E. Davidson (Eds.), *Conceptions of giftedness* (pp. 264–284). New York: Cambridge University Press.

Csikszentmihalyi, M., & Wong, M. (1991). The situational and personal correlates of happiness. In F. Strack, M. Argyle, & N. Schwarz (Eds.), *Subjective well-being* (pp. 193–212). Oxford: Pergamon Press.

Damon, W. (1983). *Social and personality development.* New York: Norton.

deCharms, R. (1976). *Enhancing motivation: Change in the classroom.* New York: Irvington.

Deci, E. L., & Ryan, R. M. (1985). *Intrinsic motivation and self-determination in human behavior.* New York: Plenum.

deVries, M. (1992). *The experience of psychopathology.* Cambridge: Cambridge University Press.

Dewey, J. (1913). *Interest and effort in education.* Cambridge, MA: Riverside Press.

Dewey, J. (1933). *How we think.* Lexington, MA: Heath.

Dewey, J. (1938). *Experience and education.* New York: Macmillan.

Dewey, J. (1980). *Art as experience.* New York: Perigee. (Originally published 1934)

Dirac, P. A. M. (1978). *Directions in physics.* New York: Wiley.

Dornbusch, S., Carlsmith, J., Bushwall, S., Ritter, P., Leiderman, H., Hastorf, A., & Gross, R. (1985). Single parents, extended households, and the control of adolescents. *Child Development, 56,* 326–341.

Dossey, J. A., Mullis, I. V. S., Lindquist, M. M., & Chambers, D. L. (1988). *The mathematics report card.* Princeton, NJ: Educational Testing Service.

Drake, S. (1978). *Galileo at work: His scientific biography.* Chicago: University of Chicago Press.

Dunn, S. E., Putallaz, M., Sheppard, B. H., & Lindstrom, R. (1987). Social support and adjustment in gifted adolescents. *Journal of Educational Psychology, 79,* 467–473.

Eccles, J. S., & Harold, R. D. (1992). Gender differences in educational and occupational patterns among the gifted. In N. Colangelo, S. G. Assouline, & D. L. Ambroson, *Talent development: Proceedings from the 1991 Henry B. & Jocelyn Wallace National Research Symposium on Talent Development* (pp. 2–30). Unionville, NY: Trillium Press.

Eccles, J. S., & Midgely, C. (1989). Optimal classroom environment in adolescence. In C. Ames & R. Ames (Eds.), *Research on motivation in education: Goals and cognitions* (Vol. 3, pp. 139–186). San Diego: Academic Press.

Erikson, E. H. (1968). *Identity: Youth and crisis.* New York: Norton.

Evans, K. M. (1971). *Attitudes and interests in education.* London: Routledge & Kegan Paul.

Fagen, R. M. (1981). *Animal play behavior.* New York: Oxford University Press.

Feldman, D. H. (1986). *Nature's gambit.* New York: Basic.

Fimian, M. J., & Cross, A. H. (1986). Stress and burnout among preadolescent and early adolescent gifted students: A preliminary investigation. *Journal of Early Adolescence, 6,* 246–267.

Frandsen, A., & Sorenson, M. (1969). Interests as motives in academic achievement. *Journal of School Psychology, 7,* 52–57.

Gadamer, H. (1986). *The relevance of the beautiful.* New York: Cambridge University Press.

Galbraith, J. (1985). The eight great gripes of gifted kids: Responding to special needs. *Roeper Review, 8,* 15–18.

Gardner, H. (1983). *Frames of mind: The theory of multiple intelligences.* New York: Basic.

Geffert, E. (1985). Motivationale Grundlagen der mathematischen Begabung. *Zeitschrift für Psychologie, 193,* 431–441.

Getzels, J. W., & Csikszentmihalyi, M. (1976). *The creative vision: A longitudinal study of problem-finding in art.* New York: Wiley Interscience.

Gilligan, C. (1982). *In a different voice.* Cambridge, MA: Harvard University Press.

Goertzel, V., & Goertzel, M. G. (1962). *Cradles of eminence.* Boston: Little, Brown.

Green, K., Fine, M. J., & Tollefson, N. (1988). Family systems characteristics and underachieving gifted adolescent males. *Gifted Child Quarterly, 32,* 267–272.

Greenberger, E., & Steinberg, L. (1986). *When teenagers work: The psychological and social costs of adolescent employment.* New York: Basic.

Griessman, B. E. (1987). *The achievement factors.* New York: Dodd, Mead.

Griffin, N., Chassin, L., & Young, R. D. (1981). Measurement of global self-concept versus multiple role-specific self-concepts in adolescence. *Adolescence, 16*(61), 49–56.

Groos, K. (1898). *The play of animals* (E. L. Baldwin, Trans.). New York: Appleton.

Hansen, R. A., & Neujahr, J. (1976). Career development of high school students talented in science. *Science Education, 60,* 453–462.

Hart, L. H., & Goldin-Meadow, S. (1984). The child as a non-egocentric art critic. *Child Development, 55,* 2122–2129.

Harris, I. B. (1990, October). Child development and the cycle of poverty. Keynote address, American Academy of Child and Adolescent Psychiatry Annual Meeting, Chicago.

Harter, S. (1978). Pleasure derived from optimal challenge and the effects of extrinsic rewards on children's difficulty level choices. *Child Development, 49,* 788–799.

Hasher, L., & Zacks, R. T. (1979). Automatic and effortful processes in memory. *Journal of Experimental Psychology: General, 108,* 356–388.

Hauser, A. (1951). *The social history of art.* New York: Knopf.

Hauser, S. T., Powers, S. I., Noam, G. G., Jacobson, A. M., Weiss, B., & Follansbee, D. J. (1984). Familial contexts of adolescent ego development. *Child Development, 55*(1), 195–213.

Henderson, B. B., & Gold, S. R. (1983). Intellectual styles: A comparison of factor structures in gifted and average children and adolescents. *Journal of Personality and Social Psychology, 45,* 624–632.

Henry, J. (1965). *Culture against man.* New York: Random House.

Hersh, R., & John-Steiner, V. (in press). A visitor to Hungarian mathematics. *Mathematical Intelligencer.*

Hidi, S. (1990). Interest and its contribution as a mental resource for learning. *Review of Educational Research, 60,* 549–571.

Hidi, S., & Baird, W. (1986). Interestingness – A neglected variable in discourse processing. *Cognitive Science, 10,* 179–194.

Hill, J. P. (1987). Research on adolescents and their families: Past and prospect. In C. E. Irwin (Ed.), *Adolescent social behavior and health.* San Francisco: Jossey-Bass.

Hodgkinson, H. L. (1985). *All one system: Demographics of education, kindergarten through graduate school.* Washington, DC: Institute for Educational Leadership.

Hoffman, J. E., Nelson, B., & Houck, M. (1983). The role of attentional resources in automatic detection. *Cognitive Psychology, 51,* 379–410.

Holton, G. (1988). *Thematic origins of scientific thought* (rev. ed.) Cambridge, MA: Harvard University Press. (Originally published 1973)

Hormuth, W. E. (1986). The sampling of experience in situ. *Journal of Personality, 54*(1), 262–293.

Inghilleri, P. (1986). La teoria del flusso di coscienza: Esperienza ottimale e sviluppo del se. In F. Massimini & P. Inghilleri (Eds.), *L'esperienza quotidiana: Teoria e metodo d'analisi* (pp. 85–106). Milan: Franco Angeli.

Irwin, C. E. (Ed.). (1987). *Adolescent social behavior and health.* San Francisco: Jossey-Bass.

Jackson, D. N. (1984). *Personality Research Form manual.* Goshen, NY: Research Psychologists Press.

James, W. (1917). *Selected papers on philosophy.* London: Dent.

James, W. (1950). *The principles of psychology.* New York: Dover. (Originally published 1890)

Janos, P. M. (1990). The self-perceptions of uncommonly bright youngsters. In R. J. Sternberg & J. Kolligian (Eds.), *Competence considered* (pp. 98–116). New Haven, CT: Yale University Press.

Jenson, A. R., Cohn, S. J., & Cohn, C. M. (1989). Speed of information processing in academically gifted youths and their siblings. *Personality and Individual Differences, 10,* 29–33.

Jones, L. R., Nullis, V. S., Raizen, S. A., Weiss, I. R., & Weston, E. A. (1992). *1990 science report card: NAEP's assessment of 4th, 8th and 12th grades.* Washington, DC: National Center for Educational Statistics, U.S. Department of Education.

Jung, C. (1958). A psychological approach to the dogma of the Trinity. In H. Read, M. Fordham, & G. Adler (Eds.), *Collected works* (Vol. 11). Princeton, NJ: Princeton University Press.

Kahneman, D. (1973). *Attention and effort.* Englewood Cliffs, NJ: Prentice-Hall.

Klein, G. (1990). *Om kreativitet och flow.* Stockholm: Brombergs.

Klint, K. A., & Weiss, M. R. (1986). Dropping in and dropping out: Participation motives of current and former youth gymnasts. *Canadian Journal of Applied Sport Sciences, 11,* 106–114.

Konner, M. (1991). *Childhood.* Boston: Little, Brown.

Kubey, R. (1984). *Leisure, television, and subjective experience.* Unpublished doctoral dissertation, University of Chicago.

Kubey, R., & Csikszentmihalyi, M. (1990). *Television and the quality of life.* Hillsdale, NJ: Erlbaum.

Kuhn, T. S. (1970). *The structure of scientific revolutions* (2d ed.). Chicago: University of Chicago Press.

Langer, S. (1957). *Philosophy in a new key.* Cambridge, MA: Harvard University Press.

Larson, R., & Csikszentmihalyi, M. (1978). Experiential correlates of solitude in adolescence. *Journal of Personality, 46*(4), 677–693.

Larson, R., Mannell, R., & Zuzanek, J. (1986). Daily well-being of older adults with family and friends. *Psychology and Aging, 1*(2), 117–126.

Lorek, P. (1989). *Family structure and academic achievement in talented adolescents.* Unpublished doctoral dissertation, University of Chicago.

Maccoby, E. E., & Martin, J. A. (1983). Socialization in the context of the family:

Parent–child interaction. In E. M. Heatherington (Ed.), *Handbook of child psychology: Vol. 4. Socialization, personality, and social development* (pp. 1–101). New York: Wiley.

MacIntyre, A. (1984). *After virtue: A study in moral theory.* Notre Dame, IN: University of Notre Dame Press.

Marr, D. B., & Sternberg, R. J. (1986). Analogical reasoning with novel concepts: Differential attention of intellectually gifted and nongifted children to relevant and irrelevant novel stimuli. *Cognitive Development, 1,* 53–72.

Maslow, A. H. (1968). *Toward a psychology of being.* New York: Van Nostrand.

Maslow, A. H. (1971). *The farther reaches of human nature.* New York: Viking.

Massimini, F., & Inghilleri, P. (Eds.). (1986). *L'esperienza quotidiana: Teoria e metodo d'analisi.* Milan: Franco Angeli.

Matas, L., Arend, R. A., & Sroufe, L. A. (1978). Continuity of adaptation in the second year: The relationship between quality of attachment and later competence. *Child Development, 49,* 547–556.

Mayers, P. (1978). *Flow in adolescence and its relation to school experience.* Unpublished doctoral dissertation, University of Chicago.

McCormack, J. (1984). *Interpersonal influences and the channeling of goals in adolescence.* Unpublished doctoral dissertation, University of Chicago.

McKnight, C., Crosswhite, F., Dossey, J., Kifer, E., Swafford, J., Travers, K., & Cooney, T. (1987). *The underachieving curriculum: Assessing U.S. school mathematics from an international perspective.* Champaign, IL: Stipes Publishing for International Association for the Evaluation of Educational Achievement.

Miller, P. J. (1982). *Amy, Wendy, and Beth: Learning language in South Baltimore.* Austin: University of Texas Press.

Mohan, J., & Jain, M. (1983). Intelligence and simple reaction time. *Asian Journal of Psychology and Education, 11,* 1–4.

Nakamura, J. (1988). Optimal experience and the uses of talent. In M. Csikszentmihalyi & I. S. Csikszentmihalyi (Eds.), *Optimal experience: Psychological studies of flow in consciousness* (pp. 319–326). New York: Cambridge University Press.

Nesselroade, J. R., & Baltes, P. B. (1974). *Adolescent personality development and historical change: 1970–1972.* Monographs of the Society for Research in Child Development, *39*(1, Serial No. 154). Chicago: University of Chicago Press.

Newland, T. (1976). *The gifted in socio-educational perspective.* Englewood Cliffs, NJ: Prentice-Hall.

Nicholls, J. G. (1990). What is ability and why are we mindful of it? A developmental perspective. In R. J. Sternberg & J. Kolligian, Jr. (Eds.), *Competence considered* (pp. 11–40). New Haven, CT: Yale University Press.

Oden, M. H. (1968). The fulfillment of promise: 40-year follow-up of the Terman gifted group. *Genetic Psychology Monographs, 77,* 3–93.

O'Donnell, J., & Andersen, D. G. (1977). Decision factors among women talented in math and science. *College Student Journal, 11*, 165–168.

Offer, D. (1969). *The psychological world of the teenager.* New York: Basic.

Offer, D., & Offer, J. B. (1975). *From teenager to young manhood: A psychological study.* New York: Basic.

Offer, D., Ostrov, E., & Howard, K. I. (1978). *The Offer Self-Image Questionnaire for Adolescents.* Chicago: Michael Reese Hospital & Medical Center.

Offer, D., Ostrov, E., & Howard, K. I. (1981). *The adolescent.* New York: Basic.

Offer, D., Ostrov, E., & Howard, K. I. (1982). Family perceptions of adolescent self-image. *Journal of Youth and Adolescence, 11*, 281–291.

Ogbu, J. U. (1978). *Minority education and caste: The American system in cross-cultural perspective.* New York: Academic Press.

Ogbu, J. U. (1990). Cultural mode, identity, and literacy. In J. W. Stigler, R. A. Shweder, & G. Herdt (Eds.), *Cultural psychology* (pp. 520–541). New York: Cambridge University Press.

Olson, D., Bell, R., & Porter, J. (1982). *Family adaptability and Cohesion Evaluation Scales II.* St. Paul: University of Minnesota Publications, Family Social Science Department.

Olson, D., Sprenkle, D., & Russell, C. (1979). Circumplex model of marital and family systems: I. Cohesion and adaptability dimensions, family types, and clinical applications. *Family Process, 18*, 3–28.

Osgood, C. E., Suci, G. J., & Tannenbaum, P. H. (1957). *The measurement of meaning.* Urbana: University of Illinois Press.

Piaget, J. (1977). *The development of thought: Equilibration of cognitive structures.* New York: Viking.

Pivik, R. T., Bylsma, F., Busby, K., & Sawyer, S. (1982). Interhemispheric EEG changes: Relationship to sleep and dreams in gifted adolescents. *Psychiatric Journal of the University of Ottawa, 7*, 56–76.

Plihal, J. E. (1982). *Intrinsic rewards in teaching.* Unpublished doctoral dissertation, University of Chicago.

Polanyi, M. (1958). *Personal knowledge.* Chicago: University of Chicago Press.

Prigogine, I. (1980). *From being to becoming: Time and complexity in the physical sciences.* San Francisco: Freeman.

Rathunde, K. (1988). Family context and optimal experience. In M. Csikszentmihalyi & I. Selega Csikszentmihalyi (Eds.), *Optimal experience: Psychological studies of flow in consciousness* (pp. 342–363). Cambridge: Cambridge University Press.

Rathunde, K. (1989a). The context of optimal experience: An exploratory model of the family. *New Ideas in Psychology, 7*, 91–97.

Rathunde, K. (1989b). *Family context and optimal experience in the development of talent.* Unpublished doctoral dissertation, University of Chicago.

Rathunde, K. (1991a, April). *A path with a heart: The role of interest in the development of talent.* Paper presented at the American Educational Research Association Annual Meeting (Motivation in Education Program), Chicago.

Rathunde, K. (1991b, April). *Family influences on student interest and talent development.* Paper presented at the American Educational Research Association Annual Meeting (Motivation in Education Program), Chicago.

Rathunde, K. (1992a). Playful and serious interest: Two faces of talent development in adolescence. In N. Colangelo, S. G. Assouline, & D. L. Ambroson (Eds.), *Talent development: Proceedings from the 1991 Henry B. & Jocelyn Wallace National Research Symposium on Talent Development* (pp. 320–324). Unionville, NY: Trillium Press.

Rathunde, K. (1992b). Serious play: Interest and adolescent talent development. In A. Krapp & M. Prenzel (Eds.), *Interesse, Lerner, Leistung* (pp. 137–164). Münster: Aschendorff.

Rathunde, K. (in press). The experience of interest: A theoretical and empirical look at its role in adolescent talent development. In P. Pintrich & M. Maehr (Eds.), *Advances in motivation and achievement* (Vol. 8). Greenwich, CT: JAI Press.

Rathunde, K., & Csikszentmihalyi, M. (1991a). Adolescent happiness and family interaction. In K. Pillemer & K. McCartney (Eds.), *Parent–child relations throughout life* (pp. 143–162). Hillsdale, NJ: Erlbaum.

Rathunde, K., & Csikszentmihalyi, M. (1991b). *Family context, interest, and adolescent school performance.* Manuscript submitted for publication.

Redding, R. E. (1989). Underachievement in the verbally gifted: Implications for pedagogy. *Psychology in the Schools, 26,* 275–291.

Rimm, S. B. (1991). Parenting the gifted adolescent: Special problems, special joys. In M. Bireley & J. Genshaft (Eds.), *Understanding the gifted adolescent* (pp. 18–32). New York: Teachers College Press.

Robinson, N. M., & Robinson, H. B. (1982). The optimal match: Devising the best compromise for the highly gifted student. *New Directions for Child Development, 17,* 79–94.

Rogers, C. R. (1961). *On becoming a person.* Boston: Houghton Mifflin.

Rossi, A. S. (1987). Parenthood in transition: From lineage to child to self-orientation. In J. B. Lancaster, J. Altmann, A. S. Rossi, & L. R. Sherrod (Eds.), *Parenting across the life span.* New York: Aldine De Gruyter.

Roth, J., & Sussman, S. (1974). *Educating gifted children.* Toronto: York Borough Board of Education.

Runco, M. A., & Okuda, S. M. (1988). Problem discovery, divergent thinking, and the creative process. *Journal of Youth and Adolescence, 17,* 211–220.

Schiefele, U. (1988). Motivationale Bedingungen des Textverstehens. *Zeitschrift für Pädagogik, 34,* 687–708.

Schiefele, U. (1991). Interest, learning, and motivation. *Educational Psychologist,* *26*(3–4), 299–323.

Schiefele, U., Winteler, A., & Krapp, A. (1991). *The measurement of study interest and its relation to other motivational variables and the use of learning strategies.* Unpublished manuscript, University of the Bundeswehr, Munich.

Schlick, M. (1934). Ueber das Fundament der Erkentniss. *Erkentniss, 4.* (English translation in A. J. Ayer [Ed.], *Logical positivism.* New York: Free Press, 1959).

Simon, H. A. (1969). *Sciences of the artificial.* Cambridge, MA: MIT Press.

Simon, H. A. (1978). Rationality as a process and as product of thought. *American Economic Review, 68,* 1–16.

Sjoberg, L. (1984). Interests, effort, achievement and vocational preference. *British Journal of Educational Psychology, 54,* 189–205.

Snow, C. E., Barnes, W. S., Chandler, J., Goodman, I. F., & Hemphill, L. (1991). *Unfulfilled expectations: Home and school influences on literacy.* Cambridge, MA: Harvard University Press.

Spence, J. T., & Helmreich, R. L. (1978). *Masculinity and femininity: Their psychological dimensions, correlates, and antecedents.* Austin: University of Texas Press.

Stanley, J. C., & Benbow, C. P. (1983). Extremely young college graduates: Evidence of their success. *College and University, 58,* 361–371.

Stanley, J. C., & Benbow, C. P. (1986). Youths who reason exceptionally well in mathematics. In R. J. Sternberg & J. E. Davidson (Eds.), *Conceptions of giftedness* (pp. 361–387). New York: Cambridge University Press.

Stanley, J. C., Keating, D. P., & Fox, L. H. (Eds.). (1974). *Mathematical talent: Discovery, description, and development.* Baltimore: Johns Hopkins University Press.

Steinberg, L., & Silverberg, S. B. (1986). The vicissitudes of autonomy in early adolescence. *Child Development, 57*(4), 841–851.

Stigler, J. W., Lee, S., & Stevenson, H. W. (1990). *Mathematical knowledge.* Reston, VA: National Council of Teachers of Mathematics.

Subotnik, R. F. (1988a). The motivation to experiment: A study of gifted adolescents' attitudes toward scientific research. *Journal for the Education of the Gifted, 11,* 19–35.

Subotnik, R. F. (1988b). Factors from the structure of intellect model associated with gifted adolescents' problem finding in science: Research with Westinghouse Science Talent Search winners. *Journal of Creative Behavior, 22,* 42–54.

Tamir, P., & Lunetta, V. N. (1978). Cognitive preferences in biology of a group of talented high school students. *Journal of Research in Science Teaching, 15,* 59–64.

Terman, L. M. (1925). *Mental and physical traits of a thousand gifted children.* Stanford, CA: Stanford University Press.

Tetlock, P. E. (1983). Accountability and complexity of thought. *Journal of Personality and Social Psychology, 45*, 74–83.

Thornburg, H. D., Adey, K. L., & Finnis, E. (1986). A comparison of gifted and non-gifted early adolescents' movement toward abstract thinking. *Journal of Early Adolescence, 6*, 231–245.

Tidwell, R. (1980). A psycho-educational profile of 1593 gifted high school students. *Gifted Child Quarterly, 24*, 63–68.

Tiger, L. (1992). *The pursuit of pleasure.* Boston: Little, Brown.

Torrance, E. P. (1978). Images of the future of gifted adolescents: Effects of alienation and specialized cerebral functioning. *Gifted Child Quarterly, 22*, 40–54.

United Nations Children's Fund (UNICEF) (1990). *The state of the world's children 1990.* New York: Oxford University Press.

Van Tassel-Baska, J. (1989). The role of the family in the success of disadvantaged gifted learners. *Journal for the Education of the Gifted, 13*, 22–36.

Walberg, H. J. (1984). Improving the productivity of America's schools. *Educational Leadership, 41*, 19–27.

Walters, J., & Gardner, H. (1986). The crystallizing experience: Discovering an intellectual gift. In R. J. Sternberg & J. E. Davidson (Eds.), *Conceptions of giftedness* (pp. 306–331). New York: Cambridge University Press.

Weiss, I. (1990). *Report of the 1988–89 National Survey of Science and Mathematics Education.* Research Triangle Park, NC: Research Triangle Institute.

Weisskopf, V. (1991). *The joy of insight.* New York: Basic.

Werner, H. (1957). The concept of development from a comparative and organismic point of view. In D. Harris (Ed.), *The concept of development.* Minneapolis: University of Minnesota Press.

West, J. D., Hosie, T., & Mathews, F. N. (1989). Families of academically gifted children: Adaptability and cohesion. *School Counselor, 37*, 121–127.

Whalen, S., & Csikszentmihalyi, M. (1989). A comparison of the self-image of talented teenagers with a normal adolescent population. *Journal of Youth and Adolescence, 18*(2), 131–146.

White, R. W. (1959). Motivation reconsidered: The concept of competence. *Psychological Review, 66*, 297–333.

Whitehead, A. N. (1929). *The aims of education.* New York: Free Press.

Wilson, W. J. (1987). *The truly disadvantaged.* Chicago: University of Chicago Press.

Youniss, J., & Smollar, J. (1985). *Adolescent relations with mothers, fathers, and friends.* Chicago: University of Chicago Press.

Index

299